Poetic Culture

Poetic Culture

Contemporary American Poetry between Community and Institution

CHRISTOPHER BEACH

Northwestern

University Press

Evanston

Illinois

Northwestern University Press
Evanston, Illinois 60208-4210

Library of Congress Cataloging-in-Publication Data

Beach, Christopher.
Poetic culture : contemporary American poetry between community
and institution / Christopher Beach.
p.   cm. — (Avant-garde & modernism studies)
Includes bibliographical references and index.
ISBN 0-8101-1677-4 (cloth : alk. paper). — ISBN 0-8101-1678-2
(paper : alk. paper)
1. American poetry—20th century—History and criticism.
2. Authors and readers—United States—History—20th century.
3. Reader-response criticism.   I. Title.   II. Series: Avant-garde and
modernism studies.
PS325.B43   1999   99-27504
811'5409—dc21   CIP

FOR MY PARENTS

                    are we putting
each other to sleep
or waking each other up;
& what do we wake to?
Does our writing stun
or sting? Do we cling to
what we've grasped
too well, or find tunes
in each new
departure.

    —Charles Bernstein, "Artifice of Absorption"

Contents

Acknowledgments

There are a number of people I would like to thank for contributing their time, knowledge, and enthusiasm to the making of this book. Marjorie Perloff, Robert von Hallberg, Alan Golding, Charles Bernstein, Michael Bérubé, and Stuart Culver each read part or all of the manuscript and offered valuable advice at various stages of the book's development. Bob Holman, Maggie Estep, Shutup Shelley, Joshua Blum, Philip Fried, and others too numerous to mention supplied essential firsthand knowledge of the poetry scene, poetry slams, and poetry-related media. I also thank my graduate students and colleagues at both the University of Montana and the University of California, Irvine, for their input and support. The University of Montana gave me a research grant which allowed me to spend the summer of 1995 in New York City, and both UCI and the Claremont Graduate University have kept me gainfully employed while I finished writing it. Special thanks, as always, are owed to my wife, Carrie, for all her love, intelligence, and generosity.

The book is dedicated to my parents, Northrop and Myrtle Beach. And since this is a book about poets, I send it out to a few of those who have enriched the culture for me and many others: William S. Burroughs (1914–97), Denise Levertov (1923–97), and Allen Ginsberg (1926–97).

Chapter 3 first appeared in *Contemporary Literature* 38, no. 1 (spring 1997), and a shorter version of chapter 2 was published in *Western Humanities Review* 50, no. 1 (spring 1996).

I gratefully acknowledge permission to quote from the following poetic works: "Chopped-Off Arm" and "One Thing Leads to Another," from *Mother Said* by Hal Sirowitz, copyright © 1996 by Hal Sirowitz, are reprinted by permission of Crown Publishers, Inc.; "Faces," "White Thighs," and "Black Dog, Red Dog," from *Velocities* by Stephen Dobyns, copyright © 1994 by Stephen Dobyns, used by permission of Penguin, a division of Penguin Putnam Inc.; "Tap Tap on Africa" from *Joker, Joker, Deuce* by Paul Beatty, copyright © 1994 by Paul Beatty, used by permission of Viking Penguin, a division of Penguin Putnam Inc.; "Long Point Light" from *Atlantis* by Mark Doty, copyright © 1995 by Mark Doty, reprinted by permission of HarperCollins Publishers, Inc. The following poems from the television series and series book *The United States of Poetry* are used by permission of Bob Holman and the authors: "Democracy" by Leonard

Cohen; "The X Is Black" by Amiri Baraka; "Winter Place" by Genny Lim; "Boulder Valley Surprise" by John Wright; "Sold Out" by Vess Quinlan; "I'm an Emotional Idiot" by Maggie Estep.

You will fear that a discussion of conditions under which works of art
have come into being, and their subsequent effects, must impertinently
preempt the place belonging to the experience of those works as such; that
sociological orderings and relatings will suppress all insight into the truth or
falsity of the objects themselves. . . . Such a method becomes most
distressing when applied to lyric poetry. The tenderest, most fragile forms
must be touched by, even brought together with, precisely that social
bustle from which the ideals of our traditional conception of poetry have
sought to protect them.

—Theodor Adorno, "Lyric Poetry and Society"

Introduction

The study of poetry can move simultaneously in two directions that are,
or at least often appear to be, polar opposites: these poles are, to put it
reductively, the aesthetic and the sociological. Yet the question that is at
the center of much recent debate concerning the state of contemporary
American poetry is one that cannot easily be answered by either aesthetics or sociology alone: What contribution does contemporary American
poetry make to contemporary American culture? It is a question that until
recently was almost never asked in so direct a form. There was little need
to question poetry's importance or its relevance, since the literary "canon"
of which poetry was an essential part was seen as both inviolable and
unavoidable. Poetry was not read as a socially contingent practice whose
purposes and conditions of production varied from society to society and
historical era to historical era, but as a universally relevant and respected
art, the terms of whose gradual change were formal or aesthetic rather
than material or economic.

Today, however, we are beginning to question on a deeper level the
cultural significance of poetry, both as a canonical system and as a contemporary practice. We are also increasingly made aware—through the
intervention of new historical and sociocultural theories and methods—
of both the means of (material) production that are responsible for the
creation of poetic texts, and of the fields of (symbolic) cultural production
that sustain, promote, and disseminate such texts.[1]

This book is a study of the cultural dynamics of poetry in the United
States today. Though there exists a significant body of work dealing with

the social practices of writing and reading American literature, remarkably little has been written about the ethnographic, sociological, or cultural dimensions of contemporary poetry. Those few studies that address twentieth-century literary production and reception (Janice Radway's work on the romance novel and the Book-of-the-Month Club, James West's work on the American literary marketplace, and Richard Ohmann's analysis of the canon of contemporary American fiction, for example) have by and large dealt with the novel rather than with poetry. The work that exists on the everyday lives and practices of poets today has consisted primarily of anecdotal or biographical discussions, rather than attempts to provide some kind of comprehensive or analytical study of poetry as a sociocultural phenomenon.[2] Two fundamental reasons can be adduced for the lack of critical work in this area: First, we still live in a post-Romantic age in which the assumption is most frequently made (and supported by the New Critical paradigm that has dominated American poetry criticism, despite some notable exceptions, for the past half century) that poetry is a type of aesthetic production with a secure status independent of historical, social, and economic contingencies. Second, because of the relatively limited numbers of poetry readers (at least in the United States), and because of the persistent perception of poetry as an exclusively "high cultural" phenomenon (cut off from, or even in competition with, such popular media as television), the methods of cultural studies that have been used to interrogate modes of "popular culture" (film, television, popular music, novels) have not yet been applied in any systematic way to poetry.[3]

Nevertheless, the study of poetry within a sociocultural context is crucial to our overall understanding of the poetic medium, in that it serves as a useful counterbalance to the critical methods that have until now been brought to bear on poets and poetic texts. Although critics have written for more than half a century of the "death of poetry" (from Edmund Wilson in the thirties to Randall Jarrell in the fifties to Joseph Epstein, Dana Gioia, and Vernon Shetley today), there are a larger number of serious poets publishing today than ever before. The *American Poetry Annual* lists some six thousand actively publishing poets, more than a thousand of whom teach full or part-time in the various graduate and undergraduate writing programs throughout the country; the number of amateur and aspiring poets is in the hundreds of thousands. The range of presses and periodicals that publish poetry is itself astonishing; the *Directory of Poetry Publishers* lists over two thousand. Finally, the institutionalization of poetry, as represented by the rapid growth of university writing programs and writers' conferences; the proliferation of prizes, grants, and awards; and the emergence of specialized newsletters dealing with economic and lifestyle issues of interest to poets indicate that poetry is a distinct "culture" in much the same sense as rock music or film, and worthy of study for the same reasons that they are.

This is not to argue that quantity in itself is an adequate or even meaningful measure of a poetic culture. The presence of such institutional forces, however, does indicate the need for new critical methods that allow us to examine poetry beyond the limits of the accepted contemporary canon, and beyond the terms in which canonical poetry has been discussed and evaluated. Recently, Pierre Bourdieu has provided us with the important notion of "cultural capital." Bourdieu's model is extremely pertinent to an understanding of several aspects of contemporary poetic culture, and it allows us to move beyond the relatively narrow ways in which poetry's place within contemporary culture has been defined by both academic discourse and the popular media.

In the pages that follow, I have tried to provide a useful analysis of various ways in which poetry culture operates in the United States today, of various levels on which the field of contemporary poetry is defined. In so doing, I have also sought to articulate a "defense" of poetry, a justification for its continued vitality both as an aesthetic form and as a site for the creation of community and value. Just as poems are not written in a historical vacuum, they cannot be evaluated in a vacuum. Thus the perceived decline in poetry's importance, and perhaps of its quality as well, must be viewed within a larger context than that provided by aesthetically based discussions of poetry and poetic tradition. The most important question, it seems to me, is not whether poetry writing has suffered a decline—either in terms of its quality (Joseph Epstein) or its relevance (Dana Gioia)—but where the perception of such a decline is located and how it is articulated (or not) within various segments of the poetry culture. This broad investigation will in turn spawn more specific questions: How does the commodification and institutionalization of poetry within a given culture, like that of the contemporary United States, affect the quality of poetry produced by and for that culture? What constitutes a working definition of professionalism within the poetic field, and how are poets both co-opted by and evaluated within a professional and institutional context that often reflects class orientations and expectations?

In *Poetic Culture*, I have attempted not only to describe the cultural phenomenon of poetry in this country, but also in some measure to analyze the social and economic structures—the structures of cultural, educational, and economic capital—underlying the poetic community in question. In order to understand the operations of poetic culture, four interrelated areas of questioning have to be explored. Moving from the most specific to the most general, each of these topics is in some way applicable to all Romantic and post-Romantic poetry, but they raise particularly acute issues for American poetry since about 1960.

1. *Institutional media.* How does the poetic culture define itself through its own internal media, including both general poetry journals and specialized professional publications that provide information, opinion, and advice for poets, such as *Poets and Writers,* the *Associated Writing Programs Chronicle, Poet, Poet's Market, Poetry Exchange, Poetry Connection, Directory of Poetry Publishers, Directory of American Poets and Fiction Writers,* and columns on poetry in *Writer's Digest, Writer's Journal,* and *Byline* magazine? How do these forums work to create a sense of poetic community? How do they affect the commodification and circulation of poetry?

2. *Institutional power.* What are the systems of cultural capital at work in the poetic community? More specifically, how are questions of canon and taste arbitrated within the network of poetry writing, reviewing, criticism, teaching, and granting? What is the relationship between the social or institutional capital conferred by university teaching and other forms of professional achievement, such as publication? What is the role of journals, presses, prizes and fellowships, writers' colonies, anthologies, and *Best American Poetry* annuals in determining poetic status?

3. *Cultural legitimacy.* How do poetry and poetic culture participate in an elitist or exclusionary high cultural network that views itself as necessarily distinct from, in opposition to, and culturally superior to, popular culture? What is the nature of poetry as a cultural artifact? Must it compete with popular culture, or can it participate in areas of popular culture such as video and performance?

4. *Cultural relevance.* What is the relationship between poetic culture and American culture at large? How important is poetry to a larger society? Does the survivability of poetry as a form of aesthetic expression rest on its appeal to a nonspecialist (i.e., nonacademic, nonprofessional) readership? How large a readership does it require? In what sense does it "matter" if few people read it or care about it?

While I do not answer all of these questions in the chapters of this book, they do inform the questions I raise concerning the changing place of poetry in American culture over the past quarter century. Clearly, poetry continues to play a significant role in American culture, despite enormous changes in the technological, institutional, and demographic structure of "postmodern" society. The important fact is that there are still poets writing today who believe that, in one way or another, poetry can make a difference in the world. As Adorno suggested, poetry in its most authentic forms can serve as a response to, critique of, or protest against "a social condition which every individual experiences as hostile, distant, cold, and oppressive"; the poem "proclaims the dream of a world in which things would be different."[4] We must continue to read and to study poetry, but not with the naive belief that it is a rarefied cultural form set apart from the forces of the market and needing to be protected from such forces. Poetry is not simply a "self-constituted and irreducible activity" that makes present "the mystery of language itself," as Calvin Bedient has suggested.[5] It is also a cultural practice subject to the same forces of administration, commodification, standardization, and homogenization as the culture at large. We need to understand the cultural circumstances within which the production of poetry takes place, both on the level of the communities within which poets write and on the level of the institutions that organize and disseminate that writing.

I focus this study on a dynamic tension that informs all aspects of contemporary poetic culture—the tension between the level of the community and the level of the institution. For the purposes of this book, I define a poetic "community" as a group of poets with shared interests, goals, orientation, or background. A community can range from a local community (existing within a given city or neighborhood, or even around a particular venue such as a bookstore, bar, or coffeehouse where particular kinds of poetry are displayed, read, or discussed) to a larger regional or national community, such as that of cowboy poetry, slam poetry, or Language poetry. Ron Silliman has identified these two kinds of community structures as "scenes" (communities specific to a place) and "networks" (transgeographic communities).[6] The creation of a poetic community is also, as Stephen Fredman suggests, a gesture of "self-exile" from society at large, an attempt to "gather a group of like-minded others" into a "network for mutual support," often in an effort to "overcome some of the isolation, anxiety, and uncertainty about whether it [is] even possible to write poetry" in this country.[7]

An institution, on the other hand, is a form of social organization structured by some force outside the immediate control or jurisdiction of the poets themselves, and usually in the service of something other than their own private needs. The university, and more specifically the creative-writing program, is the most obvious form of institutional structure in the current poetry culture, but there are many other kinds of institutions that also play a role in the organization and administration of American poetry: publishing houses; literary magazines; newspapers that review poetry and cover poetry events; literary organizations such as the American Academy of Poets, American Academy of Arts and Letters, and the Poetry Society of America; granting agencies, both public and private, such as the NEA, the MacArthur Foundation, the Guggenheim Foundation, the National Book Foundation, and the Lila Wallace/Reader's Digest Fund; and institutionalized writers' colonies such as Yaddo and MacDowell. Unlike communities, which evolve organically out of the needs of particular groups of poets, institutions usually involve some form of bureaucracy. Also unlike communities, which tend to be self-sufficient (and at times highly insular) entities, institutions require a larger context, whether that context is defined in terms of readership, marketability, or a more general cultural or ideological agenda. While cultural institutions are to some degree necessary to the dissemination of culture beyond a relatively small group, they are also more likely to lead not only to the increased bureaucratization of culture, but also to the increased commodification of cultural production. As both Adorno and Bourdieu have indicated, institutions are the means by which cultural value is allocated and adjudicated. Yet the relationship between institutions of cultural administration and the productions of culture itself is a paradoxical one: on the one hand, writes Adorno, "culture suffers damage when it is planned and administrated"; on the other hand, "when it is left to itself . . . everything cultural threatens not only to lose its cultural effect, but its very existence as well."[8]

Communities are, in a sense, a mediating link between individuals and institutions; they are often the first step in the evolution toward an institutional framework. While communities generally begin as collective and egalitarian enterprises, every community will at some point in its history develop hierarchical relationships that may lead to more permanent institutional structures. Communities can also exist *within* institutional frameworks, coalescing, for example, around a particular press or magazine, or within the creative-writing workshop environment.[9] Institutions are thus in many cases a catalyst for a given community, or a means of perpetuating a community beyond the life cycle it would otherwise have had. The ubiquitous form of "workshop" poetry has certainly been sustained, as have its practitioners, by the institutional structures of the academic creative-writing program. Similarly, anthologies devoted to poetry by "experimental" or "alternative" writers represent a form of institutional intervention in the effort to sustain the sense of an active poetic avant-garde community.[10]

Communities have been of fundamental importance to American poetry throughout its history, allowing American poets to form subcultures that can address issues outside the social and artistic mainstream. Such alternative or countercultural communities have included the Transcendentalists, the Imagists, the Objectivists, the Beats, the San Francisco Renaissance, the Black Mountain poets, the New York school, and the Language poets. In recent years, communities have also evolved out of a broad range of racial, ethnic, and gender constituencies, from various feminist poetic communities to communities of poets from African American, Latino, Asian American, and Native American backgrounds. Finally, there is the largest community of all, which is really more of a constellation of smaller interlocking communities: the community of poets affiliated with academic creative-writing programs. It is the formation of this supercommunity, certainly the largest and most dominant in terms of capital, institutional access, and mainstream media exposure, that has been largely responsible for the creation of various other poetic communities at its margins: the experimental community centered around Language poetry, the community of Nuyorican slam or performance poetry (and more generally of slam/performance poetry as a national phenomenon), the community of New Formalist poets, and the communities of radical feminist poetry and poetry by other sociopolitically marginal groups.

In opposition to the community defined as a sociocultural group specific to time and place is the literary canon, which is itself an institutional structure, or at the very least an institutionally sanctioned arena of poetic validation. As Silliman suggests, canons are not "inescapable facts of a pre-existing social landscape" in the way that institutions are, and there is a significant difference between "contesting canons and contesting institutions."[11] Nonetheless, the process of canonization takes an institutional form in providing a privileged status to poets whose work, over time, gains an aura of legitimacy, a legitimacy that becomes increasingly difficult to challenge. Even the creation of alternative canons—a project that has been in process within various sectors of American poetry since the constitutive groups of the New American Poetry of the 1950s challenged the hegemonic domination of the New Criticism and East Coast academic world—is an imperfect solution that only partially rectifies the effects of canonization, contributing to the continued polarization or even balkanization of the poetic field, and leaving many deserving poets within what Silliman calls "the ranks of the disappeared."[12] Even those poets, like Charles Olson, Robert Duncan, and Jack Spicer, who achieved the greatest importance within the alternative canon proposed by Donald Allen's 1960 anthology, have failed to make major inroads into the poetic mainstream either for themselves or for their successors, who have been largely excluded from consideration for public awards and prizes such as the Pulitzer, the National Book Award, the Guggenheim, and the NEA.

These facts are not a matter of dispute. What is a matter of dispute, however, is the way in which the poetic field should be mapped or carved up to reflect differently situated communities within it. Can we still define the poetry culture as divided between an academic mainstream of "workshop" orientation and an experimental, oppositional, or countercultural poetry with an avant-gardist aesthetic and political agenda? Or have such polarized accounts become a less accurate description since the emergence of a variety of multicultural poetries, each seeking its own place in the overall poetic field? What is the status of a "resistant" or "marginal" avant-garde at a time when many Language writers and other experimental poets are gaining academic recognition and moving into positions within the academy? As I hope to demonstrate in the chapters of this book dealing with the question of canonicity in contemporary American poetry, the formation of canons is not as simple an issue as either the proponents of the existing canon or its opponents would have us believe. In fact, the relationship between canons, institutions, and communities is an area of inquiry that is as much as ever fraught with controversy and clouded by biased and misleading accounts.[13]

In recent years, academic literary criticism has paid increasing attention to the issue of canonicity as it relates to factors such as class, race and ethnicity, and gender and sexuality. The groundwork for a sociology of canon formation has been laid by the theoretical work in the sociology of culture, especially Bourdieu's sociocultural analysis of taste, distinction, and cultural capital as they operate within the field of cultural and literary production. Informed in part by Bourdieu's analysis, scholars have begun to show an interest not only in the academically controlled cultural biases that govern the formation of canons, but more generally in the concept of class as it relates to both the production and the reception of literature.[14] Yet the sociological and institutional dimension of canon formation, while it has been of growing concern to literary and cultural scholars, remains a relatively underdeveloped field of inquiry, especially, as Alan Golding has pointed out, within discussions of American poetry.[15]

Cary Nelson's critique of the modernist canon in *Repression and Recovery* constitutes the single most significant attempt to redefine the canon debate as it relates to American poetry in the twentieth century. Nelson's is the most sustained argument to this point for a more pluralistic, inclusive, and multicultural approach to American poetic history. His approach stresses the ideologically and culturally motivated choices that underlie any attempt to define a single canon of poets; he incorporates within his polemical argument hitherto marginalized groups in an effort to challenge or perhaps even to undermine the very idea of a canon as such. Nelson concurs with both Barbara Herrnstein Smith and Jane Tompkins in positing the "contingency" of literary canons and, more generally, of literary value. Praising Smith for her claim that "validation [in literary study] often takes the form of privileging absolutely—that is 'standard'-izing—the particular contingencies that govern the preferences of the [dominant] group and discounting or . . . pathologizing all other contingencies," Nelson argues that "literary works become, for all practical purposes, different texts under different cultural conditions."[16]

Yet despite the importance of his argument concerning the social constructedness of existing canons, Nelson's treatment of the issue of canonicity is an incomplete one. Nelson pays insufficient attention to the aesthetic claims or values of the poems from the alternative canons he proposes, and he does not adequately theorize the complex systems of cultural legitimation that contribute to the construction of literary canons. While he does pay brief attention to the formal and aesthetic qualities of noncanonical experimentalists such as Mina Loy, Else von Freytag-Loringhoven, Abraham Gillespie, Marsden Hartley, and Harry Crosby, Nelson provides little discussion of the aesthetic or formal innovations provided by these poets, and he fails to speculate on the factors that may have prevented them from entering the canon. Instead, he concludes simply that there are many "obviously experimental poets whose work has been substantially forgotten," as if either their forgotten status (whether deserved or not) or their experimentalism should itself guarantee them a greater degree of attention in the present day. In seeking to overturn several generations of academically generated and passively received ideas about the modernist poetic canon, Nelson relies almost exclusively on what Golding has called the "institutional" model of canon formation, as opposed to the "aesthetic" model that has until recently predominated in discussions of American poetry. According to this "institutional" model, canonicity is determined not so much by the tastes and abilities of poets themselves as by the interventions of institutions such as publishers, anthologies, informational media, universities, and the discipline of academic literary study itself.

It is this institutional model, rather than the "aesthetic" model of canonicity, that has come to hold sway in most academic discussions of the literary canon. But as Charles Altieri has suggested, arguments such as those of Smith and Nelson apply a reductive principle that produces a circular and self-substantiating logic. If taken to their logical extreme, such arguments of contingency tell us only that Homer is in the canon because Homer is in the canon, or, to put it another way, that Homer is considered to be an important poet (only) because the values contained within Homer's works are those shared by, ratified by, or privileged by the literary and educational institutions of subsequent Western civilization.[17] On the other hand, poets *not* currently in the canon, whether intentionally passed over or inadvertently ignored, were excluded (only) because their values or contingencies failed to match those of the society in which they wrote and those that came after. Such arguments, while superficially persuasive, fail to acknowledge the evident fact that some works succeed better than others *not* because of the particular values or contingent functions they embody but because they embody those values and functions more substantially, more clearly, more profoundly, more systematically, or with greater complexity than other works. If Vachel Lindsay's poetry—to cite one modern example provided by Nelson—has been judged less successful than T. S. Eliot's, it may be less a matter of our culture's preference for "the self-sufficient status of literariness" over "the fantasy of a truly public and participatory poetry" than a matter of how compellingly the poets in question carry out their respective projects.[18] Nelson's avoidance of such aesthetic questions—or his trivializing of those questions as merely part of the institutional politics of canon formation—begs the important issue: Does all poetic writing have an equal claim to canonical status, or are certain works more likely to achieve such status (or perhaps in a broadly cultural sense even more "deserving" of such status), based on the aesthetic, emotional, ethical, and intellectual work they perform within given societal contexts?

Nelson acknowledges in a footnote the power of Altieri's defense of the "existing canon," but he takes issue with Altieri's characterization of the social and psychological effects of the canon as it operates within culture.

For Nelson, the canon tends to be "coercive and restrictive rather than generally broadening," and can be articulated with equal success by both "liberating and repressive projects."[19] This is no doubt true, but it has less to say about the canon per se than about the ends to which any work of literature can, with admirable or questionable intentions, be put. Certainly not all works celebrated by "repressive" regimes are inherently "bad," just as not all works celebrated by more enlightened or "liberating" political systems are inherently "good." To reduce literature or the canon to such ethical or ideological categories is to greatly diminish its scope and importance, and to open literature up to the potential for even greater rhetorical manipulation in the service of a given ideological end. One important function the canon *does* perform over time is to transcend the immediate functions dictated by its historical context. This is evidenced by the fact that Homer and Shakespeare have remained at or near the center of the European canon despite the vicissitudes of historical and political change, and that their works have been called upon to support a number of claims with which they might not have initially been associated.

If critics like Nelson err on the side of emphasizing the contingent and institutional nature of canons, other critics go too far in applying a set of purely aesthetic or evaluative criteria to the making of canons. While Golding uses the terms "aesthetic" and "poet-centered" to describe the model adopted by critics such as Helen Vendler, Harold Bloom, Hugh Kenner, Charles Altieri, and Christopher Ricks, I prefer the term "evaluative," which places greater emphasis on the process whereby poets are placed in the canon: that is, in a selective process through which the critic (or later poet) evaluates the relative "strength," "importance," "greatness," or "individual talent" of a given poet.

In all evaluative approaches to the canon, critics base their critical judgments quite explicitly on the belief that aesthetic criteria, or some notion of personal "taste" (either that of other poets or of the critic), should in itself determine the canon's formation. Vendler, in fact, denies the relevance of anything *but* aesthetic criteria for canonicity. In her review of Robert von Hallberg's *American Poetry and Culture, 1945–1980,* for example, she criticizes von Hallberg's attempt to make civic and ethical value a central concern in the poetry he treats. Vendler writes of her own predilection to consider "aesthetic value, properly understood, quite enough to claim for a poem."[20] Yet in making such claims, Vendler does not appear to recognize the fundamentally problematic nature of appealing to a universally accepted notion of "aesthetic value, properly understood," as a test for the relative importance or centrality of a poem or a poet. How do we "properly understand" claims for aesthetic value without some reference to a wider ethical, cultural, or sociohistorical context? Even if we are to accept the questionable proposition that poets "are elevated to canonical status by the envy and admiration of their fellow poets" and that "it is poets—and not anthologists and professors—who eventually decide which poets are read after their own generation has disappeared," who is to decide which poets' judgments we are to pay most attention to? Certainly, if we want to appreciate the importance of Milton, Keats, or Stevens, there is an accepted and well-delineated tradition of "envy and admiration" to which we can turn in framing our own sense of the canon. On the other hand, if we wish to understand and appreciate the diversity of poetry by African Americans or Native Americans during the past half century, Vendler's aesthetic criteria for poetic excellence and her model of poet-based canon formation may not be the most useful or illuminating ones. Likewise, the particular set of aesthetic criteria that we would need to apply in order to appreciate a poem by Elizabeth Bishop, A. R. Ammons, or John Ashbery may not be adequate to understanding the sociocultural context that made possible the modernist and postmodernist avant-garde of Dada, Objectivism, or Language poetry. As Golding has observed, Vendler's argument for a purely aesthetic or evaluative model of the canon is a somewhat disingenuous one, since only an institutional model can explain the suppression of alternative canons carried out in Vendler's *own* work. "In her position as an institutionally well-placed critic," Golding remarks, "Vendler promotes one poet-derived canon . . . over another, exercising her canonizing power without acknowledging it."[21]

In an ideal world, we might be able to view the poetic canon through the lens provided by Vendler: not as an interlocking set of aesthetic and ideological turf battles motivated in large part by differences of education, class, gender, race, and ethnicity, but as a collective representation of the consensus that could be reached by well-informed writers, teachers, and readers in a genteel assessment of the country's most important or most talented poets. In practice, however, the historical record has established that it is extremely difficult to arrive at anything like critical or aesthetic consensus unless the participants in the consensus-building process are a highly centralized group with relatively similar cultural, socioeconomic, and educational backgrounds. Such a consensus can exist to a greater extent in societies where more centralized systems of cultural authority hold sway both in the media and in academic life—as they did in postwar America and to some degree still do in both Britain and France—but it has little chance of prevailing in a pluralistic and culturally decentralized society such as the contemporary United States. To demand such a consensus in today's literary culture, or to apply one's own taste as surrogate for such consensus, is to reject as "inappropriate, irrelevant, [or] extrinsic" to the "true nature" of poetry all forms of poetic expression which depart from one's own expectations and desires for the genre in question.[22]

The dangers of applying such a rigidly evaluative paradigm to the canon of contemporary American poetry can be seen in a recent study like J. D. McClatchy's *White Paper*. A self-styled cultural conservative and an eminent member of the poetic establishment, McClatchy presents his book as a "position paper" for the rejection of a middlebrow aesthetic that he believes has adversely affected contemporary poetry. It is also a position paper against various other forms of poetry, including virtually any writing that emerges from racial or ethnic diversity or from alternative or marginal status within the mainstream poetry culture. McClatchy echoes aspects of both Vendler and Bloom, first in his reliance on an unexamined notion of what he believes to be superior "taste," and second, in his effort to cast poetry as "the defense of the self against everything," including "ideology," "history," and "cultural force." While at the opposite extreme from Nelson's, McClatchy's argument is even more clearly illogical: if the poem were only about the poetic and personal "self," and that "self" was to be defined only in a nonideological, nonhistorical way (if such an autonomous state were even ontologically possible), any grounds for the evaluative selection of one poet or poem over another would become narrowly aestheticizing principles that would not allow for any consideration of the larger cultural and historical context from which literature in large part derives its value. Further, such claims for an aesthetic purity of design can be, and have often in the past been, mere smoke screens for other social or ideological agenda.[23]

In her book *At the Dark End of the Street: Margins in Vanguard American Poetry*, Maria Damon provides a potential alternative to the either/or scenario provided by Nelson and McClatchy. Damon's book takes up both explicitly and implicitly the question of canonicity by examining the current place of marginalized poetries in the United States. Damon concerns the "transgressive" forms of pleasure that can be derived from the "marginal imagining" of those poets who in one way or another stand outside the poetic and cultural mainstream, those who challenge the boundaries of the canon rather than attempting to define them. As Damon explains, the work of such poets "continues to occupy nonrespectable places in a shadow-canon, a kind of indeterminate halo of experimentalism that surrounds the 'real' canon like an aura that waxes and wanes with the literary weather, highlighting and simultaneously cluing us in to the illusory nature of the central canon."[24] The poets Damon discusses—the African American Jewish Beat poet Bob Kaufman, three teenage women poets from the projects of South Boston, the gay San Francisco poets Robert Duncan and Jack Spicer, and the Jewish lesbian experimentalist Gertrude Stein—combine race, gender, sexual orientation, subcultural affiliation, and formal experimentation in such a way as to place them radically outside the process of legitimized high cultural canon formation.

Unlike proponents of the evaluative canon such as McClatchy and Vendler, Damon foregrounds the role of socioeconomic factors such as race, class, and economic situation in determining canonical status. She deliberately counters the idea of a "central canon" and replaces it with a largely nonwhite group of mixed gender and sexual orientation, possessing little academic capital and little status within the institutional poetry scene. Yet as Damon's study also makes clear, an interest in questioning or critiquing the canon does not necessitate avoiding questions of aesthetics and literary innovation. Damon differs from a critic like Nelson, and from most other critics of multicultural or marginalized poetries, in giving greater attention to the avant-garde potential of marginalized writers, stressing the avant-garde's status as "writing that pushes at the limits of experience as well as the limits of conventional form." As Damon asks, in a powerful if overly neat formulation: "Who is better equipped to push literature and sensibility to its limits than the dispossessed, those whose material and social resources are themselves constantly strained to or beyond their limits?"[25] By juxtaposing poets from very different cultural spheres (i.e., Robert Lowell and "three unknown teenage women writing from the D Street Housing Projects of South Boston"), by challenging canonical boundaries and hierarchies, Damon marks her project as very different from McClatchy's. Yet she also differs from Nelson in recognizing poetry's other, more subversive power, a power to transgress not only through overt statement, identity politics, or personal narrative, but through the manipulation of language: the use of puns by Spicer and Duncan to focus on gay culture as a "crossover culture," or of "doggerel

Yiddish" by Stein to indicate her own status as a Jew and a woman while "deterritorializing" the English language.[26]

In examining the interrelation of poetic communities and literary institutions, and in attempting to situate the "canon debates" within the context of this relationship, my book differs sharply from recent books, including McClatchy's, that have discussed the "situation" or "fate" of contemporary poetry.[27] These books have all followed a fairly similar pattern, combining provocative but unrigorous debate with formal (i.e., New Critical) readings of individual poets in order to ask questions about poetry's role in contemporary society. The questions they raise are of two fundamental kinds: *cultural* (what is the problem with the current sociocultural position of poetry, and what can we do to resuscitate it?) and *aesthetic* (what kinds of poetic writing will make possible a revitalization of the poetic art)? While these studies are of some value in highlighting the crisis in contemporary poetry—or at least the common perception of that crisis—they are generally unsatisfying in several respects. First, their discussion of the place of poetry remains within the realm of "high" or traditionally literary culture, leaving unexamined and unproblematized the significant relationship between poetry and other forms of culture and discourse. Second, their analysis of contemporary poetic culture is generally unsystematic, depending on anecdotal evidence and textual examples taken from the work of a few poets to stand as synecdoches for larger trends and issues, rather than providing any kind of statistical or historiographical basis for their claims. Finally, despite differences in the "canons" they represent, each of these books has tended to espouse a narrow spectrum of American poetic writing, usually of a relatively traditional or conservative bent, as not only exemplary but normative of the overall poetic orientation in contemporary America.[28] Each of them has also proposed a "solution" to the problems facing contemporary poetry: for Jonathan Holden, it is the more engaging use of subject matter; for J. D. McClatchy, the recuperation of the aesthetic norms of the previous generation; for Dana Gioia, the better marketing of poetry for the general reader; and for Vernon Shetley, the reinvestment of poetry with a kind of difficulty, intellectual engagement, or "skepticism" characteristic of a midcentury poetic.[29]

These critics have proven decidedly unwilling to consider work from alternative traditions, treating with an undue lack of seriousness work that is either formally experimental, politically radical, or representative of writing by marginalized groups. Gioia, for example, dismisses radically experimental writing such as Language poetry; such poetry has been "pushed off to the fringes of literary culture where it has either been ignored by the mainstream or declared irrelevant."[30] Shetley, who does consider Language poetry in part of one chapter, ends by trivializing such experimental writing and dehistoricizing both the Language movement and the larger postmodernist avant-garde in which it participates. Neither of them pays any attention to radically political poetry or to poetry that foregrounds race, ethnicity, class, gender, or sexual orientation. McClatchy, in some ways the most conservative of the group, presents a canon of poets that is so predictably white, Northeastern, and genteel as to be banal: Warren, Lowell, Bishop, Berryman, Plath, Snodgrass, Merrill, Howard, Hollander, Clampitt, and Hecht. As Hank Lazer has pointed out in his critical review of *White Paper,* McClatchy "eliminate[s] from consideration most of the challenging work of the day," including poets of color and poets who engage in any kind of formal innovation.[31] McClatchy's dehistoricized and essentializing claim that "poetry is the most conservative of the arts" is supported only by his own examples: his map of American poetry essentially follows that of the most influential poetry critic of our time, Helen Vendler, but is if anything even more conservative than hers, since she at least admits Ashbery and Ginsberg into her anthology of contemporary verse. More seriously, McClatchy betrays his own class and ideological biases, calling for "a recovery from poetry's boom" and a rejection of "workshop" poetry—none of the poets he treats are under the age of fifty, and thus few would have attended workshops—not realizing that, as Lazer astutely points out, "his own position is that of the academic par excellence (or, more discriminately, the high academic, with the workshop/middlebrow being the low or populist academic)."[32] Like the other purported studies of the situation of contemporary poetry, McClatchy's book does little justice to the breadth and vitality of current poetic production.

What is most disturbing in this current crop of books about American poetry is not that a few critics have neglected, or even rejected, alternative modes and traditions, but that they portray their own critical tastes and canonical definitions as self-evidently normative and universal, refusing to acknowledge that they are highly polarized toward a particular kind of poetic writing. The article "The Year in Poetry" in a recent yearbook of the *Dictionary of Literary Biography* (1992) is symptomatic of this tendency to define as "poetry" only poetry that challenges no boundaries of taste, form, or genre. In this thirty-three-page article—included in what is advertised as a "reference" guide for the general reader and student—there is hardly any mention of alternatives to the mainstream (academic) tradition as it has existed more or less unchanged for the last twenty years. There is only one parenthetical reference to Language poetry, by most accounts the most significant mode of experimental poetry today. No books of experimental poetic writing are mentioned in the article; nor are any books discussed by poets whose perspectives seriously question the dominant poetry establishment. In a year that saw important new volumes by such preeminent experimental writers as Bruce Andrews, Bernadette Mayer, Lyn Hejinian, John Yau, Leslie Scalapino, Jackson Mac Low, Ron Silliman, and Anne Waldman, such an exclusion is highly suspect and cannot be excused as simply an oversight. In fact, the author of the article, Robert McPhillips, uses this supposedly objective forum to make the highly polemical claim that "postmodernist" poets such as Ashbery and Creeley "are interested in continuing the modernist revolution in art and are content to limit their audience to an elite, usually academic, coterie (whose critical 'high priestess' is Marjorie Perloff)." Aside from the gratuitously arch reference to Perloff as "high priestess," as if modernism were to be dismissed as a somewhat odd but easily forgettable cult, McPhillips ignores the fact that Ashbery and Creeley are two of the best-selling and most widely taught poets in America today (hardly "revolutionary" in their position vis-à-vis either the poetic or the publishing establishment), and that Ashbery is one of the major prize-winners of our era. It would certainly be difficult to maintain that Creeley and Ashbery write for a smaller "coterie" than the New Formalist poets like Dana Gioia and Frederick Turner, whom McPhillips praises for their attempts to write "accessible" verse.

Particularly distressing in such narrowly biased accounts of American poetry is their seemingly shortsighted historical vision. What would the history of American poetry have been if critics earlier in the century had similarly ignored or ridiculed the work of Pound, Williams, Crane, Cummings, Moore, Eliot, Hughes, or Stevens, all of whom stretched in radical ways the conventions of Victorian and Georgian verse?[33]

As should by now be clear, I have not always attempted in the pages of this book to maintain the "objective" stance of the sociological researcher. In fact, I have at times stated my own aesthetic criteria and preferences quite strongly, as in the comparison of the "mainstream" academic poet Stephen Dobyns and the experimentalist Lyn Hejinian, and in my critiques of poetry anthologies and academic creative-writing programs. While my intent has been to write a book that is synthetic and open-minded rather than narrowly partisan, I do believe that certain sectors of American poetic culture have been more successful than others in articulating new perspectives and in generating innovative formal and cognitive structures. If the book has a polemic, it is less against the work of particular poets than against what I view as the overly conventional mindset and conservative institutional orientation governing much of the production, dissemination, and discussion of poetry in this country. This orientation, I will argue, has been in large part created and perpetuated by the growing creative-writing industry and its satellite structures (journals, presses, reading series, prizes, writers' conferences), which I discuss in chapter 2. Since this book is in a sense a retrospective look at the poetic culture of the past few decades, I will suggest that the most important contributions to American poetic practice (those that stand the best chance of being remembered decades from now) have come from the community of experimental or avant-garde poets most often grouped as Language writers and from the energy of new multicultural poets represented in a broad range of spoken-word, performance, and print formats. Were I to venture a guess, the two events of the 1990s with the most lasting cultural and aesthetic resonance may well be the publication of Paul Hoover's Norton anthology *Postmodern American Poetry* and the production and broadcast of Bob Holman's television series *The United States of Poetry*. Hoover's anthology provides a new legitimacy for the work of the innovative or avant-garde tradition originating with the New American Poets of the 1950s and 1960s; Holman's series (which I examine in detail in chapter 7) demonstrates not only the tremendous breadth of poetic expression in this country, but also the highly effective use of a nonprint medium—television—for the presentation of poetry.

1. Discussing the Death of Poetry to Death

In recent years, discussions of contemporary American poetry have often taken the form of position papers on the status of poetic culture. More specifically, the discussion has concerned the institutional structures that dominate both the production of poetry and its dissemination and consumption as a cultural commodity. In 1983, the poet Donald Hall set off the first round of debate over what has variously been called the "situation," the "fate," and the "death" of American poetry when he referred to the homogenized graduates of creative-writing programs as "McPoets" and cited careerist ambition as the primary motivation of poets who churned out mass-produced "McPoems" as fast as Chevrolets or disposable razors.[1]

Hall's essay struck a resonant chord within the poetic community, registering the latent dissatisfaction of many poets and readers with the current state of American poetry. Since the mid-1980s, poets as diverse as Greg Kuzma, Charles Bernstein, Robert Peters, Mary Kinzie, Dana Gioia, and Thomas Disch, as well as critics such as Joseph Epstein, Charles Altieri, Jed Rasula, and Vernon Shetley, have joined Hall in criticizing or even denouncing what they see as the mediocrity and homogeneity of the poetic mainstream. In 1986, Kuzma attacked what he considered the typical academic poet in a scathing article in *Poetry*, claiming that high-profile positions in creative-writing departments now counted for more than poetic talent. Epstein, comparing the contemporary generation of poets unfavorably with those that preceded it, went beyond both Hall and Kuzma in a comprehensive condemnation of contemporary poetry;

he posed the rhetorical question "Who killed poetry?" in his 1988 essay. Bernstein, an experimental poet with a very different agenda from Hall, Kuzma, or Epstein, nevertheless found himself in fundamental agreement with them when he disparaged the "official verse culture" dominating mainstream poetic practice: a hegemonic culture that includes within its parameters the major trade and university presses and the editors and reviewers of all the most prominent literary magazines.[2]

Bernstein and others, like Ron Silliman and Barrett Watten, who have analyzed contemporary poetic culture from the perspective of the contemporary avant-garde, view the issue not only as one of aesthetic decline but also as an ideologically motivated institutionalization, which becomes a means of either inclusion or exclusion based on a set of narrow aesthetic and formal criteria. In an even less flattering portrait of this same phenomenon, Robert Peters described what he called the "Onlie Beast of Poesie," a virtual monopoly of the dominant poetry culture held by writing programs, grant and prize committees, presses, and publications such as the *AWP Chronicle* and *Poets and Writers*.[3] And following in the procession of those who have invented new labels for mainstream poetic practice, Jed Rasula coined the term "PSI," or "Poetry Systems Incorporated," a "first-person singular poetry hegemony" that promotes a notion of poetry as an "innocuous artifact" that in no way seeks to challenge the status quo, a "home movie" poetry as easily produced and consumed as cable television and supported by meaningless reviews and flattering blurbs.[4] Perhaps most famously, Dana Gioia—a poet affiliated with the New Formalism—revisited the issue in his polemical essay "Can Poetry Matter?" first published in the *Atlantic*, and subsequently republished in a book-length collection of the same name.[5] Titles of other recent books, such as Vernon Shetley's *After the Death of Poetry*, Mary Kinzie's *The Cure for Poetry in an Age of Prose*, and Donald Hall's *Death to the Death of Poetry*, indicate that these concerns still exercise a strong fascination for those in the community of poets and poetry critics.

Such fears of poetry's diminishment, or even its demise, are hardly new: Edmund Wilson posed some of the same questions asked by Gioia and other recent commentators in his 1934 essay "Is Verse a Dying Technique?" However, the stridency, specificity, and urgency of the debate has intensified in recent years. Where Wilson's essay was more a cry in the wilderness than a statement of consensus, the current chorus of voices registers a deeply felt dissatisfaction of various sectors of the poetry community both with the current state of American poetry and with the cultural structures that produce that poetry. By the late 1990s, Gioia's question ("Can poetry matter?") seems almost a cliché. Yet the amount of attention paid to this alleged death is in itself an indication of how deeply the need for poetry, or at least for talk about poetry, permeates our national consciousness. From a sociological perspective, the validity of the claims made by Hall, Kuzma, Epstein, Bernstein, Peters, and Gioia during the past decade is less important than the fact that such arguments represent a significant self-reflexive discourse about the current practice of poetry. Unlike the 1950s and 1960s, when the academic poetry "establishment" came under fire from the emerging countercultural avant-garde, this new attack seems to have come from all angles: the postmodern left (Bernstein), the traditional left (Peters), the Eastern literary establishment (Hall, Epstein), the self-styled midwestern iconoclast (Kuzma) and the disaffected neo-traditionalist (Gioia). The demonization of mainstream American poetry, and especially of the creative-writing culture and its affiliated network of presses, journals, prizes, and reading series, has become almost as endemic as the poetry itself.

In historical terms, the United States has a greater abundance of poets and of poetry than ever before. It also has a healthy supply of presses and journals of various kinds to publish that poetry. The question is, are there enough readers of poetry to sustain or justify such an output, in either economic or cultural terms? It has become a cliché to state that more people write poetry today than read it. The preeminent journal *Poetry,* with a circulation of seven thousand, receives roughly seventy thousand submissions a year; magazines like the *New Yorker* and the *Atlantic* receive hundreds of thousands of submissions annually. Even small journals of modest reputation, such as *Iowa Review* and *Poetry Northwest,* handle many times more submissions than they sell copies. Close to a thousand manuscripts a year are submitted for poetry competitions of the Yale and Pittsburgh University Presses. And yet the number of people who actually read these books is minuscule when measured on a national scale: of the roughly three thousand copies printed by Yale and the two thousand printed by Pittsburgh of a given prizewinning book, relatively few are bought by independent readers, and many end up permanently uncracked on library shelves.

Notwithstanding the popular or commercial success enjoyed by a handful of poets since World War II—Allen Ginsberg, Lawrence Ferlinghetti, and Charles Bukowski, for example—and to a lesser extent by individual volumes such as John Ashbery's *Self-Portrait in a Convex Mirror,* Adrienne Rich's *Diving into the Wreck,* and Robert Creeley's *For Love,* each of which has sold more than twenty thousand copies, the vast majority of poetry volumes published today fail to reach an audience much larger than one or two thousand, and many fall short of that. Joseph Brodsky put the limited audience for poetry in perspective when he cited the fact that "a standard commercial publishing house, printing this or that author's first or second volume, aims at only 0.001 percent of the [U.S.] population."[6] Given these figures for poetry publication and the relatively small readership for poetry relative to other genres, it would appear that poetry is a cultural commodity for which supply greatly exceeds demand; there are simply not enough readers to sustain interest in such a large output, let alone convey that interest to a wider public.

Yet despite the limited readership for poetry, so many books of poetry are published annually in the United States that it is difficult even to estimate their number with any accuracy. Over a thousand new collections of poetry are published in America annually. When chapbooks and books by little-known presses are included, the number could run as high as two or three thousand.[7] Furthermore, the presses publishing these books are constantly changing. According to a survey by Mary Biggs, some 246 American poetry publishers commenced operations just between 1980 and 1987.[8] Since no survey of poetry publishing is completely comprehensive and there is no firm definition of what constitutes a "book" of poetry (as opposed to a chapbook, pamphlet, or self-printed volume), it is virtually impossible to estimate with any accuracy the exact number of books published. The number of journals publishing poetry is even more staggering than the number of presses: the *Directory of Poetry Publishers* finds over a thousand, and their list is far from comprehensive.

As has been argued by commentators like Gioia, Kuzma, and Bruce Bawer, the overproduction of professional poets by creative-writing programs has created a glut of academically trained poets, all of whom need to publish on a regular basis in order to find or keep their positions. This requires the creation of ever more publishing outlets for their poems—new journals, new presses—which in turn create an untenable environment for critics, reviewers, editors, and readers, all of whom are swamped with a greater volume of poetry than they can possibly assimilate. What emerges from this overpopulation of poets, such critics claim, is a homogenous mediocrity: thousands of anonymous poets producing thousands of forgettable books and hundreds of thousands of disposable poems. Any literary genre that has as many practitioners as readers, they argue, risks surviving only as a culturally marginal form, an inbred clique exercising little or no significant societal role.

There is no doubt—if we take into account only the presence of poetry within the dominant print media (commercial publishers, newspapers, and nonspecialist magazines)—that poetry has suffered a decline in recent decades. Throughout the 1950s, poetry was regularly covered in magazines such as the *Saturday Review*. Even when compared with the fairly recent era of the late 1970s, poetry volumes receive far fewer reviews today, at least in the mainstream publications covered by the *Book Review Index*. In the eight-year period from 1974 to 1981, seventeen different books of poetry received at least twenty reviews each, four received more than thirty, and one, Robert Lowell's *Day by Day*, was reviewed forty-five times.[9] In the eight-year period from 1985 to 1992, however, only two books received more than twenty reviews in the year following publication: Allen Ginsberg's *Collected Poems* and Adrienne Rich's *Atlas of a Difficult World*. The recent books of John Ashbery, certainly among the preeminent poets of the era, have received far less attention than his previous volumes: he now averages close to ten reviews per new volume instead of twenty-five or thirty. Even major prizes like the Pulitzer and the National Book Award, which once guaranteed a degree of renown, now provide only a meager amount of critical attention, and almost no public audience, for their recipients.

Today, the *New York Times Book Review* only infrequently reviews new books of poetry—even the bipolar division of its table of contents into "fiction" and "nonfiction" reflects this tendency—and when it does it gives them only cursory attention. Indeed, a recent survey found that volumes of poetry are almost always reviewed in groups of three books, and that these composite reviews occur on the average of less than once every two months.[10] This means that in an average year only fifteen books of poetry—or about 1 percent of the total—will be reviewed in the *Times*. The groupings of books in these reviews are fairly arbitrary, often based only on the press from which the books come and making no more generalized statement about the important trends in contemporary poetry. Further, these are not "critical" reviews in any true sense of the term: rarely do they find anything but praise for the volumes they review, and seldom do they use the review as an opportunity to debate larger issues confronting American poetry.

The other dominant print media are even more blatant in their exclusion of poetry. The *New York Review of Books*, perhaps the most influential organ for the dissemination of literary culture in this country, almost never reviews poetry by living American authors.[11] Vehicles of mainstream culture like the *New Yorker, Commentary,* the *Nation,* the *New Republic, Harper's,* and the *Atlantic* only rarely cover new poetry, even though they do publish individual poems.

For Joseph Epstein, the reasons for this decline in poetry's general importance are clear. Epstein's essay "Who Killed Poetry?" focuses on what he sees as a qualitative decline in American poetry since the modernist generation of Pound, Eliot, Stevens, Crane, Williams, Moore, Cummings, and Auden. These poets, Epstein claims, were "true" artists, whatever their actual "profession" happened to be. Their work was memorable: "[O]nce read, it never is quite forgotten." Contemporary poets, on the other hand, are "professional" without being imaginative, talented, or even particularly competent: "[T]he entire enterprise of poetic creation seems threatened by having been taken out of the world, chilled in the classroom, overproduced by men and women who are licensed to write it by degree if not necessarily by talent or spirit."[12] Epstein's article can easily be criticized for its tendentious rhetoric about the decline in standards and its almost completely subjective rationale. His arguments about the increasing dominance of the university in poetic life, about the overprofessionalization of poets, about the breakdown of language use in our society generally, and about the gradual weakening of post-Romantic lyric modes may be facile and unsupported, but they are not easily dismissed. Despite his conservative modernist bias, Epstein makes some trenchant observations about the state of contemporary poetry. He identifies a generic problem: an overemphasis on the short lyric as the focal point of contemporary poetry since the New Criticism. While a good deal of recent work has been done in other poetic forms (the existence of which Epstein seems largely unaware), it is clearly the personal post-Romantic lyric that continues to receive the lion's share of attention in the mainstream poetic community, and that remains the basis of workshop practice in the vast majority of creative-writing programs.

Perhaps of more interest than Epstein's essay itself, however, is the reaction to the essay by various members of the poetic community. In two consecutive issues of its official publication, the *AWP Chronicle,* the Associated Writing Programs ran a "special symposium" devoted to Epstein's essay, including both a reprint of the essay itself and responses by some thirty poets, editors, and administrators. These ranged from extremely negative assessments to favorable reviews by those who agreed wholly or in part with Epstein's position. What is sociologically significant in the range of responses is that Epstein appears to have succeeded in dividing the poetry world into two opposed camps: a small group of those who feel similarly disaffected by the status quo, and a larger group who either dismiss Epstein's criticisms (one poet calls them "just plain silly") or who feel personally affronted by them.

One of the more vocal commentators in the symposium was Dana Gioia, who used the opportunity to frame his response to Epstein's piece as a point of departure for his own essay of two years later. Gioia is essentially in agreement with Epstein's essay: while he distinguishes himself somewhat from Epstein in emphasizing the fact that he "care[s] passionately for contemporary American poetry," he admits that Epstein's "pessimistic assessment of the literary situation is all too sound." In his *Atlantic* essay, later reprinted in his book *Can Poetry Matter?* Gioia may be more even-handed than Epstein, but his conclusions concerning the state of the poetic mainstream are no less negative. Gioia, in fact, goes beyond Epstein in identifying a more fundamental concern with the demographic fact of what he considers an overpopulation of poets in this country. Gioia finds paradoxical the fact that "the engines that have driven poetry's institutional success—the explosion of academic writing programs, the proliferation of subsidized magazines and presses, the emergence of a creative-writing career track, and the migration of American literary culture to the university—have unwittingly contributed to its disappearance from public view."[13] This disappearance has been the result of several key factors, Gioia argues: the failure of the mainstream print and other media to provide adequate coverage of poetry; the creation of a poetry subculture that publishes magazines, books, and anthologies that present mediocre work and make little attempt to reach out to a larger audience; the lack of more public venues for poetry, such as readings on radio or presentations that combine poetry with other arts; the decline in the quality of poetry reviewing; and, finally, the professional homogeneity created by academic writing programs. In several of these respects Gioia's critique echoes Epstein's; but Gioia casts his net more broadly, condemning the sociocultural and economic infrastructure of American poetry as well as its individual practitioners and critics.

Gioia's essay may not have received the instant notoriety of Epstein's piece, but it has over time achieved the even greater status of a cause célèbre; *Can Poetry Matter?* even garnered a nomination for the National Book Critics Circle Award. Partly because Gioia is himself a practicing poet, partly because of the less elitist, even populist tone of his essay, and partly because his criticisms are by now so familiar as to hardly raise an eyebrow in the poetic community, his work has attracted less negative reaction than Epstein's, although reviews have for the most part been more critical of the book than favorable. Lance Dean's brief review in *American Literature*, for example, sums up the major problems with the book, pointing to its "view of poetry [that] is rather narrow and too often self-righteously proclaimed," and to Gioia's evident enjoyment of "being contrary" for the sake of contrariness.[14]

In denouncing academic poetry criticism, Gioia ignores the fact that academics such as Charles Altieri and Charles Molesworth have already discussed with far greater critical finesse many of the same issues he raises. One wonders, given the lack of a critical apparatus in his book, how much academic poetry criticism Gioia has actually read, but one also wonders at times how much *poetry* he has read, beyond the poets he discusses in the book. Steven Yenser and Calvin Bedient, both "academic" poets who have published distinguished books of criticism as well as poetry, point out in their reviews the numerous contradictions and inaccuracies of Gioia's argument. Bedient is particularly sharp on the subject of Gioia's problematic relationship to modernism: how can Gioia simultaneously reject the "mandarin aestheticism" of modernism and celebrate the poetry of both Eliot and Stevens? As Bedient suggests, Gioia may favor a return to a premodernist sensibility of simplicity and "structural integrity," but he offers little insight into what kind of poetry could effectively replace the modernist and postmodernist mode: "His historical sense is too conservative, too complacent, to open the question of what new art might be needed now, in view of a recent cultural shift."[15] Though less harsh than Yenser—who disparages almost everything about Gioia's book—Bedient suggests real problems with Gioia's critical abilities, especially with his "tolerance for mediocrity" and insufficient understanding of the modernist project.

In a review in the *American Book Review*, Marjorie Perloff also takes issue with the major points of Gioia's essay, though from quite a different perspective from Bedient's. While it at first appears surprising to see Perloff—herself a champion of the avant-garde and an unabashed critic of the poetic mainstream—defending contemporary poetry against Gioia's attacks, one can well understand why she would want to challenge his claims. What Perloff appears to find most objectionable is not the conclusions Gioia draws but the smugness of his critical stance and the largely unsupported hyperbole of his rhetoric. After all, Gioia's attack on contemporary poetic culture assumes the value of a traditional canon of older white male poets—including Donald Justice, Anthony Hecht, Donald Hall, James Merrill, Louis Simpson, William Stafford, and Richard Wilbur—which is antithetical to the experimental canon Perloff espouses. Perloff's rebuttal of the points made by Gioia's book seems at times more a reaction to the sententiousness of his tone than to the substance of his critiques of mainstream poetry, many of which she agrees with. While she readily concurs, for example, with Gioia's basic premise that "nine-tenths of the so-called 'poets' that teach at this or that university have very little talent," she draws very different conclusions from this fact. For Perloff, it is not clear that any correlation exists between the quality of poetry written by these creative-writing professors and their ability to teach students, an assumption at the heart of Gioia's discussion.

More important, Perloff identifies in Gioia's essay, and in his book as a whole, both a latent conservatism often masked as a kind of progressivism, and an unrigorous and sometimes even illogical rhetoric. If much of what Gioia claims is indeed true, he weakens his argument with unfortunate examples. Gioia displays his own ignorance (or at least his lack of critical perspicacity) in claiming that Allen Ginsberg's *Howl,* one of the genuinely "popular" books of poetry published in the past forty years, is nothing more than "slogan shouting," or that John Ashbery—one of the few contemporary poets whose name actually is known to a larger reading public—is merely a "discursive poet without a subject." Further, Gioia's language and argumentation are often imprecise: terms like the "common reader" and the "decline" in poetry's audience are only weakly defined; his assumptions about what "any intelligent reader" would think are biased, patronizing, and arguably both racist and sexist; his one-sided arguments about the decreasing audience for poetry and the problems caused by the creative-writing academic culture are not sufficiently supported. As Perloff suggests, one could just as easily argue that the university, rather than destroying poetry, has created a ready-made audience for poetry such as never existed before. In theory, at least, "the campus may well be the most democratic site for [poetry's] dissemination." There is no inherent problem with having the university be the privileged site of American poetry, Perloff argues; instead, it is the promotion of inferior or uninteresting poets, both within and without academia, that has proved deleterious to American poetry. These problems are not the fault of the university itself, but of more general misconceptions about what poetry is or can be in contemporary society.[16]

While there may be a degree of truth in what Gioia says about the insularity and thoughtless self-promotion of many poets within mainstream academic culture, the motives behind his argument remain somewhat unclear. Why is Gioia so quick to condemn a creative-writing culture when a good part of the canon of poets he supports are or have been academics? And what are the aesthetic criteria by which he decides what is "good" poetry and what is not? Why are Donald Justice, Weldon Kees, and Anthony Hecht in Gioia's canon, and Ginsberg, Ashbery, and the Language poets out? As Perloff suggests, the world of contemporary poetry has become too "open, fluid [and] anarchic" for the kind of facile aesthetic judgments Gioia makes. Is the New Formalism really the last best hope for American poetry, as Gioia suggests on the final pages of his book? If Gioia supports poetry that exemplifies both an opposition to the "middle-aged generation that dominates the poetry establishment" and an "accessibility to non-specialist readers,"[17] should he not embrace poets like Ginsberg and the post-Beat urban poets of "poetry slams," or poets of the new multicultural canon such as Linda Hogan and Jessica Hagedorn, rather than a group of white male establishment writers from the highly educated elite? If American poetic culture is bankrupt, it is not because not enough people read poetry (as Gioia claims), or because too many people write it (as he also claims), but because the mainstream press prefers to cover biographies, autobiographies, and self-help books rather than serious literature.

But the degree of interest generated by Gioia's book suggests a deeper insecurity in the poetry culture. Ironically, Gioia has become far more famous as the author of *Can Poetry Matter?* than he probably ever would have become simply by writing poetry. The interest in the book indicates that anyone willing to take a strong position on contemporary poetry, however biased or imprecise, immediately stands as a beacon for the thousands in the poetry culture who are dissatisfied with the status quo yet afraid or unwilling to voice their dissatisfaction publicly.

In fact, most poets, editors, critics, and reviewers today are reluctant to articulate the formal, aesthetic, or ideational qualities of exemplary poetic writing even in the relatively imprecise way Gioia does. The present climate has discouraged not only original thinking about poetry, but any rigorous standards for evaluating that poetry. Given the decreasing visibility of poetry in our culture, the decreasing degree of consensus about what poets and what poetry journals must be read in order to keep abreast of the rapidly changing poetry scene, and the decreasing ability of critics to provide meaningful descriptions of current developments in poetry, it is understandable that very few nonspecialists follow contemporary poetry at all. Even those academics who teach and write on poetry have the time to know in detail the work of only a few poets. Torn between the exigencies of critical theory and cultural studies, the expanding literary canon required by an increasingly multicultural curriculum, an ever-growing body of critical and secondary work on canonical writers, and the demand for more specialized fields of personal expertise, academic critics and scholars find themselves with little time or energy for the kind of general discussion of poetry—or, for that matter, of *any* form of contemporary literature—that took place in American intellectual life only a few decades ago. This problem is exacerbated by the fact that fewer and fewer poetry specialists are being hired to teach in academic literature departments, and fewer poems are being taught in literature classes.[18]

In this environment, it should come as no surprise that active critical debate about poetry, except in extremely limited circles, has ceased to be of any vital cultural importance. In fact, the lack of active critical debate about poetry in this country has encouraged an insular mentality: many presses and journals have become identified with a certain kind of writing (i.e., mainstream, multicultural or experimental), to the point where there is little self-reflexivity about what they will publish, or why. Reviewers for these journals are often sympathetic only to the narrowly defined type of poetry that the journal publishes and reviews. The reviews of new poetry that appear in such journals as *Poetry* and the *Hudson Review* give a sense of the tastes and opinions of the reviewer, but they rarely provide critical insights into the current trends in contemporary poetry or landmarks to guide the reader through an unnavigable morass of mainstream verse.[19] Many of the most prominent American poets eschew writing criticism and reviews altogether, perhaps out of fear that any negative comments about a fellow poet will lead to later reprisals against their own work and careers. While such reticence may be justified in the name of professional harmony and supportiveness within an already marginalized community, it deprives contemporary poetic culture of a much needed infusion of meaningful critical debate. As Jed Rasula suggests, most poetry reviewing "makes no attempt to contextualize poetry (in relation even to other art institutions, let alone the life of a community or a group)" and the poetry review is often no more than a kind of glorified book report narrating a self-indulgent moment of readerly introspection. Literary critics who provide candid and insightful discussions of current poetic practice are increasingly rare, to the point where much criticism of contemporary poetry is "so routinely unadventurous that it amounts to in-house copy for the poetry discussed."[20] To make matters worse, the editorial statements of journals and presses are often no more than empty formulations that rely on a prior knowledge of the journal's taste: *Partisan Review* asks for "poetry of high quality" and Pittsburgh University Press for "poetry of the highest quality"; *Field* seeks the "best possible" poetry; the *Gettysburg Review* works by tautology, accepting "any poetry except that which is badly written."[21] Few presses and journals have the degree of individual identity to give a more specific description of the kind of poetry they publish: as a result, the vast majority of literary publications are virtually indistinguishable from one another. When editors of established literary magazines attempt to stretch the boundaries of mainstream taste by including more work in multicultural or experimental modes, as Marilyn Hacker did during her tenure at the *Kenyon Review,* they risk being replaced by more conservative stewards.[22]

Commentators with different and even polarized critical perspectives have characterized the decreasing quality and relevance of poetry criticism in recent years. Dana Gioia points to the clubbiness and boosterism of poets, critics, editors, and anthologists who fail to take a critical or evaluative stand on each others' works. According to Gioia, "critical prose exists not to provide a disinterested perspective on new books but to publicize them." At the other end of the critical spectrum, Alan Golding deplores the "Language-bashing" practiced by many critics and reviewers who attack poetic experimentation such as that of the Language poets without paying adequate attention to what the poems themselves attempt to do. In what Golding characterizes as a "scapegoat-hungry literary culture," challenging work like that of the Language group is superficially dismissed with "a few cracks about tedium, fragmentation, a desiccated esthetic, and dehumanization." Finally, Hank Lazer comments on the "dismal state of institutionalized criticism of poetry" today; as Lazer suggests, most contemporary criticism is "given over either to aesthetically dominated judgmental reviews (mainly short blurbs of praise written by peer-poets implicated in the literary/professional networks they are asked to judge) or to an academically sanctioned (mis)application of current critical theory to canonically (and professionally) acceptable extended readings of 'major' contemporary poets."[23]

What Lazer identifies is not only the diminished status and quality of poetry criticism and reviewing, but the increasingly apparent split between the criticism and scholarship of "academic critics" (PhD-holding professors in literature departments) and the kind of critical writing generated by MFA-trained poets who write about their fellow poets. The problem with the criticism of contemporary American poetry lies largely in the changing institutional status of both creative writing and academic criticism. As Michael Bérubé points out, the almost complete separation of these two fields, a separation that has become more marked over the past twenty or thirty years, "has created two distinct arenas of literary criticism, two distinct prestige systems, neither of which is professionally relevant to the other." These two systems are mutually exclusive not only on a professional level (*PMLA* and *Critical Inquiry* versus *Poets and Writers* and *AWP Chronicle*, PhD versus MFA, literature faculties versus creative writing faculties), but on an intellectual and cultural level as well. The issues of concern to professional academic critics are of little interest to professional poets, and vice versa: their discussions take part "in different loci, different vocabularies, and different publications." The problem, Bérubé explains, "is not that there are so few poet-critics, but that there are so few poet-critics who are read and cited in both kinds of contemporary criticism, the kind published in *Antaeus* and the kind published in *Diacritics*." [24] Bérubé chooses extreme examples to illustrate his point, but even if we consider the academic center, there is little overlap between the readership of such journals as *Contemporary Literature* on the literary-critical side and *American Poetry Review* on the creative-writing side.

The split of creative writers and literary scholar-critics into two virtually separate communities is partly the consequence of the increasing bureaucratic and institutional framework that has grown up around the creative-writing academy and its affiliated culture. The umbrella organization for creative writers, the AWP, was created in 1967 as an institutional alternative to the MLA (Modern Language Association of America), which had given little attention to creative writing as a discipline within literary studies. [25] One index of this trend toward self-referential professionalism in recent decades has been the steady growth of publications specifically serving the creative-writing community. These include not only the *AWP Chronicle* (which serves much the same function for the Associated Writing Programs as do the various publications of the MLA for its constituents), but the bimonthly journal *Poets and Writers* (revealingly proclaiming itself the "*Wall Street Journal* of our profession"), *American Poetry Review* (a bimonthly geared primarily to a readership of creative writers), regional newsletters like *Poetry Flash* (serving the West Coast, the San Francisco Bay Area in particular), and magazines such as *Poetry Exchange, Poetry Connection,* and *Poet.* They also include annual anthologies that claim to present the "best" of American poetry, as well as guides, now deemed indispensable to practicing poets, like *Poet's Market, Directory of Poetry Publishers,* and *AWP Official Guide to Creative Writing Programs,* "how-to" books and magazines with titles such as *Writer's Digest, Writer's Journal, Byline* magazine, *The Art and Craft of Poetry, Creating Poetry,* and *The Poet's Handbook.* The reason for the appearance of such publications is clear: they respond both to the rapidly expanding numbers of poets, poems, and books of poetry, and to the increasing professionalism of poetry in this country. In emphasizing the practical aspects of writing and marketing poetry over the more aesthetic and intellectual aspects of poetry, these guides contribute to the idea of poetry as a technique, craft, or hobby rather than an intellectual discipline with a highly complex cultural history.

Barrett Watten has offered one of the most trenchant critiques of the "stultification of literary process" that has resulted from the ideological division between intellectual life and contemporary literary practice in this country. According to Watten, the "marginalization of the avant-garde" has been perpetuated and encouraged in large part by the spread of creative-writing programs within the academy. As a result of the "professionalization" of creative writing as a separate discipline from English literature, both the study and the funding of contemporary literature have been abandoned to the creative-writing programs, which are more interested in reinforcing "the poetics and politics of [a] threatened petit-bourgeois personal life" than in engaging any deeper form of literary or cultural politics.[26]

Other critics have commented on this same phenomenon. As Sandra Gilbert argues, criticism written by those contemporary poets who attempt it is "largely technical and confessional, as though most of these writers fear that they're ill equipped to make large judgements of either tradition and the individual talent." On the other hand, as Patrick Parrinder reminds us, contemporary critical and cultural theory is at least partly responsible for encouraging the discursive gap, since "the major critical theorists of the present day would rather reinterpret the established classics, from Plato to Virginia Woolf, than discuss contemporary poetry." Marjorie Perloff has demonstrated the almost complete lack of attention to modern or contemporary poetry on the part of academic criticism: "The [critical] drive to move 'Beyond the New Criticism' does not, it seems, prompt the desire to learn about the poetry, indeed any of the fictive discourses, of one's own world."[27] As a result of this dissociation of sensibilities, we find an increasing tendency to insulate contemporary criticism and theory from any understanding of the basic production practices of literature.

The disappearance of both the poet-critic who is still read by literary academics and the academic poetry critic who is still read by practicing poets reflects deep institutional changes in the structure of American literary criticism. Professional poets ignore most academic criticism, which they see as either too narrow or too theoretical, and the literary academy excludes or marginalizes the critical work of those poets—like Ron Silliman and Amiri Baraka—who pose a challenge to its highly systematized critical vocabulary. Yet academic critics, with few exceptions, seem relatively unconcerned with this state of affairs. Jonathan Culler acknowledges contemporary criticism's "lack of connection to a recognized literary avant-garde," but rather than working toward rectifying the situation, he uses it as an occasion to celebrate contemporary academic theory as a replacement for the (apparently extinct) literary avant-garde.[28]

If Culler is correct in his analysis of the change that has taken place—the shift from the New Criticism of Brooks, Ransom, Tate, and Warren to structuralist and poststructuralist modes, which cannot as easily be seen as "explicating or promoting" contemporary literary practice—he is wrong to claim that criticism or "theory" can replace the function of the avant-garde. While it is true that criticism shares with avant-garde art the function of "generating questions about discursive knowledge" and of pursuing "contestatory" strategies, we must question what happens when criticism relinquishes its role as an explanatory or corollary practice and attempts to assume the creative or political role of the literary avant-garde itself. For one thing, the place of academic critics within the institutional structure of the university makes any real sociopolitical critique ineffectual, or at best highly contextualized; it is pure narcissism to see academic criticism or theory as having any significant impact outside the academy. More important, criticism's appropriation of the space once held by avant-garde literary practice would consign all contemporary literature to a second-class status. If "today the avant-garde simply *is* literary theory and criticism," as Culler suggests, then all experimental movements that attempt to articulate a genuine avant-garde practice are marginalized in the academy with respect to the "real" avant-garde (the theory of Derrida and

Baudrillard).[29] Contemporary poetry and fiction, when they are discussed at all within the academy, are assumed to be conventional expressions of bourgeois aesthetic ideology with no discursive agency except as revealed by "theory." Culler's argument has the effect of de-emphasizing the important formal and ideological differences *between* literary practices, collapsing Kathy Acker's work into John Updike's, or Susan Howe's into Philip Levine's. Culler's apparent ignorance of an active avant-garde practice in both fiction and poetry is disturbing in that it indicates the isolation of innovative literary practices from the discourses of academic criticism and theory. Contemporary poetry has thus suffered not only from its own institutional practices, but from its neglect by the very readers—those highly trained in the critical reading of texts—best qualified to understand it.

Perhaps American poetry will never again achieve the level of high cultural status it enjoyed in the 1950s and 1960s, when poets like T. S. Eliot and Robert Lowell were lionized as cultural heroes. Nevertheless, it can only be seen as ironic that the prognostications of poetry's imminent death have coincided with a general resurgence of popular interest in poetry. The 1990s have seen the incipient signs of a reawakening of nonacademic interest in poetry. Poets appear in movies—from *Poetic Justice* (1993), with Janet Jackson reciting poems by Maya Angelou, to *Love Jones* (1997), a love story involving a hip young poet from Chicago's open mike bar scene, to *Slam,* the winner of the Grand Jury Prize at the 1997 Sundance Film Festival, in which a black street poet (played by poet Saul Williams) is jailed on a drug charge and finds release for his rage in the prison's spoken-word movement. Poets participate in open mikes and poetry slams at local bars and coffeehouses in every city in America. They meet to hear readings and attend workshops at literary centers like Poets House in New York City, the Loft in Minneapolis, the Literary Center in Seattle, Beyond Baroque in Venice/Santa Monica, and the Writer's Center in Bethesda, Maryland. They attend large gatherings of "cowboy poetry" such as that held annually in Elko, Nevada, and events like the annual Poetry Circus of readings and performance contests held in Taos, New Mexico. They use electronic media such as the Internet to "publish" poetry (via electronic journals), to create poetry archives and Web sites, and to build communities of poets who can exchange ideas and information about poetry and poetics. They appear on television in such programs as *Words in Your Face, MTV Unplugged, The United States of Poetry,* and *The Language of Life,* and on ads for Nike. Poets now experiment with various "crossover" formats between poetry and other media, including video, rap, MTV, and contemporary music. These crossovers include the experiments in spoken performance by such poets as Anne Waldman, Bob Holman, Miguel Algarin, Jessica Hagedorn, Quincy Troupe, Victor Hernandez Cruz, Wanda Coleman, Michele Clinton, Emily XYZ, Luis Alfaro, Matt Cook, and Dana Bryant; the intermedia work of young poet/musicians like Maggie Estep, John S. Hall, Reg E. Gaines, Everton Sylvester, Michael Franti, and Tracie Morris; the multimedia/video poetry of Walter Lew and Gloria Toyun Park; the hypermedia/hypertext poetry of Benjamin Friedlander, Robert Grenier, Lee Ann Brown, Christopher Funkhauser, and Susan Brenner.

Significantly, all of these are signs *not* mentioned by Epstein or Gioia of the surprisingly strong interest in poetry in this country, a popular interest not dependent either on a return to literary formalism (Gioia) or on a neomodernist aesthetic (Epstein). Things are changing rapidly in the landscape of contemporary American poetry. It may be too soon to judge whether poetry is in a state of decline or in the early phase of a new renaissance, but the best places to witness poetry's vitality are no longer the pages of *Poetry* and the *New Yorker*. Cultural critics' assumptions of the "decline" or "death" of poetry dismiss changes in poetic practice all too easily, categorizing them according to an anachronistic set of aesthetic and cultural criteria.

The revitalized nonacademic poetry scene represents the convergence of several cultural developments: the cross-cultural popularity of rap; the reemergence of a "cafe" scene more conducive to poetry (largely replacing the disco and club scene of the 1970s and early 1980s); the growth of computer and communications technology; and the growing impact of multiculturalism. Perhaps the growth of the nonacademic poetry scene can also be read as the contrarian legacy of the Reagan-Bush years, a period during which ethnic and racial minorities, gays and lesbians, and artists and writers felt increasingly disenfranchised from and disillusioned with mainstream American life, and during which freedom of expression in the arts came under increasing pressure from the forces of political and moral conservatism. Poetry, especially in the form of slams and open readings, provided disempowered groups with a social forum both for political venting and for creative display. Finally, we might read the almost instantaneous popularity of the slam, spoken-word, and open-reading phenomenon as the reaction of a younger generation of poets against the encrusted and insular system of mainstream academic poetry that has constituted the only context for poetry most poets and readers under forty have ever known. In fact, the beginnings of the slam coincided with the waning of academic creative writing as a growth industry in the late 1980s and early 1990s, and the simultaneous downturn in spending on individual writers' grants by the NEA.

The current poetry and spoken-word scene can be found in various manifestations throughout the United States and Canada. In Chicago, where the slam was invented in the late 1980s, poetry emerged as a working-class phenomenon, creating a blue-collar poetic community in opposition to the more genteel academic milieu that had dominated Chicago's poetry scene. In New York, both the St. Mark's Poetry Project and the Nuyorican Poets Cafe have been crucial sites of nonacademic poetry, as have various reading venues such as the Ear Inn, Biblio's and Jackie 60. Los Angeles has quietly emerged as an important center of West Coast poetry, where a form of populist performance poetry variously called "Standup Poetry," "Easy Poetry," or "Long Beach Poetry" has combined stand-up comedy and the post-Beat poetry exemplified by the work of Charles Bukowski. In 1995, Long Beach hosted the "When Words Collide" spoken-word festival, with performances by over a hundred poets and spoken-word artists, including Patti Smith and Laurie Anderson. Harvey Kubernick's LA-based New Alliance record label has issued numerous spoken-word collections, as well as recordings by individual artists such as Luis Alfaro, Michelle Clinton, Wanda Coleman, and Linda Albertano. Spoken word has blossomed in Canada and in the Pacific Northwest as well: Portland's Tim Kerr Records has released the spoken-word CD *Talking Rain,* and Virgin/EMI's Canadian division has produced *Word Up,* a CD compilation of Canadian and U.S. poets.

Clearly, poetry is not dead, though some poets and critics may be temporarily confused about poetry's place within the destabilized field of contemporary culture. All the evidence suggests that poetry—if defined in its widest parameters—is very much alive. Clearly, poetry *can* matter in all sorts of ways and to all sorts of people. It can matter to poets if they can move beyond their factionalism and begin to appreciate the tremendous energy and variety of contemporary poetic expression. It can matter to academics and intellectuals if they can once again be made to see the value of poetry as a cultural practice with significant avant-garde, communitarian, and pedagogical potential. And it can matter to readers and listeners if they can be exposed to the most innovative and challenging poetries through whatever forms of media prove most effective in spreading both the spoken and the written word.

Within five years there will be a creative writing program available for everyone in America within safe driving distance of his home.
—Greg Kuzma, "The Catastrophe of Creative Writing"

2. Careers in Creativity
The Poetry Academy in the 1990s

The movement of poetry writing into the university, and more specifically into the institutional context of the creative-writing program or workshop, has been the single most significant demographic phenomenon in American poetry since World War II. In recent years, the rapid growth of a creative-writing culture and the emergence of a poetry academy of unprecedented size and influence have made creative-writing programs the object of a vociferous and often hostile critique. If writing programs are not criticized for their ethic of small-minded careerism, their trivializing techniques of poetic writing, or their homogenizing tendencies, they are chastised for producing too much poetry too quickly and for emphasizing quantity at the expense of quality. J. D. McClatchy, for example, has criticized the poems written by the workshop faculties and their students, "whose unversed minds became the measure of all things," largely by stressing what he sees as the everyday banality of their topics ("urban chanties, epiphanies around the backyard barbecue, work songs for the twice-divorced kitchen brigade"), the "slackness" and "poverty" of their technique, and the "unrelieved tedium of speechliness," in which "a deliberately 'anti-poetic' rhetoric turns into the formulaic slogans of reportage."[1] For McClatchy, such programs have a strong tendency to homogenize the poetry produced not only in the individual workshop or department, but multiplied ad infinitum on a national scale.

The rapid growth in academic creative writing is not an altogether surprising phenomenon, given the fact that the university has come increasingly to be the only viable center of American cultural life. The system of higher education has become the single most important source of cultural capital, and the single most powerful agent in legitimating that capital. American poetry, to an even greater extent than fiction and other forms of literary writing, has come to depend on the university for its primary economic and cultural base. The university system now functions as the major screening mechanism for the poetry culture, as a means of including some poets and excluding others; it also functions more subtly as a mechanism for making hierarchical distinctions concerning the most prestigious programs and poets. The growth of university creative-writing programs, which expanded professional opportunities for poets throughout the 1960s, 1970s, and 1980s, has now created a difficult situation for those poets not already securely employed within the system.[2] The number of unemployed and underemployed MFAs living in America's university towns grows every year. The inflation of poetic résumés in recent years is a direct response to this situation: today a published book of poems, in addition to the MFA, has become a virtual prerequisite for poets who wish to be employed at the university or college level.

Several reasons for this rapid growth can be proposed: (1) a relatively flat economy, with fewer career opportunities for a highly educated population in their twenties and thirties; (2) a widespread need for modes of individual self-expression, manifested in everything from the growing number of television talk shows to the number of aspiring creative writers; (3) a geographic dispersion and democratization of poetic practice that has moved the centers of poetic influence away from large urban areas such as New York, Chicago, and San Francisco, and beyond such universities as Harvard, Columbia, and Stanford; (4) the dominance of more accessible forms and genres of poetry (confessional, free verse, narrative lyric), which can be written without a strong sense of poetic tradition or a high degree of technical mastery, and which can be easily taught in a classroom or workshop environment; (5) the need on the part of the university to find a new growth area as enrollment in more traditional fields such as English literature, foreign languages, philosophy, and art history have declined; (6) the abandonment, within literature departments, of more traditional literary authors and approaches, leaving the study of such authors and approaches increasingly in the hands of creative-writing departments.

Clearly, the rapidity and extent of the growth in creative writing has been a source of consternation to many in the poetry culture; according to some, it has produced a state of crisis in the American poetry academy at the very moment of its seeming success.[3] Critics like Greg Kuzma, Bruce Bawer, and Dana Gioia comment sardonically, and perhaps hyperbolically, on the overpopulation of creative-writing programs and the disappearance of individual creativity in a workshop process that relies on academic assignments and functions in a spirit of bureaucratic professionalism. Even R. V. Cassill, the founder and first president of the AWP, has argued for the deinstitutionalization of creative writing and the disbanding of the AWP itself.[4] Is academic creative writing, then, an idea that has served its function, an institution whose time has come and gone? Does the entrenched network of academic poetry constitute an elitist and reactionary front, a wall of vested power and institutional status that marginalizes alternative poetic cultures and discourages the participation of groups from outside the academic mainstream? Has the "industry" of creative writing reduced the production of poetry and poets to simply another "job," a job no different in kind from that of any other professionally trained worker? Does the "workshop" model that characterizes the vast majority of programs lead to a homogenization of technique and a silencing of alternative paradigms and approaches?

The fact that critics of the current academic poetry culture have been more numerous and more rhetorically persuasive than its defenders should not in itself be seen as a proof that their claims are more valid. Yet this imbalance in discursive power raises an important question: how does the current creative-writing poetry culture justify itself—its objectives, its aspirations—beyond the immediate goal of responding to an apparent demand on the part of students who believe they have the talent to be professional poets and the corresponding need for academic poets to earn a living teaching poetry writing?

This question has not been answered in any rigorous way, since the creative-writing program as a postwar cultural phenomenon is rarely mentioned in literary-historical studies of the period, either in terms of its effect on the poetry written or in terms of its relationship to critical or scholarly activity within literature departments. David Perkins never mentions the emergence of creative-writing programs in his *History of Modern Poetry*, and even Robert von Hallberg's *American Poetry and Culture, 1945–1980* fails to address the impact of such programs in any direct way. Sociocultural studies of the literary profession, such as Grant Webster's *The Republic of Letters* and Gerald Graff's *Professing Literature*, are also silent about the phenomenon. The dearth of critical discussion and even of documentation (with the exception of Stephen Wilbers's book on the Iowa creative-writing program) undermines any definitive understanding of the cultural dynamics of the postwar academic literary scene.[5]

One way of attempting to gain a better understanding of these dynamics is to examine the ways in which the poetry academy has affected both the means of poetic production and the status of poetry within the larger field of cultural production. It is important to remind ourselves that the institutionalized system of academic poetry I have been discussing is still a fairly recent phenomenon. Aside from the poets who attended the Iowa program in the 1930s, 1940s, and 1950s, and the relatively small number of other programs in the 1950s and 1960s, the professionally oriented MFA program in poetry became a significant demographic force only in the 1970s, and a dominant institutional structure only in the 1980s.[6] It may be too early to reach any final conclusions about the effect the academization of American poetry has had, or will have, on poetic practice. What *is* clear is that American poetry has undergone a very significant paradigm shift. In the three decades from approximately 1955 to 1985, American poetic culture transformed itself from a system virtually independent of academic creative-writing programs to a system extremely dependent on such programs. The MFA has become universally accepted as the terminal degree in poetry writing—the full equivalent of the PhD for literary academics—and virtually a prerequisite for teaching positions. The vast majority of those winning the major awards for younger poets over the past two decades (Guggenheims, Lamont prizes, and National Poetry Series, for example) have held graduate degrees in creative writing.[7]

It is also clear that before the creative-writing program became the dominant site of poetic production in the 1960s and 1970s, poets received a very different training and followed a markedly different career path. From the 1920s until the 1950s, most poets had literary careers that remained largely independent of the institutional framework provided by the academy. The path to poetic success may have been just as predictable as that of today's poets, but it followed a different set of rules: acceptance of one's work by the literary magazines, especially *Poetry;* publication of a first "thin book" of poems, preferably by a reputable trade press; and, finally, for the lucky few, favorable reviews in one of the larger circulation journals that covered poetry and some measure of renown and support within literary circles. The typical poet of the prewar and immediate postwar eras would have had a college degree but no formal training in the craft of poetry itself. Without the ready-made structure of the creative-writing network, a poetic career was more difficult to construct than it is today—following a less clearly articulated set of guidelines—and it involved a positive reception by a far smaller coterie of writers, critics, publishers, and readers.

In the 1950s, for example, many of the poets who were later to become major figures in postwar American poetry wrote for ephemeral magazines, small presses, and extremely limited readerships. They also had diverse educations and worked in a wide range of jobs before achieving any kind of mainstream poetic success. A. R. Ammons worked as an elementary school principal and business executive. John Ashbery went to Paris on a Fulbright and worked there as an art critic for most of the next decade. Robert Creeley worked as a farmer in New Hampshire, lived in France and Mallorca, and taught at schools in Albuquerque and Guatemala. Allen Ginsberg worked for a military sea transport, as a book reviewer for *Newsweek*, and as a market researcher, before publishing *Howl* in 1956. W. S. Merwin worked as a tutor in France, Portugal, and Mallorca, and as a freelance translator in London, before *A Mask for Janus* was chosen for the Yale Series of Younger Poets in 1952. Amiri Baraka (Leroi Jones) served in the U.S. Air Force as a climatographer and aerial gunner, founded *Yugen* magazine and the Totem Press, coedited *Floating Bear*, and worked as a jazz critic and reviewer. Gary Snyder followed his studies in anthropology with Buddhist study in Japan, and worked as a logger, fire lookout, and merchant seaman. While the trend of poets studying at places like the Iowa Writers' Workshop and the University of Washington was already beginning to affect the careers of poets in the 1950s and early 1960s—as seen in the examples of Richard Hugo, James Wright, David Wagoner, and Donald Justice—poets with formal academic training in "creative writing" were still in the minority. The historical shift from the paradigm of the generation of poets who emerged in the 1950s to the succeeding generation of largely MFA-trained poets who emerged in the late 1960s and 1970s represents a significant change in the cultural definition of poetry as an institutional practice.

Written in 1965, Harrison and Cynthia White's *Canvasses and Careers* remains one of the benchmark studies of institutional changes in the art world, and of their effects on the kind of art produced. The Whites trace the emergence of a dominant institution in French nineteenth-century painting—which they call the "Academic" system—and the decline of that system in the later part of the century. The Whites' book provides a seminal model for understanding the institutional networks that exist in any artistic or literary profession, and an interesting analogue for the current growth of the academic poetry network. Their study is especially significant because it was one of the first to document not just the lives and contacts of the "major" artists, but the situation of the "run-of-the-mill" artist as it is reflected in an "institutional system of organizations, rules, and customs."[8]

The first poetry critic to note the parallels between the French academic painters of the 1850s and the current institutionalization of poetry was Charles Altieri, who set in relief the way in which, in both cases, "extraordinarily skillful artists created a climate skeptical of any intellectual role for the medium, hence trapping it within a narrow equation of lucidity and elegantly controlled surfaces."[9] Institutionally, too, the systems appear similar: both creating a form of "inbred professionalism" by relying too much on the praise and support of other professionals within the same network rather than directly seeking sources of patronage among a consuming public. The Whites' study would seem to support Altieri's comparison of the academic system as it emerged in France in the late eighteenth and early nineteenth centuries and the academic workshop system of American poetry as it evolved in the 1970s and 1980s. Indeed, the parallels are striking. Among the most salient are (1) the rapid growth in the number of official academies and academic painters, similar to the accelerating increase in the number of poetry MFA programs and academic positions; (2) the geographic dispersal of artists from the center of cultural power (Paris) to local academies in cities throughout France, similar to the dispersal of poets from literary centers in Boston, New York, and San Francisco to creative-writing programs in cities and small university towns all over this country; and (3) the centralization of the systems of power and influence within the art culture through contests, stipends, commissions, salon exhibitions, and academic positions that created an "official route to success" within the world of painting, similar to the currently sanctioned "official verse culture."

Ironically, the success of the academy in producing painters would also be its downfall. By the 1860s, there were more than three thousand professional painters in the system, producing at least twenty thousand canvases a year: far too many to be supported by a country the size of France in either cultural or economic terms. As the Whites comment, "the true talent of the Academic system became obscured in the unprecedented mass of painters and paintings it had generated, and this flood choked its earlier ability to adapt to and moderate nuclei of radical art."[10] This glut of art produced not only a sense of satiation in the market and in the popular taste, but also a stultifying effect on painters attempting to achieve anything outside the prescribed bounds of academic decorum. It was this situation that ultimately led to the creation of a new system that would allow, and even encourage, more innovative paintings, such as those of the Impressionists. The new paradigm that emerged, the "dealer-and-critic" system, played an increasingly central role after the 1860s, and resulted in the most important paintings of Manet, Renoir, Monet, Degas, and others.

Altieri's analogy of the current poetic culture with French academic painting raises important questions. What were the sociohistorical conditions that allowed the current system of American poetry to emerge? Is the academic system of "creative writing" likely to meet the same disastrous fate as the nineteenth-century academic system described by the Whites? Given the still-rising popularity of creative-writing programs, it might seem premature to make any such prognostications; however, Thomas Disch has recently predicted just such a demise of the poetry workshop. In a recent *Hudson Review,* Disch not only calls for "the disestablishment of poetry workshops as an academic institution," but prophecies that such programs "will, in [his] own lifetime, self-destruct."[11]

While Disch may be correct in his assessment of the difficulties in sustaining the growth of creative writing as an academic discipline, the entrenchment of the poetry establishment within academia, as well as a continuing supply of interested students, makes it highly unlikely that any such "self-destruction" of the creative-writing system will occur in the near future. Though the total number of writing programs is no longer growing as rapidly as it was in the 1980s, applications to the most prominent programs continue to mount. When economic opportunities for "twenty-somethings" change, however, or when two years of study in writing poetry no longer appears a viable alternative to more practical or mainstream pursuits, we may see a dramatic exodus from the creative-writing system. It is likely that the same economic pressures that have affected the rest of the humanities over the past twenty years will eventually begin to impinge on the competitiveness and viability of creative-writing programs. Further, the extremely limited academic job prospects for graduates of these programs—even worse than for scholarly jobs requiring the PhD— may eventually have a discouraging effect on future applicants.

But the more important question concerns the effects of creative writing on poetic practice. Like Altieri, we are tempted to ask whether the emphasis on a particular kind of academic training in poetry writing has narrowed the aesthetic possibilities within the field of mainstream poetry, just as the overacademization of French art in the nineteenth century resulted in a more homogenous and "inbred" professionalism. Has the learning of a certain skill in putting together a particular kind of lyric poem come at the expense of a larger or more radical aesthetic, intellectual, or even social vision? Has the sheer growth in numbers within academic poetry, rather than supplying greater diversity, actually encouraged homogeneity and worked to marginalize alternative or experimental practices?

Jonathan Holden has been one of the few academics who have attempted in print to defend the creative-writing system. Yet Holden seems a particularly ineffective spokesman for mainstream academic poetry, weakening his own argument with unsupported assertions and spurious logic. For example, in his response to Altieri's observation that the situation of academic poetry today is not unlike that of French academic painting of the 1850s, Holden finds it sufficient merely to assert that "American poetry in the 1990s is immeasurably more vigorous and varied than nineteenth-century French academic painting," without suggesting the grounds on which an argument for such variety might be based, and without providing any particular evidence of such vigor.[12] Similarly, in responding to assertions about the general mediocrity of academic verse, Holden makes a misleading claim about the mediocrity of most work produced in any art form at any given time:

> When an art form is produced en masse, most of it will conform to the fashion of the moment, be merely competent. But why feign surprise or disappointment at this? Mediocrity is present in every human endeavor. Indeed, it is prevalent *by definition,* it is a statistical fact: In every statistical sample, there is a "median," "the value, equaled or exceeded by exactly half of the values in a given list." To decry mediocrity in any list—a list of restaurants, baseball players, attorneys, poets—is redundant.[13]

Holden's argument contains several logical fallacies. First, he begs the question of whether poetry should be produced "en masse," a question that lies at the heart of several critiques of the current academic culture. Second, he avoids what is perhaps the central issue for most critics of contemporary poetry: the concern not with the decline of the average poet, but with the decline in the literary or aesthetic standard of even the strongest mainstream poetry being produced, by academic poets like Philip Levine, Sharon Olds, and Rita Dove.

It is no doubt the case, as Holden maintains, that mediocre poems were always written; the difference today is that the sheer volume of mediocre verse that reaches print makes it more difficult for the most challenging or innovative poetry to find its way to a wider public venue. According to Len Fulton, editor of the *Directory of Poetry Publishers,* the publishing volume of poetry in America today exceeds that of 1965 by a magnitude of ten to one. Much of this increase is the direct result of creative-writing programs, which have produced poets at a far greater rate than ever before. What appears to incite many of the workshops' opponents is the sense that creative-writing programs act as an artificial stimulant to the poetry culture as a whole, creating both a supply of poetry and a demand for publishing outlets that reflect neither normal market forces nor the independent motivation of individual writers, far fewer of whom might emerge from the channels of traditional higher education than do from creative-writing programs.

According to Pierre Bourdieu's analysis of the sociocultural dynamics involved in different artistic and literary fields, poetry, at least since the mid–nineteenth century, has been defined as a highly elite genre, one in which cultural legitimation comes neither from bourgeois taste nor from a popular audience: in other words, it is defined a priori as a form of "high art." Poetry's traditional status has been that of the "disinterested activity par excellence," one that, in the post-Romantic tradition in particular, is dependent on a "charismatic legitimation" granted "to only a few individuals, sometimes only one per generation." [14] With a smaller and less diverse readership than either fiction or drama, poets traditionally compete for fewer places at the top of the pyramid of success. Poetic history over the past two centuries can in fact be characterized as a struggle for poetic legitimacy carried out either by individuals or by small and elite groups of writers who engage in a succession of successful or abortive revolutions. The situation of contemporary American poetry reflects a deep underlying tension between the cultural paradigm identified by Bourdieu and the very different paradigm represented by the world of academic creative-writing programs. On the one hand, many poets and critics still adhere to the post-Romantic ideology of the poet as an autonomous artist receiving legitimation within an elite world of personal and aesthetic contacts. It is exactly in these terms that the poetic process is defined both in the Bloomian model of one or two "strong" poets per generation who do battle with their predecessors, and in the paradigm of experimental modernism, where a series of closely defined movements—imagism, vorticism, objectivism, projectivism—attempt to revolutionize the poetic act in each historical era. On the other hand, we find the current poetic mainstream invested in the very different ideological and cultural practice of the creative-writing program. In this practice, legitimation comes not from an elite band of fellow poets, but from the institutional network of the university system, one in which poets are produced in previously unimagined numbers, in which the poetic act is defined less as a formal or aesthetic revolution than as a careful step toward the goal of impressing a teacher or enhancing one's career, and in which poetry is sold as a marketable commodity through MFA programs, university presses, journals, and reading series. The university, traditionally the "legitimating institution" that has been consigned the conservative function of restricting, consecrating, and preserving works of art, is now cast in the very different and even at times opposed role of *producing* that art. Thus two functions that have normally been kept separate—the cultural field of production and the institutional field of preservation and legitimation—are brought together in a rather tense *ménage*.

As Bourdieu's theoretical analysis suggests, there exists both in theory and in practice an uneasy relationship between the poet as independent producer and the poet as legitimator of poetic success or eminence. When Joseph Epstein criticizes the academic "workshop" poet for caring more about attending conferences and building résumés than about writing poems, he is pointing to a professional confusion between two separate spheres: what Bourdieu would call the "producers of symbolic goods" and the "legitimating institutions" that sanction them.[15] Unlike successful fiction writers, who can remain to some degree separate from the university network by virtue of their larger readership and economic autonomy, poets within the academy are completely dependent on the institution as a provider of their economic security as well as an index of their relative success. It is for this reason that the sociocultural divide between academic and nonacademic poets (the "establishment" and the "counterculture") has always been more pronounced and more contentious in the field of poetry than in other literary fields. In the 1950s and 1960s, this split became almost total, as the groups of countercultural and avant-garde poets writing outside the university—the Beats and New York Poets, for example—were virtually ignored by poets within the academy. Today, the "new academy" of the creative-writing program has similarly raised a kind of iron curtain of poetic writing, walling in a mainstream practice while excluding from its borders the work of an experimental, countercultural, or critical mode.

As Bourdieu argues, the relationship of artists and academics has always been a hierarchical one, based on unequal cultural advantages: the world of poets has traditionally been conferred a greater amount of symbolic capital in order to offset a lesser amount of economic and institutional power. It is a relationship in which the producers of poetry must denounce the "professional routine" of academics, while at the same time recognizing "that it is these [academics] who will have the last word, and that ultimate consecration can only be accorded them on an authority whose legitimacy is challenged by their entire practice, their entire professional ideology."[16] Bourdieu describes perfectly the feeling many poets and other "creative writers" express concerning their own ambivalent status within the academy, as they find themselves part of the very system their predecessors so strongly opposed. As Ron Tanner puts it in his revealingly titled "How to Be an Artist in the Anthill of Academe," many creative writers are ideologically torn: "[T]hey are so defensive—that, in order to save face among themselves they openly disdain their places as teachers, as if embarrassed, shrugging off their duties with such comments as, 'Well, teaching's a drag but it pays the bills.'" These writers, Tanner adds, "believe themselves a 'sell-out' because they are in the pay of one of the most formidable authoritarian institutions in America, the university." In some cases, these same writers go to the extreme of isolating themselves "physically and administratively from their departments," thus attempting to deny the resemblance between themselves and other kinds of university faculty.[17]

Such reactions are hardly surprising. In fact, the academic institution and the field of artistic producers are, and always have been, two separate ideological systems with very different interests. The merging of the academy with writers under the rubric of "creative writing" is hardly a "natural" one, as some have suggested, but a subordination of a cultural practice traditionally low in economic capital and institutional power to a more dominant field of power and prestige within the overall field of class relations. In the particular case of the American creative-writing academy, it is in large part a willing subordination or co-optation, in which the stakes of writing poetry are understood by all involved to be different from what they would be without the mediation of the university. As Ron Silliman suggests, there is an important difference between poetry written by an academic "workshop" poet who receives a salary from the university based on the production of poems and that written by a poet "forced to labor as a cab driver or waitress or carpenter in order to create it, with no reasonable prospect for later remuneration."[18] In other words, it is not the university that will change as a result of this merger, but the social conditions that affect poetic practice. The university may represent itself as an enlightened institution that allows and even encourages intellectual and artistic autonomy, but in fact it can serve as a cultural link to the larger interests of the state, and might not survive without that link. If poets within the academy worry about their status as functionaries obliged to meet certain professional standards that are not of their own choosing, and if poets outside the academy accuse these same poets of a "sell-out" to the institutional mentality, it is because the line between artists and academics has become, in the case of professional creative writers, very fuzzy indeed. The final paragraphs of Tanner's article reflect this same sense of confusion: while on the one hand he urges creative writers to "take stock of their own autonomy," to recognize academic institutions as the "anthills" they inevitably are ("every mandible locked onto a sizeable scrap of literary lunch"), he also urges them "to join the Department, because surely we have more to gain from collaboration than from alienation."[19]

Articles like this and others in *AWP Chronicle* are intended only in part to be informative; they also serve the purpose of uniting the creative-writing establishment around a set of issues and concerns, and of assuaging the battered egos of the much maligned academic novelist or workshop poet. And while it may be true that English departments have misunderstood the role of creative writers, putting perhaps unreasonable pressures on them to conform to a mode of conduct based on the very different model of academic critics and scholars, creative writers themselves are not totally blameless in contributing to an antagonistic atmosphere. The defensive and at times vituperative reactions to literary theory and the attempts to isolate themselves, both administratively and ideologically, from their fellow academics, are only two examples. After all, no one is forced to pursue a career as an academic poet, and those who do so need to be very aware of the contradictory implications of their position. Yet creative writing, as a system, has continued to perpetuate the split between its own practice and that of others in academic departments, even while enjoying the cultural and economic benefits such an allegiance provides. In a 1987 statement of its own policy suggestions, the AWP, the governing body for creative-writing programs, demanded a greater autonomy for creative writers within academic English departments:

AWP believes that writing program faculty, who as creative writers are best qualified to make assessments of a candidate's work, should be given the responsibility of making professional decisions about their peers, and that their evaluations of the candidate, and their recommendations, should be given the utmost weight in the review process. . . . AWP believes that writers should have the major voice in decisions concerning the hiring and retention of creative writing faculty, admissions of students to the writing program, the awarding of degrees in writing, the writing program's budget, and the allocation of physical resources.[20]

Not only is this statement problematic on several levels, but it is hard to see what purpose such an editorial could possibly serve other than further isolating creative-writing programs and antagonizing university administrators and English departments. First of all, the statement assumes incorrectly that "creative writers" are by definition better qualified to judge the quality of literary writing than critics and scholars who have devoted years of their lives to the study of literature. Second, the implied division between "writers" and "nonwriters" ignores the many kinds of writing that go on within both literature departments and society at large. As Chris Semansky indicates, "it becomes apparent that the label 'creative writing' serves both as an institutional convenience and as a generic barricade against the onslaught of discursive forces that threaten to dissolve the distinction between the creative and other kinds of writing."[21] Creative writers want to hold a monopoly on what they consider their own kind of activity ("creative") while still acquiring the kinds of professional credentials, socioeconomic advantages, and cultural identity previously available only to "scholarly" or "critical" writers.

Given this ambivalent attitude, it is not surprising that in many cases creative writers have managed to antagonize their colleagues and isolate themselves by arrogating the dual status of literary producer and expert, thus excluding the non–creative writer from any participation in contemporary literature. As Eve Shelnutt writes, "MFA programs are sending two clear messages to English departments: 'We will define writing' and 'Stay off our turf.'"[22] But since academic scholars often take a wider historical view of literature than their "creative" counterparts, and a wider generic view than most practicing poets, the denial of their part in the process will have the effect of further restricting the kinds of literary forms, genres, and stances adopted by writers in creative-writing programs, who in turn pass these narrower options on to their students.

What creative-writing programs really provide is a training in a particular kind of professionalism. Many MFA students come to realize that they are learning not so much how to write or understand poetry as how to be academic poets: they are acquiring the socialization necessary to mold themselves as professional poets, as well as the networking skills and connections they will need to pursue a career in an increasingly tight academic market. This greater professionalization can be both a positive and a negative influence on younger poets. The most appealing aspect of the professional code adopted by creative-writing programs is the sense of empowerment it can instill in young writers, a social and economic as well as individual and aesthetic confidence. The least appealing aspect, however, and the inevitable trade-off of greater socioeconomic security, is a narrow view of literary production and an antitheoretical bias that at times seems downright anti-intellectual. Indeed, Shelnutt, a professor of creative writing, warns of "a growing climate of anti-intellectualism among writing students," themselves usually the protégés of teachers who are former MFAs. As she suggests, writing programs can serve as a "haven" not only from the harsh world of economic reality, but also from "intellectual discourse" itself.[23] Symptomatic of this trend among university-affiliated creative writers are articles, like that of Peter Stitt, that attack the growth of theory in the academy. Deriding literary theorists as "people who read weird texts while riding on hobby horses of their own devising," Stitt suggests that poets should take it upon themselves to distinguish between "bad" critics (those who use jargon and don't enjoy literature) and "good" critics (those who love literature and subject literary texts to "serious, intellectual scrutiny"). In the latter category, Stitt's most prominent example is Oliver Wendell Holmes, that prototypical nineteenth-century "man of letters" who "offered a perfectly balanced and good-natured commentary on the books that came his way," without the need for "science" or "organized method."[24]

But as Marjorie Perloff points out in her response to Stitt's piece (also published in the *AWP Newsletter*), Stitt's championing of a figure like Holmes as exemplary of literary criticism, aside from being hopelessly anachronistic, works against his own interests as an exponent of "creative writing" as a discipline. Holmes himself—who, like all the "fireside poets," considered writing less a "profession" (he was a professor of anatomy) than a gentlemanly avocation—would have no doubt been appalled by the extent of professionalization and institutionalization that have entered the field of American poetry through the creative-writing program. In fact, the idea that creative writing can be taught is itself a "theoretical" one: it is based on particular theories of pedagogy and composition. Furthermore, as Perloff suggests, the most important writers at any given moment have never closed themselves off from the theoretical discourse of their time. Only since the postwar creation of a distinct creative-writing poetry establishment have poets attempted to argue "that poetry writing should remain untouched by . . . intellectual change":

> Even as theory became more and more sophisticated, poetry moved in the opposite direction. . . . To be a poet became to avoid all truck with Big Ideas and to keep one's hands clean of ordinary journalism of the sort Yeats had to write to make a living. One earned one's salary, after all, in the university and so there was no compunction to write a book of prose, critical or otherwise. Rather, the sensitive and "real" poet brought out, at regular intervals, a slim volume that would be judged, if judged at all, by fellow poets, applying such standards as "Is it real?" "Is it authentic?" "Is it deeply felt?" "Does it move us?" [25]

According to Perloff, the big losers in this process of removal from intellectual life are not the current generation of poets but their students, who are taught to believe "that theory doesn't exist or that it's just some arcane nonsense being taught on the other side of the corridor."

It is on this unfortunate situation that Shelnutt focuses her essay. MFA students, she argues, "are largely separated from the broader intellectual life of the university," whether as a result of indoctrination by their teachers or of the very structure of the English department and MFA program, which tend to separate, contain, and pigeonhole different kinds of students within different subspecialties. Not only is it difficult for MFA students "to discover how they may use various theories to think and write about imaginative writing," but it is also more difficult for them to find jobs when they leave.[26] Trained in little other than their own "craft" and the work of other contemporary writers, and entering a field with hundreds of similarly trained poets, they are unable to compete with PhDs, and in many cases even with MAs, for positions teaching literature and composition. Unless they are among the lucky few who land jobs as career poets, they become second-class citizens of the academic world. More and more graduates of creative-writing programs are now opting to begin work toward a PhD, or at the least an MA in literature, rather than attempting to go out into the world with only the MFA in hand.

Shelnutt ends the essay by suggesting that "bigger" is not necessarily "better," and that programs would do well to work toward training, not more poets, but more interesting poets, poets who "envision themselves in a community of intellectuals—a global community of writers who are able to question American publishing practices and their effects on literature."[27] Unfortunately, however, most MFA programs have little interest in upsetting the status quo as represented by the largest university, trade, and independent publishers. Despite the efforts of Shelnutt and a few others like her, the energy needed to transform or radicalize the creative-writing world will undoubtedly have to come from outside that network— whether from conservative spokesmen of the "New Formalism," such as Gioia, who see the propagation of creative-writing programs as an erosion of literary and cultural standards, or from the radical population represented by the Language writers, who view academic creative writing as overly commodified and aesthetically stultifying.[28]

Presumably, those most genuinely committed to writing poetry would continue to do so without the institutional structure of the workshop system. Without the ready-made context of an "official verse culture" the creative-writing network provides, the reified distinctions between "establishment" and "counterculture" would have to be seriously rethought. Over time, the number of actively publishing poets would no doubt decline substantially, as would the number of presses and journals, especially since many of them are currently affiliated with universities. The amount of poetry produced and published annually would once again approach, if not its pre-1975 levels, at least a more reasonable facsimile of what the poetry-reading audience can be expected to consume. As George Garrett argues, the current level of "waste" in creative writing—one that has accumulated "to almost toxic levels"—would be significantly reduced.[29]

While defenders of institutionalized creative writing like Dave Smith attempt to dehistoricize the creative-writing workshop by claiming that "[c]reative writing is no more or less than all writing" or by constructing for the workshop a "historical pedigree" that includes the pre-Socratic philosophers, the eighteenth-century Scriblerians, the New Critical Fugitives, the Harlem Renaissance, the Beats, and Black Mountain, it is clear that they are discussing a very particular institutional practice with specific and fairly recent historical roots.[30] It is also clear to most critics and teachers of poetry that the workshop tends to produce certain kinds of poetry and not others. It is highly unlikely, for example, that Charles Olson's *Maximus*, Ginsberg's *Howl*, or the blues-inspired poems of Langston Hughes would have been written in a workshop environment, or that the acerbic social satires of Pope and Swift would have appeared in the context of a creative-writing program. To take more recent examples, it is less than likely that the highly political and politicizing poems of Amiri Baraka, Audre Lorde, or Adrienne Rich would have survived the workshop process. The workshop as it exists in most American universities not only tends to homogenize what has traditionally constituted authorial style— substituting a notion of personal "voice" or "authenticity" for more inventive linguistic or stylistic manipulation—but it also tends to breed a conformity to certain established patterns of verse, in particular, the self-contained, narrative, lyric, first-person poems that have dominated mainstream American poetry for the past twenty years. Poets like Smith, whose training and sensibilities match the requirements of the workshop poem, may prosper in such an environment, but most students at the age of twenty-two have little sense even of what possibilities exist, much less of what kinds of poetic composition they would be most interested in pursuing. Given the need for exploration, especially at the relatively unformed stage of most students entering MFA programs, it is particularly strange that Smith advocates "teach[ing] our students to write what they will not be ashamed of having done in ten or twenty years," as if their possible later embarrassment about their juvenilia should outweigh the importance of uninhibited exploration and experimentation.[31]

Even this staunch defender of creative-writing programs acknowledges the system's inherent deficiencies: students do not study "the history of our language, let alone the history of criticism"; their critical responses to other poems are not as much their own as "formed by the model of their instructor and passed on when they become instructors"; and they have "little knowledge of the origin, nature, or real utility of the aesthetic ideas which they fuzzily articulate as gospel." Yet the cumulative effect of these shortcomings does not seem to bother Smith as much as it might, in part because he has become something of a crusader for the writing program. The workshop system, he believes, does far more than serve the immediate goal of teaching competent writing. Among its more grandiose objectives: "to reveal, test, and reaffirm the values by which men have found it possible not merely to survive but to live with dignity"; to instill "an appetite for excellence in the dramatic images of man"; to resist "the shallow and delusionary images" propagated by popular culture; and even to reject "the anarchists and polemicists of fringe culture."[32]

It is not altogether clear what Smith intends by "fringe culture." There was a time when most poets would have considered themselves to be part of such a culture, whether defining themselves as "bohemians," "avant-gardists," or Whitmanesque free spirits. If creative-writing programs wish to be seen as the guardians of an embattled literary and cultural tradition (Western, nonpolemical, socially and intellectually conservative), Smith's prescription would seem to be the best one. In practice, however, their failure to acquire historical and aesthetic knowledge makes it difficult for MFA students to shoulder such a responsibility.

Poetry will continue to be written and taught within the university, and creative-writing programs will no doubt thrive for some years to come. The question today is not whether such programs should exist, but how and where they can most effectively exist within the academic structure of the English department and the university as a whole. If we are to understand poetry as a commodity—something that can be bought, sold, and traded on within an institutional setting—we must also recognize that the post-Romantic ideology of artistic autonomy that still haunts creative writing is a problematic one. In other words, poetry cannot retain its charismatic privilege, its unique symbolic capital, within the institutional structures of the American university.[33] Creative writers must work with others in the intellectual community of the university rather than adopting an adversarial role or erecting a bastion against current academic trends. Only when the creative-writing academy engages these issues in a meaningful way will it take the next step in its evolution, acknowledging that careers and creativity are at best an uneasy mixture, and accepting the challenges posed by a multidimensional and constantly evolving university.

Until now, the amount of invective and polemic concerning the creative-writing program has far outweighed any serious attempt to analyze the phenomenon from a historical, sociological, pedagogical, or even philosophical perspective. Important questions remain to be asked about both the history and the institutional structure of the workshop system. Why were so many writing programs created, especially in the late 1970s and early 1980s? Is there a viable alternative to such programs? What is the future of creative-writing programs, and how does that future correlate with the future of American poetry as a whole? Can more diverse approaches to poetry, such as experimental writing, oral and performance poetry, or other alternatives to the workshop lyric, be more fully integrated into the MFA curriculum? Only when we reexamine, as poets and as critics, the place of the academy in American poetry, can we begin to move beyond slogans and mudslinging and toward a meaningful dialogue about both the state of the poetic art and the future of American poetry.

3. Poetic Positionings

Stephen Dobyns and Lyn Hejinian

in Cultural Context

It has become a critical commonplace in recent years to proclaim the end of the avant-garde. According to Andrew Ross, Andreas Huyssen, and other theorists of postmodern culture, the lines between popular culture and avant-garde (high) culture and between mainstream and oppositional aesthetics have been blurred in all the arts. Not only has postmodernism, they claim, revealed the "high modernist dogma" of avant-gardism as fundamentally sterile and outmoded.[1] It has also erased the line that existed earlier in the century between avant-gardist counterculture and academic culture, thus rendering suspect any attempt on the part of contemporary writers or artists to formulate an avant-garde project. This definition of postmodern art might lead us to ask whether we can usefully describe as a meaningful oppositional poetics the mode of poetic experimentalism most usually identified with the contemporary avant-garde: the movement best known as Language poetry.[2]

My aim in this chapter is to show that "avant-garde" remains a salient term, that it delineates a sociological as much as an aesthetic or ideological category. In doing so, I compare both the work and the reception of two contemporary American poets—Stephen Dobyns and Lyn Hejinian—who operate within poetic subcultures often viewed as diametrically opposed. While critics such as Charles Altieri, Marjorie Perloff, and Alan Golding have defined in general terms the differences between mainstream and avant-garde poetries, few attempts have been made to compare in more systematic terms the ways in which particular practices circulate within the more general sociocultural economy of American poetry. In fact, the relationships *between* different poetic communities or subcultures in the United States have remained relatively unexplored. Most often the poetic "mainstream," identified by Charles Bernstein as the "official verse culture" and the "experimental" poetry of the Language writers and related movements are considered to be literary and cultural spheres that can be treated only in isolation from each other.[3] Yet, as Ron Silliman suggests, the struggle carried out in American poetry today "is as much one between audiences as between poets." What is most concretely manifested as a stylistic difference between poets or poetic schools (mainstream, experimental) is equally a difference between larger social formations, between the ways in which "audiences are composed around individual authors" and in which these audiences understand or interpret the "attitude toward reception" formulated by a particular poetic text.[4]

In this chapter, I look both at the underlying formal and aesthetic premises that determine the kind of poetry written within these respective communities and at the sociological formations—the field of cultural practices and institutional structures—that create a context for the production and the reception of each group. A more thorough understanding of these formations will, I hope, make clear the continued importance, and the continuing sociocultural reality, of the poetic avant-garde in the United States today.

While there is clearly no completely "typical" poet from either camp, Stephen Dobyns's work embodies many of the principles laid forth in the mainstream, or "workshop," anthologies in which he is included (such as the *Morrow Anthology of Younger Poets,* edited by David Bottoms and Dave Smith, and *New American Poetry of the Nineties,* edited by Jack Myers and Roger Weingarten). On the other side, Lyn Hejinian's writing in many respects typifies the poetry included in representative anthologies of the experimental poetic counterculture associated with Language poetry (such as Ron Silliman's *In the American Tree* and Douglass Messerli's *From the Other Side of the Century*). The terms "mainstream" and "experimental" (or "official" and "avant-garde") are by no means monolithic; rather, they reflect sociocultural formations as they exist within a particular cultural field at a particular time. I do not mean to suggest, by counterposing Dobyns and Hejinian in this way, that the entire contemporary scene falls into such a binary opposition. Various commentators, including Michael

Greer and Jeffrey Nealon, have warned against the facile binarism of defining Language poetry "as the repressed 'other' of a dominant 'workshop' poetic."[5] Nonetheless, such oppositional terms can have validity when applied within specific social, historical, and institutional contexts. Since at least the early 1960s, when the polarization of two distinct kinds of poetry and two distinct cultural positions within the field of American poetry were reflected in the opposition between the rival anthologies *New Poets of England and America* (Hall, Pack, Simpson) and *The New American Poetry* (Allen), the demarcation between a poetic practice of mainstream, usually academic orientation and one of alternative, experimental, and largely countercultural orientation has been firmly in place.[6]

As Bernstein and others have noted, the latter group of poets have maintained a marginal status within the centers of literary capital in this country, and have enjoyed only limited access to the institutional centers of financial and symbolic power in the poetry world, such as trade and university-sponsored publishing houses, the larger literary magazines, teaching positions in university creative-writing programs, university-sponsored reading series, and the system of prizes, grants, fellowships, conferences, workshops, and writers' colonies sponsored and supported by the poetry establishment. With the growth of the creative-writing system, the two groups of poets have if anything become even more isolated from each other, as each has sought to define its own clearly articulated community: one within the academic creative-writing or workshop environment, a self-sustaining network of over three hundred programs; the other in a more limited engagement with the creative-writing academy and more skeptical of its institutional premises, yet in concert with recent developments in literary theory and in some cases supplementing its poetic production with an equally significant production of critical discourse. In order to define the specific sociocultural positions of Dobyns and Hejinian within these two spheres, I consider such factors as academic background and career path, critical reception, readership, and publication record, as well as the textual evidence of the poetry itself.

I chose to compare these two particular poets for several reasons. First, they are from the same generation; in fact, they were born in the same year, 1941. Thus the differences in their poetic orientations cannot be explained as generational differences: growing up in the United States of the 1940s and 1950s, they were subject to the same large-scale cultural and societal influences.[7] Second, they are similarly positioned within their respective communities, equally successful although in entirely different domains. Their success, as will become apparent, takes very different forms, reflecting both the different forms of cultural capital they possess and the different systems of accreditation within their respective cultural fields. Thus part of what I am attempting to define (or interrogate) in this essay is the idea of "success" as it functions in the social field of poetry. Poetic success is never measured in primarily financial terms, although a degree of success, in the right circles, can lead to the kind of academic affiliation that guarantees a measure of economic security. Since poetic success is more a matter of symbolic capital than of economic gain, the question of success or eminence is a particularly contested matter within American poetry culture. While to one community of poets or readers Dobyns might appear a highly successful poet (even a model for prospective or emerging poets) and Hejinian a completely marginal figure, to another group Hejinian might seem a central poet and Dobyns but a forgettable mainstream writer.

Dobyns's success, like that of all mainstream poets, is defined primarily in terms of his acceptance by the poetry establishment, as measured by such factors as academic position, publication record, inclusion in anthologies, and literary awards and prizes. Hejinian's achievement, on the other hand, must be seen in terms of her reception within a very different section of literary academia, one that follows and supports the poetic avant-garde. Since she lacks the attention of the officially sanctioned academic poetry network, as represented by publications such as *Poetry, American Poetry Review, Poets and Writers,* and the *AWP Chronicle,* Hejinian's success must be measured in largely symbolic terms: critical discussion of her work by a particular academic scholar, for example, or her inclusion in a group of poets respected by a rather rarefied intellectual milieu. As Andrew Ross has indicated, Hejinian and others associated with the Language group have written, usually quite deliberately, "outside of the institutional circuits of the poetry scene," and they have published "in their own magazines and presses" as a way of "examining the everyday social relations which underpin the production, distribution and reception of their work."[8] It may be true that, despite her status as an "outsider" in official poetry circles and Dobyns's status as a career academic professional, Hejinian has achieved a degree of academic recognition Dobyns has not. It is this ironic inversion of the expected categories of academic and nonacademic, brought about in large part by the growth and balkanization of creative-writing departments, that constitutes one of the salient features of the current poetry culture. Yet despite her greater cachet among literary academics, Hejinian's form of avant-garde poetics remains on the margins of the larger literary culture. Where Dobyns publishes in journals with fairly large circulations, such as *American Poetry Review* (20,000) and *Poetry* (7,500), and has a built-in audience of more than three hundred creative-writing programs (of which over two hundred offer graduate degrees), Hejinian publishes in experimental "little mags" with circulations generally under a thousand, and depends for her constituency on a handful of university programs (such as those at SUNY Buffalo and the University of California, San Diego), where avant-garde poetry and poetics are taught and encouraged. Where Dobyns published his recent book of selected poems with Viking-Penguin, one of the leading trade publishers of contemporary literature, Hejinian continues to publish her books with Sun & Moon, an independent press specializing in the literary avant-garde.

The final area of significant difference in the cultural position of these two poets involves their place within an international or transnational community of poets, scholars, and critics. Where Hejinian's translations of the Russian poet Arkadii Dragomoschenko and her more general participation in an international avant-garde are more typical of the Language poets, Dobyns's career is centered within a relatively self-contained creative-writing culture that is much less connected to movements and practices in other parts of the world. This difference has important implications for their respective poetics. Hejinian's experimental writing is strongly influenced by the French notion of *écriture*, the idea, theorized in much poststructuralist discourse, of a "postmodern" writing that draws attention to its own procedures. Dobyns relies much more heavily on a traditional notion of poetic technique, or craft, which owes more to the process of workshop evaluation than to any post–New Critical theory. This difference in sociocultural orientation vis-à-vis the contemporary international avant-garde conditions very different approaches to the writing of poetry and the conception of poetic practice.

Stephen Dobyns grew up in various parts of the eastern United States before receiving his MFA from Iowa in 1967, and his poetic career began in earnest when he won the Lamont Poetry Prize for his first book, *Concurring Beasts*, in 1971. Dobyns's career has been a steady climb up the ladder of mainstream academic success; he held teaching positions at Boston University, the University of Iowa, the University of New Hampshire, Goddard College, and Warren Wilson College before taking his current position as a professor in the creative-writing faculty at the University of

Syracuse, one of the more prestigious and well-established programs in the country. Although he has yet to win any of the most prestigious awards, such as the Pulitzer or the National Book Award, Dobyns stands securely in the ranks of successful mainstream academic poets. His books are reviewed regularly in visible journals like *Georgia Review, Poetry,* and the *New York Times Book Review.* He has received two NEAs and a Guggenheim and has been a regular visitor at the well-known writer's colony at Yaddo. His book *Black Dog, Red Dog* was a National Poetry Series Selection in 1984, and he has published all seven of his books of poetry with trade presses: Dutton, Atheneum, Holt and Rinehart, and Viking. His 1987 volume, *Cemetery Nights,* was chosen for the Poetry Society of America's Melville Cane Award, and the recent publication of a volume of selected poems represents the highest approbation.

Dobyns's poems have most often made their first appearance in the larger and more established literary journals, such as *American Poetry Review, Poetry, Ploughshares,* the *New Yorker, Antaeus, Iowa Review, Paris Review, Gettysburg Review,* and *Virginia Quarterly Review.* In fact, of the new poems in his last four volumes, thirty-two have appeared in *APR,* thirteen in *Poetry,* and sixteen in *Ploughshares;* overall, roughly a third of Dobyns's poems appeared in these three journals alone. This percentage, though high even among mainstream academic poets, is not all that unusual, since many of the writers I would define as "precanonical mainstream poets" publish in these same journals.[9] Although there are some individual differences concerning the forum for publication, the differences are outweighed by the similarities: these organs of the "official verse culture," along with smaller but officially sanctioned journals such as *Field, Ohio Review, Sewanee Review, Georgia Review, Southern Review, Kenyon Review, Pequod, Parnassus, Antioch Review, Mississippi Review, Yale Review,* and *Black Warrior Review,* tend to define the poetic mainstream as much as the major trade and university presses.

Since *The Balthus Poems* (1982), Dobyns's first "mature" volume, his books have become increasingly longer, but it is arguable that they have retreated from the ambition of what is still his most formally coherent and conceptually innovative collection.[10] Dobyns's early work shows the surrealist influence of writers like Neruda and Cortázar. In *Black Dog, Red Dog* (1984), the volume chosen by his contemporary Robert Hass for the National Poetry Series, Dobyns moves toward a more explicitly discursive, narrative, or scenic mode, and in doing so abandons some of the linguistic and figurative richness of his earlier poems. However, it is only in Dobyns's most recent volumes, *Cemetery Nights* (1987) and *Body Traffic* (1990), that he demonstrates a consistency of style and subject that we can identify as a recognizable, if not highly differentiated, authorial voice.

Dobyns's average poem is of middle length (about thirty-five lines), sometimes arranged in unrhymed stanzas of three, four, or five lines, but more often in the loosely organized form characteristic of much academic free verse. Within each poem, the length of the lines is varied, usually from about ten syllables to twelve or thirteen; similarly, no particular prosodic pattern is at work in most of the poems, which have a relaxed, almost proselike feeling generated by an undefined rhythm and a good deal of enjambment. Thus what has traditionally been the first level of close reading—formal analysis of the poem—appears to be of little consequence in Dobyns's work: reviewers seldom speak about his use of form, if they mention it at all.

There is also little in the way of verbal or syntactic complexity, of intellectual difficulty, or of figurative density in Dobyns's poems. What is left, and what most reviewers comment on, is either the interest of the narratives themselves (Dobyns is said to be "one of our finest narrative poets"), the "craft" of the poem, or the unpretentious simplicity of the diction and expression. While many of Dobyns's poems do contain an element of fantasy or surrealism that goes beyond the "scenic mode" described by Charles Altieri in the work of poets like William Stafford, Stanley Plumly, and Charles Wright, the poems that are most often praised by reviewers and included in anthologies are voice-based lyrics very similar to the contained lyric mode that for Altieri defines the dominant academic style. This same poetic mode is described even more unfavorably by Jed Rasula as the "levelling national idiom in American poetry," a writing distinguished only by "its stylish ease, its contrived version of relaxed address in faceless blank verse." Even at its best, such poetry acts as "an invisible agent that drags down the imagination of many good poets who feel constrained to sound 'natural.'"[11]

In order to analyze the critical predicament posed by a poet like Dobyns, let us examine two of the poems in *Cemetery Nights* most highly praised by reviewers: "Faces" and "White Thighs." "Faces" begins with an image of the speaker's daughter lying on her back on the sheepskin rug, "jerking her arms and feet / like a turtle stuck upside down in the dirt / struggling to get up." This is a father-daughter poem in the form of an interior monologue; it can be read as a highly compressed and updated rewriting of Yeats's "Prayer for My Daughter," but it also seems to draw heavily on a tradition of confessional lyric. The lines are syllabically, if not metrically, regular, each line having eleven syllables. Yet this regularity is accomplished in a highly unobtrusive way: the amount of caesura and enjambment in the poem, and the lack of a regular metric pattern, make the regular line lengths virtually undetectable, unless one goes to the trouble of counting each line. The question, then, is why does Dobyns choose to exploit such a formal device in this particular poem? Perhaps it is to distinguish the poem from the Yeatsian pentameter mode of "Prayer for My Daughter," with its sense of aristocratic order and harmony. But Dobyns's use of the device is more likely explained by the thematic movement of the poem toward a future of fear and uncertainty.

The poem traces a comparison of the poet/speaker's infant daughter to a turtle lying on its back, unable to turn over and thus easy prey to hungry crows. As is typical of the postconfessional lyric mode in which Dobyns is writing, he uses this visual image as a centering device in this poem. Also typical is the use of voice: there is little manipulation of the speaker's voice, which maintains a personal authenticity throughout:

> But here there is no threat,
> I tell myself. The room is benign and I
> act for the best. She is just contentedly
> wriggling. It is nothing like a turtle flipped
> over while two or three crows sidle closer,
> eager to pluck her soft parts. The room is safe
> and I direct my life to keep it like that.
> How much is this a fiction I believe in?
> We are forced to live in a place without walls
> and I build her shelter with bits of paper.
> The ever attentive beaks surround us. These
> birds are her future—face of a teacher, face
> of a thief, one with the face of the father.

The tone of the poem also remains constant, and there is little verbal ambiguity to complicate the poet's own attitude toward the scene he describes. The diction is simple and straightforward, so much so that a word like "attentive," with its ironic double valence of observant (crows, thief) and considerate (teacher, father) appears all the more striking against the flat background. This semantic flatness is particularly apparent in the statements that make up most of the sentences in the poem: "But there is no threat, I tell myself," "The room is benign and I act for the best," "She is just contentedly wriggling," "The room is safe and I direct my life to keep it like that." If the repetition of these flat declarative sentences remains uninteresting on an aesthetic level, it does generate a certain psychological power in the poem, creating the feeling of an almost autistic compulsiveness on the part of the father, which matches the compulsive "jerking" of the baby daughter's arms and legs. Yet this effect is to a large extent vitiated by the ending of the poem. The rhetorical question with which Dobyns begins the final section, "How much is this a fiction I believe in?" is too much of a cliché to have real rhetorical force. The final identification of the father with the other vaguely threatening figures at the end of the poem seems a predictable punch line, the kind of ironic twist used as a standard device in many workshop poems. Like all such punch lines, "one with the face of the father" loses its effectiveness after a first reading. "Faces" is not the kind of poem that bears rereading, and its devices only work to insist upon the poem's status as a consumable object. The poem is easily assimilated into exactly the kind of mainstream poem Altieri criticizes, in which "lyric emotions are . . . motivated by loss or fear of loss, and the structure of relations in the poem mirrors that constricted space." [12]

"White Thighs" is a somewhat longer narrative scene that concerns another of Dobyns's favorite themes: male sexuality and the simultaneous sense of lust and guilt men feel in relation to it. The poem begins with a voyeuristic image of young girls, watched by an unidentified man:

> White thighs like slices of white cake—
> three pre-teenage girls on a subway
> talking excitedly about what they will
> see and do and buy downtown, while near them
> a man stares, then pulls back to look
> at the slash and jab of the graffiti.

These lines attempt a kind of stripped-down imagist style, heightened by the striking simile of the first line and the violence of the final image. Where "Faces" achieves a tonal consistency through the continuous use of the single voice, this poem appears to alternate between two points of view: that of the prurient "man" and that of the poet/narrator who observes him as he observes the girls. The central section of the poem portrays the man's thoughts:

> He sees himself as trying to balance
> on the peak of a steep metal roof

but once again he turns to watch
the girls in their grown-up dresses,
their eye-shadow and painted mouths. How
white the skin must be on the insides
of their thighs. He can almost taste
their heat and he imagines his teeth
pressed to the humid flesh until once more
he jerks back his head like yanking
a dog on a leash, until he sees his face
in the glass, gray, and middle-aged.

While lines like "White thighs like slices of white cake" and "How white the skin must be on the inside of their thighs" are clearly the voice of the desiring male persona, other lines suggest the voice of a distanced observer of the entire scene—"a man stares, then pulls back"—or that of an intermediate, recording the man's thoughts: "He sees himself as trying to balance / on the peak of a steep metal roof," "He can almost taste their heat." The problem with these tonal shifts is that the reader is never quite sure whose language we are being offered—that of the man or that of the poet himself. For example, is the observation in the middle of the poem that the girls wear "grown-up dresses" and have "painted mouths" that of the poet or the persona? By the time we reach the end of the poem, it is unclear whose voice we are hearing:

The night,
he thinks, the night—meaning not simply
night-time but those hours before dawn
when he feels his hunger as if it were
a great hulking creature in the hallway
outside his door, some beast of darkness.
And again he feels his head beginning
to twist on its hateful stalk. White thighs—
to trip or slip on that steep metal roof:
his final capitulation to the dark.

It is difficult to accept such expressions as "great hulking creature," "some beast of darkness," and "hateful stalk" as those of the man described in the poem. If they are meant to be his, they are tonally inconsistent with earlier sections of the poem; if they are merely the impositions of the poet, they seem labored, as is the rhyme "trip or slip" in the penultimate line, the synesthesia of "almost taste their heat," and the alliteration of "glass, gray." The oppositions exploited in the poem—whiteness/darkness, innocence/lust, purity/desecration—are hardly original. Perhaps the poet and the "man" are meant to be the same person, which would explain the pathos of the final line but not the tonal inconsistencies. Whether or not it is the poet speaking is less important, however, than the fact that the poem's attitude toward the fantasies of the man are unclear, leaving us with several important questions unanswered. To what extent are we to sympathize with this man or universalize his situation, and what exactly would a "capitulation to the dark" entail? What does the title, "White Thighs," suggest about the significance of whiteness and gender in our culture, beyond the obvious associations with innocence and purity? Is the poem an ironic commentary on this whiteness, as the first line would suggest, or a confessional declaration of the poet's own fantasy life? What kind of social comment does the poem make about male sexuality or the exploitation of women and girls as sex objects? The ambiguity of the poet/voyeur relationship becomes problematic from both a political and an aesthetic perspective. The poem speaks to its readers by means of an ambiguity that leads not to any real semantic plurality, but to a sense of the poem's not being adequately worked through, not carefully crafted. Dobyns's tonal inconsistency indicates that he has not fully determined his own relationship to the poem's protagonist.

On a first reading, the poem generates a certain repellent effectiveness, but on subsequent readings we are struck by the overpopulation of violent images, as well as by the obvious details drawn from idioms of everyday speech ("painted mouths," "grown-up dresses"). Rather than underscoring the poetic craft we expect to find in the work of a successful academic poet, a close reading of "White Thighs" reveals the fundamental weaknesses of its construction and execution. It would appear that "craft," for this generation of mainstream poets, denotes not the modernist aesthetic of difficulty and technical complexity, but the apparent simplicity and seemingly straightforward use of the direct personal voice. The language of such "workshop" poems suggests that the "experience" of the poem can be generated by a kind of linear narrative development that relies more on a version of personal "authenticity" than on any manipulation of formal devices ("poetic artifice") or the play of self-reflexivity.

"Faces" and "White Thighs" are fairly typical both of Dobyns's work and more generally of the workshop poem as it has evolved in the 1980s and early 1990s. Even within the mainstream canon, Dobyns remains solidly in the middle, moving neither toward a more traditional neo-formalism nor toward a more "postmodern" voice. Though in certain poems, like "Tomatoes" from *Cemetery Nights,* he is able to move away from the voice-based and mimetic narrative poems that characterize the fundamental workshop style, his work remains less verbally adventurous than the best poems of Norman Dubie or Albert Goldbarth and less conceptually challenging than the strongest work of Hass or Graham. To what, then, can we attribute his degree of success within the poetry world? Let us return to that question after we have examined the poetry of Dobyns's counterpart, Lyn Hejinian.

Hejinian has had an utterly different poetic career from Dobyns's. After growing up in Berkeley, California, and Hartford, Connecticut, she attended Harvard. Returning to Berkeley in the late 1960s, she joined the nontraditional poetry scene that had emerged from the Beat movement and the San Francisco Renaissance and that would blossom in the 1970s into the West Coast branch of Language writing. There Hejinian founded both the Tuumba Press (which published chapbooks by many poets of the Language group between 1976 and 1984) and *Poetics Journal,* which has been an influential magazine of the poetic avant-garde since 1981. As a central figure in the Language movement of the San Francisco Bay Area, she has published books of poetry with small presses that specialize in experimental poetry, such as Tuumba, Burning Deck, the Figures, Chax, and Sun & Moon. Her poems have appeared most often in small journals of the avant-garde or alternative press, such as *Sun & Moon, Networks, Writing, Bomb, Avec, Ironwood, Jimmy's and Lucy's House of K, Paper Air, O-blek, Occident, Sink,* and *Tyuonyi.*

In contrast to Dobyns, Hejinian has won no significant awards, and although there have been several critical studies of her work, she has had almost no recognition within the larger reading public. While Hejinian has many admirers within the community of readers of avant-garde poetry, she has not achieved the more widespread attention of some experimental poets, such as Michael Palmer, Susan Howe, and Charles Bernstein, all of whose books are more widely reviewed and discussed. The work for which Hejinian is by far the best known is her poetic autobiography *My Life,* first published in 1980 and then republished in a revised version, with eight additional chapters (one for each year of her life), in 1987. *My Life* is something of an experimental best-seller, already having gone into a fifth printing with its publisher, Sun & Moon Press.[13] Yet when the revised edition appeared in 1987, it received only one mainstream review, and that was in the specialized publication *Library Journal*. Another recent volume, *Oxota*, has yet to be reviewed in the mainstream press.[14]

Hejinian's work has been compared to the experimentalism of Gertrude Stein, who is clearly one of her major influences. Like other practitioners of Language writing and the avant-gardists closely associated with it—including Charles Bernstein, Susan Howe, Barrett Watten, and Ron Silliman—she reflects the influence of various experimental movements in twentieth-century art and theoretical writing as well as literary texts. Hejinian's disruption of the normal parameters of poetic language, subject, and voice is informed in part by the theoretical works of such writers as Roland Barthes, Jacques Lacan, and Luce Irigaray. Her work thus exemplifies another salient feature that distinguishes Language writing from the mainstream lyric: the interest in and, in some cases, reliance on the theoretical formulations of poststructuralist theory. As the title of her early volume *Writing Is an Aid to Memory* (1979) suggests, her writing attempts not only to transcribe or capture experience, but to interact on a textual or metatextual level with that experience and the process of remembering and re-creating that experience. Her work foregrounds language's own capacity for a multiplicity of meanings and contexts, such that, as she puts it, "where once one sought a vocabulary for ideas, now one seeks ideas for vocabularies."[15] In other words, in contrast to mainstream poets like Dobyns, who proceed from the assumption that reality precedes language, and that poetry is a means of describing real (or imagined real) events, Language poets such as Hejinian assume that language precedes reality, that poetry can only represent the intersection with a level of experience that is always relived textually or verbally. Language does not present a mirror to "real" experience: as Hejinian puts it in her most important essay to date, "The Rejection of Closure," the idea that "there is an essential identity between name and thing, that the real nature of a thing is immanent and present in its name," must be rejected in favor of the idea that no such "perfect identity" exists between word and object, that what "naming" provides is only "structure," not "individual words" that correspond to actual things.[16] Like other Language poets, Hejinian tests the "enunciative limits" of her texts by pushing the poem beyond the conventional rules of form and content to a "minute consideration of the shape of the individual sentence and of the import of each individual word within that statement's semantic economy."[17]

Such an essential difference in orientation implies not only a very different idea of the possibilities of poetic practice but a different conception of the form of experience itself. One of the primary ways in which this difference is articulated is in terms of poetic voice: Dobyns attempts a consistent voice predicated on the idea of the unified individual (or, in ideological terms, of the bourgeois subject), an idea most clearly descended from the confessional poetry of Lowell and Plath but implicit in the post-Romantic lyric as it is practiced by most mainstream poets. Hejinian, on the other hand, adopts a postmodern subject position, one constituted by discursive formations that intersect within a given text, thus disrupting or interrupting any expectation of tonal consistency or of a coherent lyric subject.

Hejinian's earlier works—*A Thought Is the Bride of What Thinking* (1976), *A Mask of Motion* (1977), and *Writing Is an Aid to Memory* (1979)— already tested the limits of avant-garde poetic writing in the 1970s. In her more recent work, Hejinian has been particularly innovative in developing individualized experimental forms that overlap generic conventions: poetry as autobiography, as novelistic narrative, as diary. In *My Life*, Hejinian composes a sequence of forty-five texts, which could be described as prose poems, each of which is forty-five sentences in length (one for each year of her life at the time of writing). In *Oxota* (Russian for "the hunt"), Hejinian presents a "short Russian novel" in the form of experimental poetry; in *The Cell*, she adopts the form of a journal or diary within the generically open form of the long poetic sequence. Thus her use of form is far more self-conscious as a structuring device than that of a poet like Dobyns. As Marjorie Perloff suggests, Hejinian's use in *My Life* of the forty-five-sentence block of texts (repeated forty-five times), as well as the use of short italicized phrases placed in the white square space that begins each section, and the repetition of these phrases in various permutations throughout the text itself, emphasizes the formal artifice of text in a way that challenges the "naturalness" of genre, whether it be autobiography or poetry.[18]

Although *The Cell*, with its more thorough rejection of traditional lyricism, appears almost indecipherable to many readers, *My Life* is on many levels a more accessible text, as is apparent from its popularity within at least a segment of the poetry-reading community. According to Hejinian's "bio" for Sun & Moon Press, *My Life* "is taught annually in numerous university, college, and high school courses," an unusual reception for any text by a Language poet. In *My Life*, Hejinian experiments not only with the text's visual form, but also with its discursive structure, mixing seemingly straightforward autobiography with modes of philosophical inquiry, cultural critique, metatextual commentary, and sensory description in such a way as to challenge the barriers between autobiographical narrative, postmodern montage, and expressionist lyricism. Since sentences and images are repeated throughout the work, any passage taken at random will lack the cumulative effect produced by *My Life* in its entirety. This is already a significant difference from a poet like Dobyns, who works in what is essentially an imagist/confessionalist mode in which each poem is a discrete statement or narrative. In adopting what has been described as "procedural form" or a mode of "constructive writing" rather than a traditional lyric or narrative form, the poet sacrifices narrative clarity or voice-based coherence of subject in order to allow a freer rein to the operations of language itself. Undermining sequence, causality, connectives, and often even the basic "facts" on which narrative is conventionally based (who is speaking? where are events taking place?), this poetic "autobiography" is less interested in reproducing the self as a rationally constructed entity than in discovering the language necessary to evoke "the fullness of experiences and perceptions."[19]

I will concentrate my discussion of *My Life* on one of the early sections of the poem, the fourth, which bears the title "A name trimmed with colored ribbons." The section begins:

> They are seated in the shadows husking corn, shelling peas. Houses of wood set in the ground. I try to find the spot at which the pattern on the floor repeats. Pink, and rosy, quartz. They wade in brackish water. The leaves outside the window tricked the eye, demanding that one see them, focus on them, making it impossible to look past them, and though holes were opened through the foliage, they were as useless as portholes underwater looking into a dark sea, which only reflects the room one seeks to look out from. Sometimes into benevolent and sometimes into ghastly shapes.

Clearly, the connection of sentences here is associative rather than logical. What begins as an evocative fabric of early childhood memories merges gradually into a metatextual meditation on language or writing and its relationship to lived experience. This evolution begins in the third sentence, with the attempt to find a repeating "pattern" in the tiles on the floor. Pattern and repetition are of course central to the text of *My Life* itself, which will also take on various aesthetic qualities ("Pink, and rosy, quartz"), along with antiaestheticizing references to the world of human and natural particulars ("They wade in brackish water"). As in the following passage, the phonetic and connotative material of the words themselves suggests sequences of language not determined by narrative necessity:

> If, for example, you say, "I always prefer being by myself," and, then, one afternoon, you want to telephone a friend, maybe you feel you have betrayed your ideals. We have poured into the sink the stale water in which the iris died. Life is hopelessly frayed, all loose ends. A pansy suddenly, a web, a trail remarkably's a snails.

Here we find the syntactic breakdown of logos, as represented by thetic statements (" 'I always prefer being by myself' ") into pure image. The text constantly directs the reader toward a metatextual layer that supplements its "literal" meaning. We can make definitive statements, but only end up "betraying" them; life is not a simple or logical process, but one that is "hopelessly frayed, all loose ends." Life also ends in death, and what has appeared meaningful at one moment (the iris in full bloom), may be nothing more than "stale water" the next. Like the "brackish water" earlier in the section, this "stale water" is at least on one level a figure for the inexorable process of natural decay, a decay that may leave new life in its wake ("A pansy suddenly, a web, a trail remarkably's a snails"). We also find an implicit analogy between the cycle of life and decay and the linguistic process by which words exhaust their meanings, giving birth to new meanings. Here, the form and sound of language themselves come into play, further complicating the collage-like "web" of Hejinian's text, its "trail" of signifiers. Suddenly the conventional rules of language are confused; the logical necessity of "proper" syntax is replaced by new and evocative patterns of sound and image ("a trail remarkably's a snails").

While on one level this section of the poem is clearly filtered through the remembered experience of a four-year-old girl—and reflects the limits of her awareness—on another level it is the highly self-conscious re-arrangement of material drawn from the poet's entire life. Every arrangement of life suggested by the text is by necessity an aesthetic one, experienced through the individual consciousness of the poet. The section ends with an evocative passage that opens with an ambiguous and disturbing image:

> A urinating doll, half-buried in sand. She is lying on her stomach with one eye closed, driving a toy truck along the road she has cleared with her fingers. I mean untroubled by the distortions. That was the fashion

when she was a young woman and famed for her beauty, surrounded by beaux. Once it was circular and that shape can still be seen from the air. Protected by the dog. Protected by foghorns, frog honks, cricket circles on the brown hills. It was a message of happiness by which we were called into the room, as if to receive a birthday present given early, because it was too large to hide, or alive, a pony perhaps, his mane trimmed with colored ribbons.

Here the poet's childhood self is presented within a gender-coded environment in which she must be "protected" from the outside world, in which she will become increasingly aware of such feminine preoccupations as "fashion" and "beauty," and in which she must remain "untroubled" by societal "distortions." Hilary Clark has pointed out the way in which *My Life* functions on one level as a feminist critique of "the clichés of paternal authority . . . of femininity and social adhesion."[20] While Hejinian's poetry may be less overtly political than work by other Language writers such as Ron Silliman, Bob Perelman, or Bruce Andrews, she is clearly engaged in a critique of postwar liberal ideology in a way that a poet like Dobyns is not.[21] This ideological critique, however, is rarely univocal. In this passage, for example, there is a confusion of gender identifications rather than an explicit commentary about gender: the girl, lying prone on the ground, is associated metonymically with the urinating doll in the sand, but she is also seen playing with a "toy truck," typically the symbolic locus of a male child. In the final image of the poem, we again experience gender confusion in the form of a male animal coded as feminine: "a pony perhaps, his mane trimmed with colored ribbons."

These final sentences exemplify the sheer play of language and sound that characterizes Hejinian's multilayered poem. As Clark suggests, "soundplay creates new relations of sense."[22] Hejinian's repetitions, puns, and inversions create a poetic fabric that is simultaneously comforting and estranging. Here, the "name trimmed with colored ribbons" with which the section begins is strangely mutated into a "mane trimmed with colored ribbons." While meaning is restored to the seemingly nonsensical title of the section, the name/mane inversion also hints at a kind of dyslexic substitution. The relationship instituted by the wordplay between "mane" and "name" is left ambiguous: it comes to represent the way in which language shifts, through sonic or orthographic resemblance, into different discursive and semantic registers. The "name" trimmed with colored ribbons, perhaps something a four-year-old girl would bring home from a friend's birthday party, is transfigured into a "mane," a mark of animalism, which works in semantic opposition to the social world.

The self-conscious linguistic ambiguity as it functions in Hejinian's text is very different in kind from the tonal ambiguity of Dobyns's "White Thighs." In the sentence "Protected by foghorns, frog honks, cricket circles on the brown hills," we find a descriptive phrase—"frog honks"—clearly suggested by the sound of the previous word "foghorn" (itself suggested by the sound of "dog" in the preceding sentence), and in "cricket circles" we find a similar tonal modulation taking place at the syllabic level. Both the child of the poem and the adult poet appear to be fascinated by the onomatopoeic resemblances between word and world; both are learning how to use language in new and more evocative ways. Much like her predecessor Stein, Hejinian uses such wordplay and soundplay to emphasize the nonlinearity of speech, the creative and combinatory potential contained in language itself, outside of any communicative sequence of meaning. Where Dobyns's poem is primarily narrative and metaphoric in structure, Hejinian's text is associative and metonymic. The dominant figure in both "White Thighs" and "Faces" is the simile, the most highly foregrounded type of metaphorical construction. The verbal energy in "White Thighs" is generated by dramatic similes: "White thighs like slices of white cake" . . . "he jerks back his head like yanking a dog on a leash" . . . "he feels his hunger as if it were a great hulking creature." And the dominant image of "Faces," that of his helpless baby daughter, is introduced by the simile "jerking her arms and feet like a turtle stuck upside down in the dirt." In fact, the images that occur in Hejinian's text are not fundamentally different from those used by Dobyns; the difference lies in the form of their combination, which relies on semantic juxtaposition and metonymic association rather than metaphoric comparison. As Hejinian herself suggests, metonymic thinking "moves more rapidly and less predictably than metaphors permit . . . moves restlessly, through an associative network, in which associations are compressed rather than elaborated."[23] In Dobyns's poems, the metaphors and similes may have a certain initial shock value, but once understood they become predictable and static. Once we know that white thighs are like white cake, at least for this particular speaker, no subsequent rereading of the poem will generate more insight into such an image. Hejinian's poem, on the other hand, with its continually startling combinations and recombinations, never allows such a sense of static closure or internal sufficiency. The associative network of *My Life* occurs both on the immediate level of the individual section, where meaning is generated by metonymic association and sonic resemblance, and on the macroscopic level of the entire poem, where through repetition and chronological evolution the "life" of the speaker takes shape. Though very different from long twentieth-century poems such as Pound's *Cantos* or Duncan's *Passages,* Hejinian's poem requires a similar reading strategy, one that does not simply proceed sequentially, as in the narrative lyric, but simultaneously throughout the entire text.

A formal analysis of Dobyns's mainstream lyric and Hejinian's Language writing may provide insight into the kind of interpretive and aesthetic processes involved in reading these two types of poems, but it leaves unanswered important sociocultural questions: Who reads these poets, and what do they hope to gain from such a reading? What more specific kinds of cultural capital do these poets possess within the larger poetic community, and what are the systems of cultural production, reception, and legitimation that create this capital? Questions about the sociological reception of literary works are difficult to answer, particularly in the case of poetry, for which little readership data exists. What we *can* determine with some certainty is that there is little overlap in the audiences for these two poets: they publish in different journals and with different presses, and they are discussed in different critical forums.

Occasionally, however, mainstream journals will review experimental poetry. In the *Hudson Review,* Mark Jarman takes the surprising step of including Hejinian's *The Cell* in a group review. Unfortunately, however, Jarman has relatively little to say about *The Cell* or about Hejinian's work in general (it appears from the review that he had not read any of her other books). He prefaces his remarks with the disclaimer (perhaps for the benefit of the typical *Hudson Review* reader) that "I am not going to pretend I like this kind of thing, because I don't," and goes on to proclaim, with no substantiation, that "Hejinian is probably the most talented of the so-called Language Poets and escapes their ideological methods by sheer wit."[24] Already we find the slanted and somewhat insouciant style that typifies mainstream poets' attempts to come to terms with experimental writing: the dismissal of such poetry as "this kind of thing" (as if we all know what "this kind of thing" is, even if we've never read any of it), the condescending reference to "so-called Language Poetry," and the sweeping generalization that Language poets are uniformly and exclusively "ideological" in their methods. Jarman backhandedly disparages

Language writing in general by suggesting that Hejinian's work (which he already has implied is not very good) is better than the rest. This point is emphasized by the quotes Jarman includes from Hejinian's book, which, out of context, do not suggest the complexity and interest of her project. In order to link Hejinian with some recognizable poetic sentiment, in this case attributed to Emily Dickinson, he chooses the following passage:

> This is the way I
> want to go in and
> out of heaven—with depth
> perception.

To the reader unfamiliar with Hejinian's work, this passage taken out of context could appear either highly pretentious or downright silly. Nothing in the review suggests possible ironies in the passage, or in its relationship to other parts of the book: it appears to have been chosen almost at random. And while Jarman does credit Hejinian with a "very appealing and felicitous mind," he finally throws up his hands in confusion: "As with all such writing, I keep reading to understand until I understand that understanding may not be the reason for reading. Yet what I perceive as the soul of Hejinian's poetry is not ultimately formless, though I cannot describe it." This is not at all helpful reviewing: had Jarman wished to "describe" Hejinian's poetry more accurately, he might have made some attempt to read more of her work, to place her in the larger context of American (and indeed international) experimentalism, or at least to refer to a critical treatment by an informed reader like Marjorie Perloff. Part of the problem with the stance of a mainstream reviewer like Jarman vis-à-vis poetry like Hejinian's, or Susan Howe's, is the lack of an adequate critical vocabulary and an adequate theoretical and historical framework for discussing such work. What Jarman does most effectively, through his references to Hejinian's status as a Language poet, is to frame her project as somehow oppositional to the mainstream, as a somewhat intriguing but suspicious "other" on the margins of the poetic scene.

While Hejinian is achieving at least some recognition from poets such as Jarman, Dobyns is probably unknown to most readers of Language poetry, so separate are their spheres of influence. But if Dobyns has been ignored by most academic critics, his books have been widely reviewed in poetry journals such as *Poetry*, the *Hudson Review*, and *Western Humanities Review*, all of which function as the principal arbiters of taste for readers of mainstream American poetry. Perhaps the most affirmative appraisal of Dobyns's work to date has been that of Thomas Lux in *Western Humanities Review.* Praising Dobyns's use of voice in *Cemetery Nights* to achieve tonal control, as well as his unpretentious use of language, Lux remarks: "A lot more craft goes on in this book than meets the eye—which is the way good craft is supposed to work." Other reviews of Dobyns's recent work have been mixed. Robert Shaw complained in his review of *Cemetery Nights* about the way in which "these cranked-up narratives trundle by on their assembly-line conveyer-belts," and Ben Howard commented that *Body Traffic* is an "uneven collection" in which many of the poems lapse into a "slack discursiveness." Even Dick Allen's otherwise positive review of *Cemetery Nights* admits that for Dobyns "form . . . does not appear to be a major concern" and that the strength of the book lies more in its "damn good storytelling" than its "lasting poetry." [25]

I cite these various reviews in order to foreground the crux of the discussion over the kind of poetic writing Dobyns's work represents. What is at stake in much contemporary poetry criticism—and particularly criticism that appears in the form of book reviews—is an evaluative measure for deciding what constitutes good poetry: two critics can approach and describe the same poem, yet the standards used to evaluate that poem may vary widely. What for one reader constitutes an exquisitely subtle use of craft can for another imply a lack of formal rigor; what is praised as a lack of verbal pretension by one critic can be denounced as a fatal flatness of diction by another; the shifts in tonal quality that strike one reviewer as highly successful can strike another as banal or obvious; the "good storytelling" appreciated by one reader can be the "slack discursiveness" or "cranked-up narratives" that spoil the poem for another. In fact, the polarized sentiment concerning Dobyns's work is indicative of a more general lack of consensus about the direction mainstream American poetry is taking.[26] Dobyns provides an exemplary case study because the mainstream critical community seems to be attempting to locate its evaluation mechanisms through an exploration of his procedures.

Yet, despite the reservations of even some mainstream reviewers about his work, Dobyns has become, as Hayden Carruth writes on the jacket blurb of his latest book, "a prominent voice in American poetry, admired more and more." Though Carruth begs the crucial question of by exactly whom Dobyns is admired, Dobyns's degree of eminence within mainstream verse culture is evidenced by Viking-Penguin's recent publication of a hefty volume of selected poems, one of the few books of contemporary poetry Viking produces in a given year. The publication of this book, which contains ample selections from each of his seven previous volumes, will presumably provide an even more visible place for Dobyns on bookstore shelves: what it does for his canonical status remains to be seen, and will depend in part on the number and the kind of reviews the book receives. The packaging of the book may also tell us something about its destined audience. The handsome cover, with a colorful Mark Rothko painting (the 1955 *Yellow, Blue on Orange*) against a black-and-white background, will attract the eye of those with a vaguely modernist sensibility. The cover copy suggests (twice) that Dobyns is "one of the finest" poets writing today; he is twice called "original" (even "wildly original"), but is also "profoundly humane, poetic in the grand tradition." A cynical response to such rhetoric might be that Dobyns is being sold as all things to all people: his poems are "utterly his own," yet part of the "grand tradition"; they are "quirky" and "funny," yet also "intensely moving."

Perhaps such hyperbole is necessary to sell a book of poetry in today's highly competitive market. Hejinian's books, now published by Sun & Moon, are less ostentatious in their packaging: published in small-format paperback only, they are books to be carried around and read in cafes, rather than placed on the coffee table. Clearly, the publishers of Dobyns's *Velocities* are reaching out to what they perceive as the general poetry reader, one who might come across the book while browsing in a literary bookstore, or a reader of Dobyns's novels who is curious about his poetry. Dobyns's ideal reader is one who is likely to be impressed by the promotion of Dobyns as one of the "finest" and "most original" poets. In this sense, the packaging of Dobyns is analogous to the strategy used by the Book-of-the-Month Club, which promotes itself as an organization providing "the best new books" for "serious book readers."[27]

Hejinian's readership, on the other hand, is a more specialized group consisting of readers who take a particular interest in experimental or alternative writing, and who in many cases also share a familiarity with postmodern literary and cultural theory. With the increasing critical attention paid both to Hejinian and to Language writing in general, a potentially much wider readership for her work, and for that of the more visible experimentalists such as Bernstein, Palmer, Howe, Clark Coolidge, and Leslie Scalapino, is now emerging. This attention may ultimately result in more exposure to prizes, mainstream reviews, academic positions, and other opportunities for these poets, some of whom have already begun to reap the benefits of their notoriety as the *enfants maudits* of the poetry world. In fact, despite the differences in the makeup of their respective readerships, Dobyns and Hejinian have audiences of roughly equivalent size: certainly larger than most of their peers, but less than the most celebrated poets, such as John Ashbery, Robert Bly, Adrienne Rich, or Gary Snyder. As has been true in this country for some time, there is more than one audience for poetry; increasingly, there is more than one canon as well. As Walter Kalaidjian indicates, there now exists an "alternative continuity of American poetry," one that can be traced back through Donald Allen's 1960 "New American Poets" to the more experimental side of modernism that is associated with the work of Stein, Pound, Williams, and Zukofsky. This alternative tradition, bolstered by the publication of Norton's anthology *Postmodern American Poetry*, constitutes a canon exemplified in the new postmodern lexicon by "the structural displacement of signified reference by the play of the material signifier, of the univocal 'self' by the wayward agency of the letter, and of a work's unity and closure by textual jouissance."[28] How such a canon situates itself vis-à-vis both the mainstream canon and other canons, such as those represented by the emerging multicultural poetries, is of political as well as aesthetic importance.

If the readership of Hejinian's poetry can still be said to be "countercultural," it is certainly a very different counterculture from that represented in Donald Allen's *The New American Poetry* forty years ago, which was, as Andrew Ross points out, "generally characterized by its dominant anti-intellectualism."[29] In contrast to what Kalaidjian characterizes as the "political romanticism," the "mystificatory images of 'bardic' power," and the "theatricalization of nonconformity and anticonventionality" embodied by many of Allen's poets (and presumably celebrated by their readers), we find in the poets and readers of today's poetic avant-garde a preponderant concern with theory (as an agent of political subversion) that at times threatens to replace any consideration of the personal, aesthetic, or even the directly political qualities of the poem. Certainly one does not come to Hejinian's work for the presentation of a radically alternative lifestyle, for the mythic resonances of a vatic poetry, or for the key to a new political consciousness, as one might have approached the poetry of Ginsberg, Snyder, or Olson in the 1960s. In fact, on the level of event and overt statement, *My Life* is fairly subdued, even suggestive of a certain recuperation of everyday life. But the very difficulty of identifying an unambiguous ideological function in Hejinian's poetry reflects a well-articulated ideological position, one motivated by the desire to preserve a fundamental sense of estrangement in language and experience. Ross points to the way that many Language poets have "been intent on guarding their work, in various ways, against . . . recognition by the culture industry," against the co-optation of their work and ideas by the fields of production within both traditional high culture and popular culture (or "avant-pop," as the postmodern synthesis of pop-cultural fluidity and experimental ambition is currently labeled).[30]

Ross's argument is that even avant-garde art forms are eventually subsumed by commodity culture to the point where any oppositional response from the avant-garde comes "into conflict with the new necessity of recognizing . . . a massive commodification of experience."[31] This argument, however, denies economic and institutional distinctions bearing on the production and reception of various contemporary poetries. Ross, who posits a fundamental critique of the contemporary avant-garde similar to Peter Bürger's, fails to recognize the ways in which the contemporary avant-garde (or "neo-avant-garde"), exemplified in the literary field by Language poetry, reworks the original or historical avant-garde (Pound, Stein, Zukofsky) not only in terms of its aesthetic forms, but in terms of its contestatory strategies and cultural positionings. As Hal Foster has written, the neo-avant-garde, rather than canceling or commodifying the historical avant-garde, "enacts its project for the first time" by producing "new spaces of critical play" and prompting "new modes of institutional analysis" that the original avant-garde could not itself have envisioned.[32]

Thus the work of a poet like Hejinian participates in an avant-garde critical movement not simply because it opposes the work of the mainstream or officially sanctioned poetic culture (as well as the institutional structures that support it), but also because it indicates a resistance to entrenched ideological and aesthetic formations that have changed little over the past forty years. In other words, there are real consequences to a poetic practice that attacks bourgeois notions of the subject and this subject's relation to discursive formations. Hejinian wins no prizes and continues to publish in small presses because her poetry and that of other Language poets can occupy no already-created symbolic or discursive space within its own historical moment: such writing, as Foster suggests, "can only be read from the future."[33] As has been the case with the experimental modernists whose work has been more fully grasped only by the avant-garde of the 1970s and 1980s, the critical force of her practice will be realized only over time, as her reception evolves and makes of her texts something we cannot yet imagine.[34]

It has not been my primary intent to make judgments about the relative value of the work of these two poets, or more generally about the modes they exemplify, but such judgments are inevitable in any comparison of two such dissimilar projects. Both poets are certainly competent practitioners of the art of poetry as they see it. And while critics from the mainstream charge that all Language poetry sounds alike, and critics from the avant-garde contend that mainstream poetry is utterly homogeneous, both of these poets have voices that are relatively distinct within their respective cultures. *My Life* can definitely not be confused with any other experimental poetic text, and, at its best, Dobyns's poetry conveys a lively and tactile quality that distinguishes it from other workshop poetry. The difference between the two poets may ultimately lie in the way in which their work is subject to the pressures of commodification Ross describes in his Adornian critique. Dobyns's poetry represents the final movement in a retreat from the rigors of modernism as represented by poets like Pound, Crane, or Stevens: its simple diction, its straightforward use of metaphor and other figures of speech, and its direct and unambiguous imagery, all lend themselves to the kind of easy accessibility and aesthetic leveling Adorno identifies in his analysis of the "culture industry." A brief passage from the end of the poem "Black Dog, Red Dog," the title poem of Dobyns's 1984 volume, will provide a final instance:

Abruptly the boy steps back. When he looks again into
the man's eyes, they appear bottomless and sad; and he
wants to touch his arm, say he's sorry about his mother,
sorry he's crazy, sorry he lets urine run down his leg
and wears a dress. Instead, he gives him his paper
and leaves. As he raises his bike, he looks out toward
red sky and darkening earth, and they seem poised
like two animals that have always hated each other,
each fiercely wanting to tear out the other's throat:
black dog, red dog—now more despairing, more resolved.

The first critique that could be leveled at such a passage, from a traditional or formalist perspective, is that it sounds exactly like prose. There is in this text no sign of the defamiliarized language that readers trained in the modernist idiom have come to expect of poetry. The lack of formal rigor (as evidenced by the almost constant enjambment), as well as the lack of strongly heightened or marked language and the foregrounded diction and imagery of everyday life (the paperboy on his "bike"), is typical of workshop poetry, as is the attempt to convey a final moment of emotional transcendence. Here we find a hint of sublime diction in the "bottomless and sad" eyes of the man, and in the "red sky and darkening earth" seen by the boy as he leaves; yet there is nothing in the writing that could not just as easily be found in a piece of contemporary prose fiction. The image of the two dogs, "each fiercely wanting to tear out the other's throat," is suspended between a comic-book grotesquerie and an attempt at the kind of mythic resonance typical of a modernist literary project. Yet the relationship between these two discourses is not emphasized as pastiche or parody in the way it would be in the postmodern text as exemplified by Language writing. From the perspective of the avant-garde, then, this poetry fails because it does not interrogate its complicity in reified systems of discourse; it does not acknowledge the extent to which, to quote Ross, "dominant political codes, the system of capital and the traces of its history, are on 'display' in the language we use." [35] In other words, while traditionalists like Harold Bloom, Helen Vendler, or J. D. McClatchy might criticize Dobyns for not having a sufficiently distinctive style or voice (or, in Bloom's terms, enough "poetic strength"), avant-gardists like Rasula and Perloff would fault him for a style that is too much part of an established and homogenized postconfessional lyric. A poem like "Black Dog, Red Dog" tries to occupy an aesthetic middle ground that is increasingly difficult to maintain, demonstrating neither its high literary status as verbal art, nor its debts to popular culture.

Hejinian's project, on the other hand, is written under the sign of a self-conscious postmodernism that declares itself avant-garde despite having in a sense already passed the point of denying the separation between popular and high culture, between modernist modes of artistic autonomy and pop-art modes of openly declared artificiality and consumability. It is in this respect, notwithstanding the obvious continuities, that Hejinian differs from her modernist forebears. When Hejinian writes on the book jacket of Ron Silliman's experimental long poem *Tjanting* that "[t]he reader recognizes every word," she unequivocally departs from the Poundian or Joycian mode of semantic difficulty. Yet at the same time, she does not intend the evacuation of textual difficulty represented by a poet like Dobyns (of whom one might say instead that "the reader *understands* every word"). What Hejinian emphasizes is the way in which a poet like Silliman, or she herself, can use strategies of syntax, parallelism, repetition, combination, and deformation to force an everyday vocabulary (the language the poet *shares* with his or her sociolinguistic community) into unexpected and unfamiliar areas of thought and meaning. To *recognize* language is not merely to understand it as transparent in its meaning and reference, but to become aware of its potential for resistance to static systems of representation, and to poetic positionings that fail to challenge such systems.

So an implied notion of "American poetry" as an active contemporary praxis—instead of a corpse readily assimilable to the established canon—would be one which *takes on* such a dominant (literary and social) paradigm. In writing, in art, this national context of sense offers praxis an *outside*, a contestable horizon, the basis for a national social reflexivity and self-reflexivity.

—Bruce Andrews, "American Poetries"

4. Canons, Anthologies, and the Poetic Avant-Garde

Anthologies of American poetry published in recent years attest to a persistent split in American poetic practice. The great divide in American poetry, between a mainstream practice rooted in the professional ranks of academic creative-writing departments and an experimental or avant-garde practice of variously situated "outsider" status, has been apparent ever since the early 1960s, but it has become even more visible in the past decade. Since the appearance in 1985 of the influential *Morrow Anthology of Younger Poets,* edited by Dave Smith and Dave Bottoms, and the following year of Ron Silliman's equally influential experimentalist anthology *In the American Tree,* we have witnessed a new divergence of poetry into two opposing camps, each with an array of anthologies that seek to ensure a form of canonical status for the poets included.

The canon of the academic poetic mainstream has been defined by Helen Vendler's *Harvard Book of Contemporary American Poetry* (1985), William Heyen's *Generation of 2000* (1987), J. D. McClatchy's *Vintage Book of Contemporary American Poetry* (1990), and Myers and Weingarten's *New American Poets of the Nineties* (1991), not to mention the more general "textbook" anthologies such as *The Longman Anthology of Contemporary American Poetry* (2d ed., 1989), Poulin's *Contemporary American Poetry* (5th ed., 1991), and the *Norton Anthology of Modern Poetry* (2d ed., 1988). In the camp of the poetic avant-garde, we have seen an equally impressive array of anthologies, including Douglas Messerli's *Language Poetries: An*

Introduction (1985) and *From the Other Side of the Century* (1994), Andrei Codrescu's *Up Late: American Poetry since 1970* (2d ed., 1991), Anne Waldman's *Out of This World: An Anthology of the St. Marks Poetry Project, 1966–1991* (1992), Eliot Weinberger's *American Poetry since 1950: Innovators and Outsiders* (1993), Paul Hoover's *Postmodern American Poetry* (1993), Dennis Barone and Peter Ganick's *The Art of Practice: Forty-five Contemporary Poets* (1994), and, most recently, Leonard Schwartz, Joseph Donahue, and Edward Foster's *Primary Trouble: An Anthology of Contemporary American Poetry* (1996).

While the anthologies within each group may differ in terms of specific focus, they clearly represent two opposed paradigms under which American poetry is written, published, and read. In fact, for many readers and commentators the most concrete symbol of the respective poetic communities (and their defining practices) is the anthology. Anthologies of younger mainstream poets such as the *Morrow Anthology of Younger Poets* and *New American Poets of the Nineties* have tended to reinforce what I have called—adopting the designation of Richard Ohmann for contemporary fiction—the "precanonical" status of a group of younger poets.[1] Of the 104 poets included in Smith/Bottoms, nearly half reappear in Myers and Weingarten. Within this group appear most of the highly successful midcareer "baby-boomer" poets of mainstream or "workshop" orientation, including Louise Gluck, Robert Pinsky, Rita Dove, Norman Dubie, Stephen Dobyns, Robert Hass, Dave Smith, Albert Goldbarth, David St. John, Sharon Olds, Edward Hirsch, Jorie Graham, Michael Ryan, and Garrett Hongo.

All of these poets published their first volumes between 1967 and 1980, and they range in age from their mid-forties to their mid-fifties. They are a group that has by and large moved up the academic ladder of success to full-time positions at reputable schools.[2] Supported by the poetic establishment through anthologies, prizes and places on prize committees, favorable reviews in prominent journals, and advantageous teaching positions, these poets publish overwhelmingly with trade presses, dominating that shrinking segment of poetry publishing. Though they may not yet have achieved the canonical status assigned to poets like John Ashbery, Galway Kinnell, Adrienne Rich, and W. S. Merwin, they are the rising "stars" of the contemporary poetry world, well connected within the networks of power, prestige, and influence in the poetry culture. These poets have achieved the largely symbolic positions within the poetry world that designate a high degree of eminence: membership in the American Academy of

Arts and Sciences (Gluck, Pinsky), positions on the Board of Electors for the Poet's Corner (Pinsky, Dove), and poet laureate (Dove, Hass, Pinsky). In short, they represent the major poetry network, a network that exerts an important influence on the contemporary canon of mainstream poetry and institutional control over academic writing programs, journals and presses, and reading series. Their readings are well attended, and they generally publish with trade presses such as Viking, Knopf, and Farrar, Straus and Giroux. Their books, given the limited sales potential for poetry volumes, rank among the "best-sellers" of the poetry world.[3]

While the success of these poets is not entirely attributable to their inclusion in anthologies, that inclusion has certainly been a sine qua non for their continued rise in eminence. The historical importance of the Morrow anthology, for example, lies in the fact that it focused the attention of the mainstream poetry community on these poets nationwide; while not completely guaranteeing their future success, it did launch the careers of a number of the poets included. In putting together an anthology based primarily on generational and institutional similarities (the vast majority of the poets held positions in academic creative-writing departments and many of them were graduates of the University of Iowa Writer's Workshop), Bottom and Smith opened themselves up to charges of cronyism and academic boosterism—charges that have plagued their anthology, and the creative-writing community as a whole, ever since. It is certainly possible to read the anthology, as Dana Gioia suggests, more as a "comprehensive directory of creative-writing teachers" (complete with a photo of each author) than as a meaningful collection of literary talent. This impression is supported by the fact that the poetry is for the most part of rather homogeneous and uninspired character, predominantly consisting of first-person narrative lyrics, what Jed Rasula has called "the suburban poetry of the 1980s."[4] The poems seek a transparent simplicity that denies any rigorous sense of form or tradition, and the vast majority of them fail to make any gesture toward interpretive difficulty or tonal complexity, relying instead on generic monologues of postconfessional ennui.

What interests me more than such evaluative judgments, however, is the way in which such anthologies construct a particular aesthetic and sociocultural context for the poets included. As Andrei Codrescu suggests, the primary criterion for editing the Morrow anthology was more sociological than literary: it was in large part an attempt to gather together poets of similar social and institutional backgrounds, "young professors who have gone to the same schools, keeping up the class spirit with the conventional shorthand of the Workshop." In fact, a sociological analysis tells us a good deal about the way in which these poets and their poems are positioned within the world of poetry publishing and promotion. The book does *not* include a representative array of the nation's most talented younger poets, as the title implies, but rather a far more homogeneous and thereby less challenging sample of predominantly white, academic, upper-middle class, nonexperimental and apolitical poets, each of whom, it seems, "is married, has two children, has received a National Endowment for the Arts or Guggenheim grant, and teaches in a college where he edits a small magazine."[5] These poets are for the most part highly successful, at least if "success" denotes job security, professional advancement, regular opportunities for publication, and the possibility of prizes, fellowships, and reading appearances.

Bottoms and Smith tip their own hands in the description they provide of the "average" Morrow poet. After providing the biographical data of this average poet—male, married with children, widely published, well awarded, academic—they proceed to paint a more revealing portrait:

He is increasingly interested in traditional forms of verse yet tends to be discontinuous and irregular in his formal practices, manifesting the style of open, personal, and sometimes garrulous poetry that his senior contemporaries evolved in the seventies. Yet he has become cool in demeanor as he is haunted by a life that seems inconsequential or less than fully lived. His knowledge, while eclectic, seems focussed on the psychological and mythical resonances in the local surface, event, or subject. He is haunted by time and death yet God seems a minor problem. He is rarely a card-carrying group member, political or aesthetic, rarely an expatriate or veteran or eccentric. He speaks Williams as fluently as he speaks Eliot, Neruda and Milosz as quickly as James Wright or Elizabeth Bishop. He seems to jog more than to write literary criticism, but the poem he writes is more often stern than funny as he discovers again and again, as Louis Simpson has written, "you find yourself standing against the wall."[6]

Aside from the fact that such a description gives the impression of an even greater homogeneity among the poets represented than actually exists (the use of the pronoun "he" is especially problematic in this respect), the terms in which the Morrow Younger Poet is described suggest certain unfortunate characteristics. One is struck here by the number of words denoting either equivocation ("yet"—repeated three times—"sometimes," "while," "seems," "but," "more often") or diminishment ("inconsequential," "less than," "minor," "rarely"). This is the composite portrait of a person who has no clear sense of who "he" is, and no strong commitment to much of anything. Even the poetry he writes is not his own; he seems doubly passive in relation to the style of writing, which was "evolved" by his "senior contemporaries." We see little of the "anxiety of influence" here; even *that* anxiety seems to have dissipated into a kind of general ennui that is more conducive to jogging around suburban neighborhoods than to writing polemical critical articles or engaging in intellectually taxing reading or thinking. As Marjorie Perloff suggests, this is "the poet as boy or girl next door, cheerfully noneccentric, indeed, willfully ignorant of such things as philosophy or literary criticism."[7] There is something vaguely superficial about the phrase "speaks Williams as fluently as he speaks Eliot," as if the works of these poets are languages picked up on a semester abroad and just as easily forgotten. The failure to mention any poetry from before the twentieth century makes one wonder if it is viewed as a dead language, not to be resuscitated except on formal occasions.

Just why Smith and Bottoms would want to provide such an uninspiring, even unflattering picture, flattening out the differences between "younger American poets" in the way they do, is not altogether clear. Yet their presentation of the "younger poet" is only confirmed by the introduction written by Anthony Hecht. Hecht, who refers to the book as a "lively, intelligent, compelling, and adventurous anthology," casts himself in the role of an elder statesman, able to comment from a somewhat distanced perspective on the work of a younger generation. What Hecht finds "adventurous" about the anthology is that the editors have chosen from "a fresh field of new and ripening talent" rather than relying on the "chestnuts" identified by anthologists of earlier generations. And while he openly disagrees with some of the choices of poets, he praises the "breadth and view" represented by the volume, which contains "very little in the way of uniformity except in regard to a general excellence."[8]

When Hecht attempts to justify the anthology's poems on aesthetic grounds, however, he defines the work primarily in terms of what it does *not* do: the poems avoid the depiction of "colorful and eccentric personal lives," they are not "personal" or "confessional," and they are "disinclined to sing." At times, Hecht's own words betray a sense of the poems' limitations: as when he writes, for example, that "no identifiable poet stands behind them" or that "the quietness of some of these voices will challenge the reader's sensibilities." Hecht seems even to contradict his own claim for the breadth and representativeness of the volume, arguing, with an almost gleeful obtuseness about his own class biases, that while the volume contains the work of college professors, psychotherapists, lawyers, and editors, there is "not a bartender or safe-cracker among them." Characterizing the bohemian or avant-garde sentiments of the 1950s and 1960s as "debased pastoral sentimentalism," a "curious attitude that has long since disappeared," he writes satirically of the antiacademic stance held by many poets, including most of Allen's "New American Poets": "Poets were supposed to go out and 'live,' the more recklessly the better, and if their lives were thus abbreviated by tragic accidents or overdoses, why that was the just forfeit they were supposed gladly to pay for being geniuses and writing immortal stuff."[9] It is difficult to know just what poets Hecht is talking about here: certainly tragic accidents, overdoses, and untimely deaths were just as common among poets of the academic or quasi-academic establishment (John Berryman, Delmore Schwartz, Sylvia Plath, Anne Sexton, and James Wright, to name a few) as among poets of the bohemian poetic cultures of New York or San Francisco. In fact, the majority of the poets from the 1950s and 1960s counterculture, unlike those of the academic mainstream, are still alive today.

But the tendentious smugness of Hecht's comment implies a much deeper antipathy to a certain kind of poetry, a certain kind of poet, and, we can only surmise, a certain kind of person. While he considers the poets in Morrow "shockingly well educated," he shows no dismay at the uniformity of their social and educational milieu, and seemingly no awareness that not all writers of their "generation" are of similar educational or class background. As Rae Armantrout rightly argued in her review of the Morrow anthology, it is disingenuous to represent as typical of a "generation" of American poets tendencies shared by only a narrow spectrum of such poets.[10] Since the only ostensible requirements for inclusion were a post-1940 birth date and publication of at least one full-length book of poems, one has to wonder at the exclusion of such poets as Bruce Andrews, Steve Benson, Charles Bernstein, Mei-mei Berssenbrugge, Jim Brodey, Michael Brownstein, Abigail Child, Tom Clark, William Corbett, Victor Hernandez Cruz, Michael Davidson, Alan Davies, Tina Darragh, Ray DiPalma, Elaine Equi, Ted Greenwald, Robert Grenier, Jessica Hagedorn, Carla Harryman, Lyn Hejinian, Paul Hoover, Fanny Howe, Peter Inman, Tom Mandel, Bernadette Mayer, Douglas Messerli, Eileen Myles, Charles North, Alice Notley, Geoffrey O'Brien, Maureen Owen, Ron Padgett, Michael Palmer, Bob Perelman, Kit Robinson, David Shapiro, Leslie

Scalapino, Aaron Shurin, Ron Silliman, John Taggart, Lorenzo Thomas, George Tysh, Anne Waldman, Barrett Watten, Marjorie Welish, and John Yau, as well as Armantrout herself. These poets represent a cross-section of the American poetic avant-garde—including Language poets, second-generation New York school poets, post–Black Mountain poets, and experimentalist multicultural poets—who are every bit as productive and certainly as talented as their mainstream academic counterparts. If Smith and Bottoms really wanted to use their anthology as a forum for the most diverse representatives of a generation of younger American poets, and to find poets whose work genuinely gave them the opportunity, as they put it, to "observe the language discovering its possibilities as if for the first time," the poets they excluded would have provided a far more interesting sample than those they included. Unlike the Morrow poets, however, those excluded had won no major prizes. Certainly they could not compete with the likes of Louise Gluck, the most awarded poet of her generation, who has won more prizes than all of them combined, including three NEAs, two Guggenheims, a Rockefeller, a Pulitzer, a National Book Critics Circle Award, a William Carlos Williams Prize, and awards from the American Academy of Arts and Letters and the American Academy of Poets. In fact, the degree of consistency between the inclusion in these anthologies and the winning of prizes provides reason enough to reconsider the workings of canon-forming power within the profession.

The two cultural sites at which such interrogation takes place on a more meaningful level are those associated with multicultural or identity-based poetry and with avant-garde (Language) poetry.[11] Proponents of multicultural poetry have criticized the "American literary establishment," whose primary institutional purpose is to "reward those who push an assimilationist patriotic literature—the literature of the mainstream—and chastise those whose literature might make the target audience of mostly white consumers uncomfortable."[12] Language poets have gone beyond such questions of identity politics to examine the ways in which historical, sociopolitical, and technological developments of the postwar era have made it imperative to question previous assumptions about the constitution of the individual subject (as writer and as reader) both within the context of literary production and within American society as a whole. It is not only the "exclusionary paradigm . . . of a western European-American monoculture" that must be questioned, according to poets like Bruce Andrews and Ron Silliman, but an understanding of poetic and cultural production at the most fundamental level.[13] What, for example, are the social and ideological implications of such decisions as whether to write poetry, what and where to publish, whether to attempt a "career" in literature, whether to teach? What does it mean, in terms that are not motivated only by racial or ethnic concerns, to resist the mainstream poetry establishment? How does one work within the contested institutional field of the academy without losing the possibility of an oppositional status within the culture at large? Is it possible to avoid co-optation by those aspects of the "official verse culture" that reflect the most insidious forms of American capitalist culture?[14]

The critique of mainstream poetic culture formulated by the Language poets has in general been more fundamental and more complex than that articulated by the various constituencies of multiculturalism and identity politics. The community of avant-garde poetry most clearly identified with the Language poets has been in large measure built upon the same critiques expressed by the "New American Poets" a generation earlier, but with a greater self-consciousness about the political and theoretical stakes in adopting an avant-garde or countercultural stance. Having witnessed the assimilation of the 1950s and 1960s avant-garde into the more culturally centrist position of the 1970s, poets of the current avant-garde are far more wary of the ways in which the innovative formal practices and counterculture stances of one era (in the work of Gary Snyder or Allen Ginsberg, for example) can be reconstituted as more generally "acceptable" or even "mainstream" forms of poetic expression a decade later.

In a canonical reappropriation of the former avant-garde by critics and editors like Helen Vendler, for example, Ginsberg's poetry can be brought into line with the dominant lyric tradition with only passing attention to his "subject matter" (i.e., the "urban poor" and the "Jewish milieu"). In justifying her inclusion of Ginsberg alongside the generally more decorous poets of the Harvard anthology, Vendler manages to reduce both Ginsberg's poetic vangardism and his sociopolitical radicalism to a merely stylistic register, placing his "tragicomic" style alongside "the surreal in Plath," "the nonchalant in Ammons," "the unearthly in Gluck," and "the intense in Bidart." In a similar move, intended to elide or repress the differences in sociopoetic categories between the poets included, she lists the ways in which different poets "write within a post-Marxist clouding of the American self-image." In this catch-all category, she includes "voices of protest [that] rise from women (Plath, Sexton, Rich), from blacks (Hayden, Harper, Dove), from the dispossessed (James Wright), from the counterculture (Snyder), from self-declared homosexuals and lesbians (Ginsberg, Rich), from Americans in opposition to American foreign policy (Lowell, Merwin)."[15] Aside from the logical problem that none of these categories is obviously "post-Marxist" in orientation, we might ask whether Merwin's "opposition to American foreign policy" (a stance shared by a great many Americans, many non-Marxist liberals included) is really comparable in sociopolitical importance to Rich's radical lesbian-feminism, to Harper's racial identity, or even to Snyder's form of "counterculturalism" (a term that hardly does justice to the range of radical political and philosophical positions Snyder has expressed throughout his life).

Vendler's move is symptomatic of the phenomenon that Andrei Codrescu has accurately observed in the introduction to his anthology of alternative poetry, *Up Late*. In about 1970, the poetic mainstream (and its critics) ceased to recognize or at least to acknowledge that anything like an avant-gardist or meaningful oppositional poetic practice existed in this country: "In the 1970s the clear distinctions of the year 1960 dissolved. The confusion of political radicalism with esthetic radicalism began to destroy the sophisticated polemics within American poetry."[16] That confusion is certainly understandable. However, in the case of Vendler, or her fellow poetry critic and anthologist J. D. McClatchy, we find less an inclination to confuse two kinds of radicalism than a desire to forget that either kind of radicalism exists. Indeed, McClatchy's claim, in his Vintage anthology, that "[t]here is no need for an anthology to take sides," is not as innocent as it seems.[17] McClatchy shares with Vendler the desire to whitewash any important differences between poets that do not fall under certain prescribed aesthetic categories. Trivializing all disagreements among poets as "merely sibling rivalries" and characterizing the "angry ideologies" about poetry as artificially constructed by "dull readers," McClatchy attempts to portray American poets as one big happy family. Even Robert Lowell and Allen Ginsberg, he suggests, while from different camps, respected each other's work. What McClatchy fails to mention is that beneath the grudging respect Ginsberg might have expressed in a public forum for Lowell, or vice versa, lay sociocultural and ideological differences that went far beyond influences (which they in some cases shared) and stylistic affinities (which, except in very superficial ways, they did not).

In fact, McClatchy's capsule history of postwar American poetry merely perpetuates Vendler's attempt to place everything on the same level. Here, Charles Olson's "open field" theory is connected not only with the work of the Beats and the New York Poets, with which it has some affinity, but also with "Theodore Roethke's plunge into the preconscious," with "the dreamwork of John Berryman's poems," with "the muted psychologizing of Randall Jarrell's monologues," and, most egregiously, with "the whole confessional movement."[18] Such collapsing of categories is not only intellectually sloppy; it also does disservice to the theoretical positions and practices of the poets involved. To link Olson, whose lifelong attack on the "interference of the lyric ego" was largely responsible for the radical decentering of the poetic self in the anticonfessionalist experimental poetry of the 1950s and 1960s, with confessionalists like Plath and Sexton, who worked from a post-Romantic or Yeatsian model of the unified and mythologized lyric self as the major focus of poetic discourse, makes a mockery of Olson's poetics and detracts from any attempt to formulate a meaningful counterpoetics in the post–New Critical era.[19]

The conservatism of literary thought that dominated such discussions of American poetry in the 1980s and early 1990s had its roots, as Codrescu suggests, in the 1970s, when a nondiscriminatory ethos of poetic egalitarianism could be seen in the editorial policies of a journal like *American Poetry Review*.[20] The obvious marketing success of the assimilationist policy of *APR* (which grew relatively quickly to its current status as the largest-circulation poetry magazine in the country, with over 20,000 subscribers), can be linked to several factors. On the one hand, there was a desire on the part of many poets to put an end to the divisive "poetry wars" that had been raging for the past twenty years. At the same time, the declining influence of the postwar avant-garde, which no longer sought to define itself by refusing to be included alongside poets of the "establishment," made possible a reconciliation of mutual convenience. Finally, the ascendancy of a middle-class poetic professionalism, brought on by the growth of academic creative-writing programs in whose interest it was to de-emphasize internecine conflicts and present "poetry" as universally relevant, swept any spirit of "dissidence" into a dusty corner.[21] In fact, the editors of *American Poetry Review* promoted the magazine, in an appeal to creative-writing professors, as a "continuous text for classes studying poetry in all its forms," a kind of serialized poetic anthology "ideal for poetry writing classes."[22]

Whether a project like that of *APR* created a "false community," as Codrescu suggests, or whether it merely reflected the more centrist tendency of American poetry during the 1970s—the tendency toward the "suburban" or "scenic" postconfessional style described by Charles Altieri and others—it certainly helped to blur the distinction between establishment and counterculture, between the "raw" and the "cooked." To a large extent, it seemed that the poetic mainstream, as it was being defined by *APR* and as it would be more fully defined by anthologies such as the Morrow, had subsumed the avant-garde, depriving it of any meaningful status within American literary culture. The academic mainstream, which had been either vilified, ignored, or parodied by the avant-garde of the late 1950s and 1960s, regained a degree of hegemony it had not enjoyed for twenty years or more. While there remained pockets of resistance — St. Mark's Poetry Project in New York, the Naropa Institute's "Jack Kerouac School of Disembodied Poetics," and groups of affiliated experimental poets in Chicago, Buffalo, and the San Francisco Bay Area — the major infrastructure of the poetic mainstream had quietly gained control of prize committees, major publishing houses, university creative-writing departments and their affiliated journals. The emergence in the late 1970s and early 1980s of the avant-garde movement known as Language poetry — a movement that had its origins in the diaspora of various poetic movements of the postwar avant-garde (primarily New York school, Black Mountain, and the San Francisco Renaissance) — reestablished the possibility of a vital resistance to the modes of "workshop" or postconfessional lyric that dominated the creative-writing network. Nonetheless, programs like Naropa and St. Mark's and poets like those of the Language movement and related experimentalist groups continued to be marginalized by the mainstream, as evidenced by their not even being mentioned in either the *Norton Anthology of Modern Poetry* (1988) or the *Heath Anthology of American Literature* (1990).[23] The centrist climate of the 1980s would allow even a relatively well-informed academic critic like Robert von Hallberg to make the claim that, "[b]eginning in 1960 the poetic avant-garde was drawn into the mainstream of American literary life; since then there has been no avant-garde, though there have been poseurs."[24]

By the end of the 1980s, anthologies like McClatchy's could with relative impunity claim an unbiased presentation of "the best" of American poetry while actually providing an extremely biased selection, based more on the status of prizewinners than on any aesthetic or social criterion. McClatchy is surely aware that there are others who would strongly disagree with his choices, but he dismisses such potential dissent as a non-issue, thus ignoring entirely the sociocultural and institutional context that lies behind any instance of canon formation. As Rasula points out, McClatchy's anthology "is an affidavit that unwittingly testifies to the bankruptcy of poetry-establishment discourse in the United States: its rhetoric denies context and effaces the historical record even as it perpetuates the received canon."[25]

McClatchy's views of American poetry, however bankrupt, are nevertheless shared by a cadre of the East Coast poetry establishment, including Daniel Halpern, editor of Ecco Press and until recently editor of the literary journal *Antaeus,* and David Lehman, series editor for the *Best American Poetry* volumes inaugurated in 1988. Lehman, in fact, makes a similar argument to that propounded by McClatchy in claiming that the "distinguished poets" who have served as editors in the series have "insisted on excellence as the paramount criterion in the selection process," undertaking the task of editing such a volume "in an ecumenical spirit."[26] Yet to be truly ecumenical, it would seem, Lehman's choice of editors would have to reflect a far greater diversity than it in fact does: of the nine editors assigned the task of selecting "the best" of American poetry, all are white and all are members of the mainstream literary establishment.

This unequal distribution is in turn reflected in the poetry represented as "the best": *Best American Poetry* annuals include a far larger share of poems from the mainstream community than from the experimental community. Only one issue, that edited by John Ashbery, contains anything like an even balance of mainstream and experimental poets, and only one, that edited by Adrienne Rich, contains a strong representation of multicultural poetry.[27] A large percentage of the selected poems come from the same nexus of influential journals, a group that includes, in order of frequency, the *New Yorker, Poetry,* the *Paris Review, APR,* and *Boulevard.* In fact, the *New Yorker* has itself provided more than forty of the poems in *Best American Poetry,* reflecting a strong bias toward the East Coast literary establishment. Thus, in the case of Lehman's role as series editor, the rhetoric and the reality do not match. Once again, we find the tacit assumption not only that all poets are judged on an even playing field, but that we can all agree on who the "best" poets are, that there is an unequivocal and universally accepted standard of excellence, and that factors such as race, gender, education, class, and geographical location have no bearing on the way we read.[28] Clearly, as Charles Bernstein suggests, it is time to put an end to the myth of "a common standard of aesthetic judgment," to "get over, as in getting over a disease, the idea that we can 'all' speak to one another in the universal voice of poetry."[29]

Bernstein has not been the only poet to critique the post-Romantic vision of poetic universality and the more specifically New Critical impulse to represent the poem as an aesthetic or verbal icon unsullied by

social or political considerations. In response to those in the poetry establishment who would seek to decontextualize poetry, Ron Silliman argues
that poetry is part of a "political economy" that is every bit as real as
that existing in other segments of society. In fact, Silliman suggests, the
underlying class dynamic of American poetry has been the most unexamined aspect of poetic culture, a kind of critical taboo that has crippled the
practice of poets, critics, reviewers, and anthologists since the New Criticism. As Silliman points out, Wellek and Warren's 1942 *Theory of Literature,* considered by many the apotheosis of New Critical philosophy, was
a "thorough assault on all contextual approaches," arguing that "the real
poem must be conceived as a structure of norms, realized only partially
in the experience of its many readers."[30] Thus the poem, for Wellek and
Warren and their New Critical followers, was ostensibly dissociated from
the social context of either poet or reader: the particularity of the poetic
audience was seen as irrelevant to any "correct" reading of the "genuine
poem." Like McClatchy, who dismisses the "poetry wars" of the 1950s
and 1960s as "sibling rivalries," and Vendler, who collapses into matters
of "style" or "poetic temperament," the crucial differences in sociopoetic
orientation between Ginsberg and Gluck, the New Critics sought refuge
from the social and ideological battleground on which the struggle for literary ascendancy is inevitably fought.

The New Critics were very clear about what kinds of poetry they liked
and disliked, but they were unwilling to admit that these value judgments
were often based on criteria that were sociological as well as formal or
aesthetic. Significantly, the poetry of the 1950s and 1960s that was most
inimical to the New Criticism—represented by Allen's New American
Poets—also depended the most heavily on a specific social, cultural, or
political context. Perhaps the most dramatic example of the capacity of
the New Critics to react to poems on a purely contextual basis (despite
protestations to the contrary) was John Crowe Ransom's eleventh-hour
rejection of Robert Duncan's "An African Elegy." Ransom had already
accepted the poem for publication in the *Kenyon Review,* when he discovered that Duncan was openly homosexual. As Jed Rasula suggests, since
the "fundamental tenet of the New Critical worldview is the degeneracy of
the modern age," its "impulse to formalism is necessarily conservative."[31]
If the critical positions of the New Critics in the 1930s and 1940s were
intended to oppose "the dream of a proletarian literature" and to inocu-
late poetry "against the virus of the real," it is hardly surprising that the

poetic and critical inheritors of the New Criticism would wish to isolate the poem from its social environment and its dialectical engagement with real-world political and artistic movements.

Though it is the very nature of the literary anthology to celebrate the individual poem as decontextualized artifact, the anthologies of avant-garde, experimental, or aesthetically revisionist poetry have differed from those of the mainstream in attempting to recognize that social formations play a crucial role in determining what poems or poets are included. Rather than relying on a mystificatory and universalizing notion of "the best," as in the case of mainstream anthologies, or, as in the case of some multicultural anthologies, simply claiming an undifferentiated politics of universal "inclusion," these anthologies have made clear how they are situated within the continuing debate over the canon of American poetry, and over the question of how the field of poetry is engaged with other aspects of contemporary culture. Eliot Weinberger, for example, is quite explicit in his rejection of the claim by mainstream anthologists "that there is no ruling party, and thus no opposition; that there are only good or bad poets, publishers, literary magazines; that the others are simply those who failed to make the grade." Despite the fact that the "outsider party" of poets is "increasingly dissatisfied" with labels such as "avant-garde," "experimental," "nonacademic," and "radical" (Weinberger himself prefers the terms "outsiders" and "innovators"), these poets are excluded from the "channels of recognition" controlled by the "ruling party" of poets and by their magazines, presses, reviewers, and anthologies.[32] Paul Hoover makes much the same point, though more gently, in the introduction to his *Postmodern American Poetry:* avant-garde poetry "renews poetry as a whole" and will "influence mainstream practice in the coming decades," but it is always "belated" with respect to "publishing opportunities and literary prizes." Giving the example of William Carlos Williams, who was celebrated by the mainstream in the 1950s after having been dismissed for decades as "antipoetic," Hoover suggests that the insider/outsider dialectic is constantly changing and subject to shifts in both literary fashion and institutional power.[33]

Further, such revisionist anthologies, while they acknowledge the important differences between individual poets, do not accept the primacy of the individual aesthetic (or "individual talent") over the group-based aesthetic or dynamic. As Silliman suggests, "the collective literature of the community . . . is gradually emerging as more vital than the production of single authors." Such a communitarian or collective aesthetic certainly informs the rhetoric of the Language poets, whose work includes several literary collaborations and an important group manifesto.[34]

Finally, while mainstream anthologists such as Vendler, McClatchy, Smith and Bottoms, and Lehman have tended to emphasize the poet's unique place within a specific cultural tradition—that of lyric poetry as conventionally defined—anthologists of the poetic avant-garde have attempted to enlarge the field within which poetry is defined to include not only all of the arts, but the historical, sociocultural, and political context as well.[35] Just as the mainstream anthologies attempt to define a lyric poetry free from the larger world, alternative or avant-garde anthologies attempt to place poetry firmly within it. Allen Ginsberg's preface to *Out of This World*, for example, locates the history of the St. Mark's Poetry Project—and by extension the last three decades of the American poetic avant-garde—within the larger political battles over censorship and arts funding. Ginsberg defines the function of the avant-garde in specifically political terms, pointing out the participation by avant-garde poets of the 1950s in the early phases of the currently popular ecological movement, as well as the role of many avant-garde writers in the fall of the communist governments of Eastern Europe in the 1980s. Ginsberg castigates the Reagan and Bush governments for their role in cutting support for the NEA, and more particularly for "decentralized arts groups" such as St. Mark's, whose grant was reduced in 1989 to only five thousand dollars.

If anthologists like Weinberger and Waldman and poets like Ginsberg point out the more overt level on which the construction of the mainstream canon enacts a conservative and largely unacknowledged literary ideology, Language poets have advanced the more fundamental and more controversial claim that conventional (poetic) language is itself inherently structured by the rules of the hegemonic capitalist ideology. This theory of language, put forward in the writings of Silliman, Andrews, and Steve McCaffery, among others, is by now a familiar one, having been summarized by numerous critics.[36] Within the more specific context of anthologies, however, such theorizing plays a further role in actively defining an oppositional stance to the ostensibly neutral and putatively normative presentation of more mainstream anthologies.

As Silliman suggests in his introduction to *In the American Tree*, the world of poetry has changed dramatically over the past few decades. First, there has been an explosion of every kind of poetic writing such that, in the case of the poetic avant-garde most closely associated with Language writing, Silliman can list another eighty poets—in addition to the forty he includes—whose work would have constituted a volume of "absolutely comparable worth." Furthermore, the "pluralization" of poetic writing through geographic diversity, through the emergence of racial and ethnic communities, and through women-centered and gay and lesbian communities, has "permanently altered the face of literature."[37] One could argue that, in this new environment, the poetry anthology as such has lost much of its value, or at least much of its traditional value as a conveyer of an agreed-upon or central canon. But one could also make the argument that, under these circumstances, the anthology is of more value than ever, at least as a road map through the ever more complex terrain of American poetry. In either case, it should no longer be possible to read poetry without a sense that, as Silliman puts it, "each audience is a distinct social grouping, a community whether latent or manifest":

> It is now plain that any debate over who is, or is not, a better writer, or what is, or is not, a more legitimate writing is, for the most part, a surrogate social struggle. The more pertinent questions are what is the community being addressed in the writing, how does the writing participate in the constitution of this audience, and is it effective in doing so.[38]

The distinction between the poetic mainstream and the poetic avant-garde may ultimately reside less in matters of style—as mainstream or "workshop" poets increasingly adopt at least the superficial stylistic features of the more "experimental" or Language-based poetries—than in questions of ideological and institutional identification.[39] The "best of" or "central canon" approach to anthologies will no longer suffice in an age so clearly defined both by its plurality and by its overt institutional politics. A coherent or at least clearly articulated attempt to construct an anthology combining the mainstream and experimentalist camps, or to link either one with a more inclusive or multicultural idea of American poetry, would be of more use than continued gestures toward one predetermined and exclusive camp or another. John Ashbery may be the only poet of the past thirty years to be fully accepted by both sides, but the potential for crossovers between mainstream, experimentalist, and multicultural groupings is greater now than at any time in the recent past. Poets like Victor Hernandez Cruz, John Yau, Arthur Sze, Nathaniel Mackey, Wanda Coleman, David Trinidad, Myung Mi Kim, and Paul Beatty represent a growing body of experimentalist multicultural work. In the space between the experimental poetry represented by Language writing and the mainstream poetry represented by the personal-narrative workshop mode, we can identify such poets as Jorie Graham, Barbara Guest, August Kleinzahler, Ann Lauterbach, Donald Revell, and Forrest Gander, all of whom appear to have found a niche as either experimental mainstreamers or mainstream experimentalists.[40] The highly fractured cultural field of contemporary American poetry has made any centralized canon impossible. If this means we have no universalized model of poetic excellence such as those represented by Eliot in the 1940s or Lowell and Plath in the 1960s, it also means that the continuation of poetry as a vital social and cultural practice is far more likely. In the final three chapters of this book, I explore the cultural contours of poetry as it exists outside the academic framework, outside the parameters of the "anthology wars," and, to a large extent, outside the borders of the printed page.

5. The Life of Canons
and the Languages of Life
Poetry, Multiculturalism, and the Media

There appears to be little consensus about who, if any, are the "masters" of the current poetic age. Robert von Hallberg has argued that "it is not possible to refer to a canon of postwar poetry," and Marjorie Perloff has characterized the current situation of poetry as both "anarchic" and "chaotic," an "odd kind of scramble" in which the definition of "the new poetry" is changing with ever-increasing frequency and in which it is "virtually impossible to keep up with even the most prominent and highly praised poets."[1] Since the 1950s and early 1960s, when rival canons of poets could be collected into two relatively small anthologies, the process of establishing a contemporary canon has become far more difficult. Not only are there more poets writing and publishing today than ever before, and more journals and presses publishing their work, but there is also a far more diverse and fluid mix of poetic subcultures dividing the available attention of readers. Each region of the country now celebrates its own group or school of poets, as does each racial and ethnic group. Not only do academic "workshop" poets have their own network within the university system, but Language poets have their own "list" on the Internet, cowboy poets have their own gatherings and conferences, feminist poets have their own collectives, and "slam" poets have their own newsletter and nationally organized system of events. Allegiances are drawn along aesthetic as well as social lines: poets can choose to associate only with other poets who write formal verse, poets who are women, poets who write haiku, or poets who do "spoken-word" performance.

Such diversity and fluidity are fairly new phenomena in the poetry world. As recently as 1973, when the first edition of the *Norton Anthology of Modern Poetry* was published, the criteria for establishing critical consensus was not a matter of much debate.[2] By the time of the second edition fifteen years later, however, we find a more highly developed awareness of how the self-proclaimed "standard anthology of modern verse in the English language" participates in the construction of a changing poetic canon. No longer content to speak in general terms of the "vitality and range" represented by the poetry included, the editors now addressed specific canonical issues: gender ("many of our best poets happen to be women"), geography (i.e., "American poets whose roots are in the West"), minority status (especially African American, Native American, and Latino/Chicano), genre (the long poem), teachability ("how well the poems work in the classroom"), and alternative traditions (Gertrude Stein and Lewis Carroll as precursors of modernist poetry).[3] It is certainly clearer from this edition than from its predecessor that many of the editorial decisions are based on factors other than purely aesthetic ones, and that in many cases the individual poets selected are by no means consensus choices.

The changes in editorial attitude reflected by the second Norton anthology are supported by the most comprehensive statistical survey of contemporary American poets to date, conducted between 1982 and 1984 by Mary Biggs. In querying 139 American poets, Biggs found an almost total lack of consensus about who the most "canonical" contemporary poets were. In fact, the respondents to Biggs's survey named 405 different poets as "among the best," and no single poet was named by more than a quarter of the respondents. As Biggs remarks in somewhat understated fashion, "The sheer number of poets named implied little agreement about which, if any, were the masters of our age."[4]

This lack of consensus reflects several significant changes that have occurred within the poetry culture during the past twenty or thirty years. These changes include the increased pressure of regionalism, the growth in poetry production brought about by the expansion of creative-writing programs, and the effects of a continued polarization between mainstream and avant-garde practices. But the greatest challenge to any consensus-based approach to the canon has come from the realm of multiculturalism. Anthologies like *An Ear to the Ground* (Georgia University Press, 1989), the *Before Columbus Poetry Anthology* (Norton, 1992), *Poetry Like Bread* (Curbstone, 1994), *Aloud: Voices from the Nuyorican Poets Cafe* (Henry Holt, 1994) and *Unsettling America* (Penguin, 1994), as well as critical collections like *A Gift of Tongues* (Georgia University Press, 1987), have problematized the notion of a "central canon" by promoting a multicultural "literature of inclusion." More specific racial and ethnic groups have also been well represented: recent anthologies have been devoted to African American poetry (*Every Shut Eye Ain't Asleep, In Search of Color Everywhere,* and *In the Tradition*), Latino poetry (*Paper Dance* and *After Aztlan*), Asian American poetry (*The Open Boat* and *Premonitions*), and Native American poetry (*Returning the Gift*). Minority poets such as Asian Americans Cathy Song, Garrett Hongo, Marilyn Chin, and Li-Young Lee; African Americans Michael Harper, Rita Dove, Lucille Clifton, Yusef Komunyakaa, Cyrus Cassells, and Jay Wright; Hispanic Americans Gary Soto, Alberto Rios, and Lorna Dee Cervantes; and Native Americans Joy Harjo, Wendy Rose, and Linda Hogan have already achieved a significant degree of mainstream recognition. Poets of other ethnic identities, including Italian American, Jewish American, Irish American, and Lebanese American, are now celebrated for their alternative visions of American life, and poetic groupings are increasingly made based on such factors as sexual preference and life and work experience (poets who are Vietnam veterans, poets with disabilities, poets in prison).[5]

It is within the context of this volatile and highly contested arena of poetic culture that I will situate Bill Moyers's PBS television series and the accompanying book, both entitled *The Language of Life*. In the series, first aired in the summer of 1995, Moyers presented eighteen poets, who were featured in the book alongside sixteen poets from his previous television programs. The series itself was heavily promoted: a reading by several of the poets included was held in Manhattan's Bryant Park, sponsored by WNET, the public television network of New York City. William Baker, the president of WNET, helped launch the event by proclaiming a "renaissance of poetry here in America," and even the article in the magazine *Poets and Writers,* which devoted the cover story of its July/August 1995 issue to coverage of the series, reads more as promotional copy for the series than as a journalistic or critical essay. Vickie Karp, a "senior writer for public television," describes the site of the Geraldine Dodge Poetry Festival, on which the series is based, as "the cozy and historic village of Waterloo, New Jersey": "One, two, or three poets at a time, each episode captures and captivates the viewer with images and drama, humor and heartache, previously uncharted paths to the writers' ideals and failures, all the ruminations and beauty and language of their worlds." As Karp suggests, one of the aims of the series was that of making poetry ("once the bane of many a schoolchild's existence") approachable to the average reader or listener. The other aim appears to have been to represent as much cultural diversity as possible, from the "Alaskan poet Linda McCarriston" to "Bronx-born performance artist Sekou Sundiata"; from Latino ex-inmate Jimmy Santiago Baca to lesbian social activist Adrienne Rich; from Nicaraguan Daisy Zamora to Japanese American David Mura. It is certainly no coincidence that exactly half of the eighteen poets represented in the series are male and half are female, and that about half are from nonwhite ethnic or racial backgrounds.[6]

Moyers's book, a hefty volume published by Doubleday, was prominently displayed in bookstores, with a jacket copy proclaiming it to be based on "a thrilling new PBS series" celebrating language and "its unique power to re-create the human experience." The series would present a "dazzlingly diverse chorus of American voices," which "give hope that from such a wide variety of racial, ethnic, and religious threads we might yet weave a new American fabric." Clearly, the intent of the series, and of the book, was to reach an audience beyond those who ordinarily read poetry: while the book promises to celebrate "the importance of poetry in our lives today," it seems more concerned with presenting "fascinating conversations" with poets who will tell us about their own experiences: "falling in love, facing death, playing basketball, losing faith, finding God."

Even before the series was aired, however, Helen Vendler wrote a biting attack on Moyers's "long and unwieldy book," and by extension on the PBS series as well, in the pages of the *New York Times Book Review.* In a review entitled "Poetry for the People," Vendler lambastes the project as "well-meaning" but "almost laughably politically correct, summoning up an anxious roll call of representatives from what academics call the 'marginalized' and the 'Other.'"[7] Vendler criticizes the book on several levels, and in doing so points out the nearly irreconcilable differences between her approach to poetry and that of Moyers and his associates in the project, including his editor and poetry adviser Jim Haba.

Vendler begins by summarizing what she sees as Moyers's assumptions about poetry, assumptions that she proceeds to argue are almost entirely wrongheaded. First, she claims, Moyers presents poetry through the filter of an "identity politics" based largely on his own "cultural guilt" as a white male. Not only does he present a canon highly slanted toward certain "marginalized" groups (women, African Americans, Asians, Hispanics, and Native Americans), but he feels the need to cast the poets from such groups as victims. Even when poets, such as the African American Lucille Clifton, refuse to accept the label of "victim," Moyers "forces the conversation toward his leading ideas," ideas which too often have to do with the "hard lives" of his interlocutors.

This concern for the lives of poets, at times irrespective of the poems themselves, leads to Vendler's second major complaint: that rather than discussing "poetry itself," Moyers diverts his interviews with these poets to "human-interest topics, which usually produce statements of thoughtless banality." Moyers promotes poetry primarily as either an occasion for "fun" (the poetry reading or festival as an "original tribal and communal form of people having 'the time of their lives' "), or as a vehicle for purely narrative content that makes any discussion of language, form, or literary tradition irrelevant. According to Vendler, Moyers's "earnestly proclaimed love for poetry turns out to be a love of its human narratives, its therapeutic power and its unifying messages" rather than a love of what she loves: "an invincible rhythm, a mastery of construction, a thesaurus of cultural imagery, arresting linguistic vitality." If he would just stop asking people about their experiences with cancer, adoption, or discrimination, Vendler suggests, and begin asking them about what makes their poems work as poems, he might escape the "talk show" mentality on which the series is based. Moyers's program and book, she admonishes, tread dangerously close not only to a kind of literary voyeurism (compared unfavorably to an interviewer asking Keats about his hemorrhages or Plath about her shock treatments), but even to a "thoughtless cruelty." On the few occasions where poets do provide an opportunity for serious discussion—as in the interview with Stanley Kunitz—Moyers fails to take up the lead.

Vendler's final indictment is perhaps the most significant. Not only does Moyers go overboard in his desire for political correctness and dwell excessively on the "human interest" angle of the poets he chooses, but he fails to introduce into the discussion of poetry any sense of the larger cultural tradition within which that poetry is created. Moyers "operates in a cultural vacuum," a vacuum in which British and European poetic traditions do not exist, and in which even American poetry "takes place in a denatured space from which other artwords and artists have been excluded." It is in light of this more broad-based cultural critique that Vendler is able to promote her own canon of contemporary American poets, one that she believes is without question aesthetically superior to Moyers's. Ignoring the fact that Moyers based his project on the poets invited to the Geraldine Dodge Festival, Vendler suggests that his criteria for selection were governed by "diversity and populist intent" rather than by aesthetic quality. In Vendler's evaluative schema for constructing a poetic canon, there is no defensible rationale for including such "minor" poets as Linda McCarriston, Marilyn Chin, and Sekou Sundiata, while leaving out "major" contemporary poets such as Allen Ginsberg, A. R. Ammons, John Ashbery, Louise Gluck, Charles Wright, James Merrill, Frank Bidart, or Jorie Graham. Moyers's choices are not merely in poor taste, according to Vendler; they constitute a "misrepresentation of American poetry" by concentrating "so tediously on 'the Other'" and by emphasizing "poetry readings over books."

In the course of her argument, Vendler makes two fundamental assumptions that are left unsupported. First, she presumes that the printed word is a better or more appropriate place for poetry than the oral reading, and that by presenting poetry in a primarily oral or performative context, Moyers and his editor fail to do justice to poetry. While it is true that Moyers does not perform "close readings" or detailed textual analysis of the poems presented either in the series or in the book, he does provide in printed form most of the poems read in the series, presumably so the reader can explore the written text at greater length after having watched the live performance. Further, he highlights the work of many poets who are particularly strong readers or performers of their own work, several of whom are from ethnic or racial traditions that emphasize different qualities of oral performance: one need only compare the live performance of poems by Jimmy Santiago Baca, Victor Hernandez Cruz, David Mura, Quincy Troupe, and Sekou Sundiata with their printed versions in order to realize that their poems are greatly enhanced by their performances. In the case of a poet like Sundiata, who has recorded more of his poetry than he has published in written form, and for whom the influence of jazz and rock music are paramount, the printed poem can be seen more as a score for oral performance than as the final product. Furthermore, Moyers is very clear about his own predilection for the oral, musical, or performative aspects of poetry. In the introduction to the book, he cites Quincy Troupe's claim that poetry began as "song" and "performance," and he evokes a reading at the Dodge Festival in which "Linda McCarriston held a packed house in silent thrall." Haba continues the same theme, arguing in his "Editor's Note" that poetry should be brought off "the page" and into "the bodies of poets and audiences, thereby returning poetry to its physical roots, which nourished us long before print began to define, and in some ways to limit, our magical experience of words." Moyers's and Haba's insistence that poetry should be a primarily aural experience is naively one-sided, but it is no more reductive than Vendler's own claim that discussions of poetry should be primarily or exclusively about *written* texts. The idea of poetry as fundamentally written rather than oral is, of course, itself a historically and culturally contingent one.

Second, Vendler presumes that the poets Moyers presents are necessarily inferior or less talented than those in her canon, damning by implication the majority when she claims to "feel sorry for the good poets who joined in Mr. Moyers' efforts."

This presumption raises once again the specter of the canon debate: given the fact that all the poets Vendler proposes are white and that none, other than Ginsberg, are particularly political in orientation, one has to wonder about her dismissal of a group of poets of whom at least half are from racially or ethnically "other" backgrounds, and the majority of whom express some directly political content. What, exactly, makes Vendler's poets "better" than those presented by Moyers? After chastising Moyers for not defining his criteria, Vendler takes it for granted that even readers unfamiliar with her other criticism will understand *hers*, although she provides few specifics to support her choices. (The fact that all eight of the poets she lists appear in her own anthology, *The Harvard Book of Contemporary American Poetry*, is not in itself an adequate justification.) What we *can* glean from Vendler's general remarks in the review is that she would favor a poetry of greater density and of more complex associative patterning than she finds in Moyers's poets. However, without concrete examples of either the presence of such attributes in her poets or the absence of them in the poets of *The Language of Life*, the comparison remains an unenlightening one.

As might be expected, the reaction to Vendler's review by those involved in the project was a sharp rebuke. Jim Haba, the emcee for the Bryant Park reading, introduced David Mura as "Helen Vendler's nightmare," and Mura himself proclaimed that "America is Helen Vendler's nightmare." Lucille Clifton pointed out in an ironic reference both to Vendler's article and to her own African American poetic predecessor Langston Hughes that "[we], too, sing America." Each of these comments was greeted by the applause of an obviously sympathetic audience, a reaction made somewhat more complicated by Vendler's reputation as the quintessential academic critic and her status as the bête noire of many in the poetry community. But such institutional histories aside, it is important to recognize that Vendler's essay makes some significant points, points that cannot be dismissed in so easy a fashion. At the very least, her review of *The Language of Life* focuses attention on some of the issues in contemporary poetry that are too often swept under the rug of political correctness.

In order to evaluate the relative merits both of Moyers's book and series and of Vendler's critique, we need to separate two issues that were elided in Vendler's review. The first issue is that of Moyers's *presentation* of the poetry: having chosen (or been offered) this particular group of poets, was this the most effective means of conveying that poetry to the audience? The second issue is that of the *choice* of poets (one not made by Moyers himself), and of the canonical intervention represented by such a choice: are these poets really the best the United States has to offer, or are they selected more for their ethnic, cultural, and experiential "diversity" than for any intrinsically literary or poetic qualities? It seems clear that Vendler would have been far less unhappy with the series had much the same approach been used with poets of what she considered higher quality. It is less certain how she would have reacted if the series had featured the *same* poets but in a more challenging or critical presentation.

Indeed, there are several significant problems with Moyers's presentation. One might object first to the rather static format of the series, which goes back and forth between poets reading their work at the festival, talking with Moyers, and occasionally leading workshops. For the most part, it is the readings themselves that are the most effective part of the series; here poets are given the space to express themselves without Moyers's leading and sometimes annoying questions. But while we might wish for more variety on the level of format or cinematography, we must accept the basic premise that this is primarily a program about poets as personalities, and it is organized in such a way as to emphasize the person rather than the artist. The weaknesses of this approach, however, are underscored in interview questions so naive, trite, or banal as to render any meaningful discussion impossible. For example, Li-Young Lee's statement that the "spiritual reality of [his] family is dislocation, disconnectedness," might have prompted an interesting question about the impact of such disconnectedness on the form or content of Lee's poetry or about the greater sense of such dislocation in multicultural poetry. Instead, we have the following banal exchange:

Moyers: Yet there's a lot of joy in your poems.

Lee: I hope there is. I wouldn't want to think that I write poems that make people sad.

Some readers might be surprised to learn that poetry is meant to be a "joyful" experience, but the answer does not appear to trouble Moyers, who moves on to another topic.

This interchange suggests a more general problem with the series: a lack of critical acumen, a "feel-good" approach to both life and poetry that causes Moyers to gloss over any problems that go beyond the personal suffering of his interlocutors. In her interview, for example, Adrienne Rich asks how poetry can engage in a meaningful political or social critique by addressing the "points of stress in our society," including "the whole question of our putative democracy and what is happening to it, how it is being eroded." Moyers fails to engage her directly here, instead attempting to put his own more affirmative spin on her comment by rephrasing Rich's "points of stress" into "points of life," an unfortunate echo (given Rich's politics) of George Bush's "thousand points of light":

These [poetic] voices may be arising from points of stress, but they are giving us points of life, as you and all the other poets here are doing. Our democracy is creating a cornucopia of voices and sounds and expressions and celebration, yet you see it as a troubled democracy.

Rich continues to press her argument, even calling into question the implications of Moyers's series:

I think we're seeing a failure of the democratic dream and a cynicism toward that dream, so that the dream becomes mere rhetoric in the mouths of politicians and corporations. When people encounter a program like the one you are trying to create here on a television dominated by the messages of corporate capitalism, which has a kind of contempt for humanity . . . I have to tell you frankly that I feel skeptical about how the content and the substance of what you and I are trying to do here will be affected by this general context.

In the hands of another interviewer (or in a format other than the typical PBS interview), such questions might have formed the basis for a probing discussion of the relationship of art to mass media, or of the place of poetry within a capitalist society, but Moyers once again lets the ball drop, only asking the rather insipid follow-up question "What does poetry say to that?" prompting Rich's disappointingly vague response, "Poetry asks us to consider the quality of life." [8]

Finally, Moyers organizes his discussion of poets along certain preconceived lines having to do with multiculturalism, diversity, and personal experience. Lucille Clifton, for example, is presented as a "self-taught" writer who "turned society's limited expectations for a young black child to advantage and dared to become a poet." (One wonders how, exactly, such a background was to her *advantage* in becoming a poet.) We also learn that Clifton "acknowledges her six children as the inspiration for much of her work," a claim that can easily be read as condescending and sexist. (Would one say this about a male poet? Were her children necessarily *more* of an inspiration than other poets, writers, or artists?)

This emphasis on a kind of politically correct presentation that has little or nothing to do with the poets' writing continues throughout the participants' biographies: Robert Bly "was an organizer of Poets against the Vietnam War" and has been "a moral force in public affairs and a healing influence in individual lives"; Jimmy Santiago Baca was "an abandoned child" whose "life on the streets led to a maximum-security prison in Arizona, where he taught himself to read and write"; Marilyn Chin "has been hailed for powerfully addressing the subjugation of Asian women raised in patriarchal societies"; Victor Hernandez Cruz "has reached out to the several communities that have shaped his work and involved their residents in artistic projects" while seeking "to make Americans aware of literature often overlooked by the establishment"; Carolyn Forché has "collected works by political poets around the world as a poetic testament to the power of remembrance in a century of atrocities"; Jane Kenyon "confronts her experiences with depression, her husband's ordeal with cancer, and the trials and blessings of daily life"; Linda McCarriston deals with "the domestic violence she saw and experienced growing up in a working-class family in Lynn, Massachusetts"; Sandra McPherson "was adopted at birth" and has a "high-functioning autistic daughter."

Whether these biographical introductions were written by Moyers himself or by the book's editor, Haba, they reflect a disturbing tendency not only in the context of Moyers's project, but in the treatment of "multicultural" poetry more generally, to read poems in exclusively thematic terms and to privilege a naively biographical approach over a more complex or nuanced critical analysis. What makes these poets *good* writers, as opposed to mediocre or second-rate writers, is never addressed in the series or the book. Aesthetic issues in general are almost never mentioned, and in fact are explicitly rejected. In a quotation highlighted by the book's editors, David Mura states that "[i]f poetry gets too far towards the realm of the aesthetic, the formal, and the beautiful and doesn't acknowledge the other side of existence—the history that we live in, the changes and the darkness of history—then the life goes out of poetry, and it becomes an escape." Mura, it would seem, commits the common fallacy of confusing "the realm of the aesthetic, the formal" with aestheticism, not recognizing or at least not acknowledging that many of the most significant poets writing in the English language in this century—Yeats, Pound, Eliot, Williams, H.D., Crane, and Robert Lowell among them—were able to combine an acute aesthetic awareness with a complex treatment of history and ideology.

Issues of the canon and of the general state of American poetry are also left aside in *The Language of Life*, a strange omission given the fact that a six-part television series was being dedicated to a form of literature practically no one reads anymore. And while there is a great deal of attention paid to the personal circumstances surrounding each poet's work, there is little discussion of the broader cultural trends that influence the writing of poetry, or even, as we might expect in a largely "multicultural" anthology, of the way the differences *between* cultures influence poetic practices. On the few occasions when opportunities for such discussion arise, they are usually squandered. When Joy Harjo makes the important point that "dream reason," a kind of nonlinear logic on which her poetry depends, "has a shape that is not particularly logical in terms of Western thought," a probing follow-up question might concern the differences between Western logic and Native American logic; instead, however, Moyers asks Harjo whether she writes her dreams down, once again swerving from enlightening cultural insight to vapid personal anecdote. Such exchanges highlight what is missing in Moyers's well-meaning attempt to bring poetry to television. Moyers clearly wants to believe that poetry can play some kind of important social or political role, that it can "give us a new vocabulary for thinking about life today," but he needs to find poetry's potential for social utility in an idealized sphere where "liberals and conservatives, Republicans and Democrats, anarchists and libertarians and socialists sitting in a room . . . can discover a common experience."[9] Unfortunately, belief in an ultimate consensus about the "power" of the poetic act only trivializes poetry's other form of power: the power of poetic language to subvert, disturb, estrange, and offend as well as to revitalize, heal, and inspire. It is this more radical and dissentient dimension of poetry, one certainly exemplified by several of the poets in Moyers's program, that he fails to allow anything like its full expression. In fact, not all viewers or readers *would* approve of the poetry presented, despite Moyers's apparently earnest belief that the fact of hearing poetry read aloud is itself sufficient to persuade anyone of its beauty and insight. It is the disagreements about what constitutes good writing, relevant ideas, and appropriate discourse that makes canons necessary in the first place.

As a result of the various limitations of Moyers's series, its viewers never have the chance to examine more deeply the practice of these poets or to compare them with one another, except in the narrow terms of "life experience" set up by the interview format. Ironically, despite Moyers's emphasis on the poetry reading and the oral component of poetic language, he provides few opportunities for us to hear about that language in action. When he gives David Mura the opening to talk about rhyme in contemporary poetry, and Mura illustrates his use of internal rhyme as a way of "fiddling against the form," Moyers abruptly changes the subject. When we hear about the influence of the singer Smokey Robinson on Sekou Sundiata, we are given no illustration, even a line of poetry, that might clarify how such an intergeneric influence might work. In short, while we would like to believe that Moyers's poets are as accomplished and formally innovative as those in Vendler's more established canon, we are given little evidence on which to base such a belief. This is particularly unfortunate in the case of poets like Cruz and Sundiata, who are exemplars of a new multicultural avant-garde as much as they are representatives of a particular "identity politics."

Moyers's series could have been a productive forum for demonstrating to the American people that a poetry written by a diverse and multicultural group of writers can be interesting on every level, that the distinction between an aesthetic or evaluative model of the canon and an institutionally or ideologically based model is not necessarily a firm one. The emergence of a new multicultural canon is significant not only in that it enlarges the scope of poetry available to writers, publishers, and readers, but also in that it refocuses the discourse about poetry and canonicity in this country, challenging the diametrical opposition between mainstream and experimental poetry that has dominated the "poetry wars" throughout the second half of the century. Since the advent of multiculturalism, the conflict between "mainstream" and "avant-garde" practices no longer defines the poetic field to the extent that it once did. The most significant tensions surrounding poetry in this country—or at least those that are the most publicly displayed—are no longer those of traditionalists versus experimentalists, the binary "us vs. them" or "raw vs. cooked" mentality that characterized the "poetry wars" of the 1950s and 1960s. Instead, they involve a more radical fragmentation of the poetic field into zones of ethnicity and identity politics that mirror the fragmentation of the larger field of literary studies and of the humanities in general.

The emergence of new multicultural presses such as Arte Publico, West End, Bilingual Review, Chusma, Tia Chucha, Puerto del Sol, Curbstone, and Fuego de Atzlan, along with the publication of anthologies representing various racial and ethnic traditions, leads us to ask whether it is even appropriate to talk of "canons" in a context of inclusion rather than exclusion. Will any discussion of a multicultural, multiracial, multiethnic, feminist, experimental, or more broadly "alternative" canon that directly challenges the existing or "mainstream" canon simply repeat the gesture of exclusion enacted by the dominant group? While some critics and anthologists, such as Jerry Ward, accept the fact that the idea of a canon has been replaced by a notion of multiple canons or particular traditions of writing, others such as Ray Gonzalez, the editor of the Latino American anthology *After Atzlan,* worry that such specific anthologies will be bought and read primarily by poets and critics of their own ethnic and racial communities, failing to reach a wider audience. Even if the audience is growing within a particular community, that community risks experiencing even greater cultural isolation from the mainstream, rather than contributing to the more general development of American poetry.[10]

To this point, discussions of multicultural American poetry have been hindered by the reliance on an impoverished critical apparatus that relies almost exclusively on institutional forms of analysis (i.e., the effects and implications of racial and ethnic "difference") rather than on aesthetic evaluation or formal explication. In the new Penguin anthology of "contemporary multicultural poetry," *Unsettling America,* for example, the editors present the poems in exclusively thematic terms: the poems chosen were those that "directly address the instability of American identity and confront the presence of cultural conflict and exchange within the United States." In her introduction, Jennifer Gillan virtually negates any defining qualities of the work included that might identify it as poetry rather than fiction or autobiography, referring to the way in which "the poems . . . tell American stories [and] proclaim the complexity of American identity." Aside from a general reference to "the power of [the poets'] writing," there is no reason to think that the various forms the anthology's poems take on the page is of any consequence to the book's editors, publishers, or potential readers.[11]

This tendency is consistent with most of the critical essays on multi-cultural poetry contained in Marie Harris and Kathleen Aguero's critical anthology *A Gift of Tongues*. With the exception of Carmen Tafolla's essay on Chicano poetry, these essays pay disappointingly little attention — either in their general remarks about the poetry of different groups or in their readings of specific poems — to formal, stylistic, or semiotic qualities. While some of the essays make gestures toward formal or rhetorical analysis, they too often remain on the level of generality, failing to explore in more concrete ways the craft, technique, or linguistic manipulation of the poets involved, or their relation to both canonical and noncanonical poetic models. Raymond Patterson describes, for example, how Al Young "capture[s] the style and attitude of the quintessential blues singer," and how Calvin Hernton "strip[s] language to its essentials," but we have no more detailed account of how this works in the poems themselves. Similarly, Roberto Marquez suggests that the incorporation of Spanish words and phrases into English in poetry by Latino poets adds "something to the language that was not there before" but remains rather vague about exactly what that "something" is.[12]

In part, this lack of close textual analysis comes from an understandable desire to present the work of as many previously neglected poets as possible in the hope of bringing them some critical attention. Harris and Aguero themselves seem almost embarrassed by the prospect of validating one particular poet as opposed to another. In their multicultural anthology *An Ear to the Ground*, for example, despite their expressed desire to recognize and promote "authentic claimants to a place in [the] American canon," and to "explore the ways in which aesthetics are related to cultural backgrounds," they also assert that essays on specific poets "are intended to serve [only] as examples of the kind of detailed consideration necessary to acquaint readers with 'uncanonized' poets and not meant to promote one writer to the exclusion of others." These statements appear to be at cross-purposes. If the goal is, as they claim in the preface, to "appreciate the possibilities such diversity presents" by "abandon[ing] narrow definitions and assumptions and evaluat[ing] the poem from the inside out," they need to articulate more clearly what their new, more flexible definitions will be (in aesthetic as well as cultural terms) and how those new definitions will expand the possibilities of poetic practice.[13]

Harris and Aguero's reluctance to make any specific evaluative or aesthetic claims about the poetry discussed is typical of much multicultural criticism. The problem with such an approach, despite its democratic intentions, is that treating *all* poets as equally deserving of critical attention will not succeed in bringing *any* of them to the kind of prominence needed for a place in the canon. Harris and Aguero's collections of multicultural poetry and poetics give us a sense that there are a lot of American poets writing (especially if we accept their claim that "a dozen such anthologies" could have been collected), but does not help us to decide which poets from among that multitude deserve our particular attention. Like Moyers, they seem more interested in exploring the way in which poems grow from "experiences and stories other than those that have dominated the classroom textbooks" than in their professed desire to present "the best of many aesthetics," and their rather defensive claim to not "consciously" have chosen the most "ethnic" work leaves us wondering what the rationales for their choices *were*.[14]

In evaluating both the criticism and the anthologizing of multicultural poetry, other important issues need to be addressed as well. We need to move beyond reductive studies of race, gender, and ethnicity to look more closely at a wider range of sociocultural factors. How do educational background and current academic affiliation affect the canonical success of poets from various traditions? How do the institutional histories of minority poets differ from those of their mainstream counterparts, in terms of grants, prizes, publication, inclusion in anthologies, attendance at writers' colonies, teaching positions, and participation in reading series? In larger terms, we need to examine how accurate race and ethnicity really are as indicators of poetic diversity, especially if they are not linked with such factors as class, region, and educational background. We should not simply take for granted, as Harris and Aguero do, that minority or ethnic poets write from "cultural histories" whose "notions of the nature and functions of art . . . differ from those enshrined in the academy."[15] Can we assume that because a poet is Latino or Native American he will have a particular politics, a particular stylistic orientation, a particular relation to the poetic canon, or a particular social, economic, or educational background? Is the poet's racial and ethnic identity necessarily more relevant to an understanding of her work than factors such as where she studied creative writing, in what neighborhood or region of the country she grew up, or who her most significant poetic influences are? In Garrett Hongo's recent anthology of Asian American poets, *The Open Boat*, for example, the majority of the poets represented hold either MFAs or MAs in creative writing. While this is somewhat less true of the poets represented in anthologies of Latino, Native American, and African American writing, the trend appears to be toward a greater integration of minority groups into the workshop environment and, by extension, into the officially sanctioned mainstream poetry network that surrounds it. In fact, the work of an Asian American poet like Hongo (Irvine MFA, tenured professor at the University of Oregon), an African American poet like Rita Dove (Iowa MFA, national poet laureate, and poetry chair at the University of Virginia), a Latino poet like Martin Espada, or a Native American poet like Linda Hogan manifests a greater affinity with the conventions of a mainstream confessional, lyric, or narrative tradition than do the works of many white male poets writing today.

The answers to these questions are not simple. Clearly, grouping poets according to a particular "identity politics" has an important function, not only in legitimizing or empowering the writers of those groups, but also in creating a sense of solidarity within an ethnic or racial community that can lead to greater cultural awareness and greater cooperation between writers, publishers, booksellers, and readers. At the same time, however, poetic groupings based solely on race or identity politics can give a misleading impression of political, thematic, or stylistic uniformity. Even more important, they risk "ghettoizing" the selected poets further, encouraging their reception as "ethnic" poets read primarily by those within their own groups rather than being integrated with poets from other backgrounds into a canon of exceptional work. Yet, in an irony noted by Harris and Aguero, it may only be by being placed into racial or ethnic categories that minority poets can gain recognition "as authentic claimants to a place in a real American canon."[16]

In 1993, a critical symposium at the University of Virginia posed the question, "Does literary value supersede other kinds of value?" The papers given in the symposium and later published in the multicultural journal *Callaloo* raise a number of questions that are germane to the issues of multicultural diversity and canon formation that I have raised. Can or should a critical discussion of multicultural literature, or for that matter of any literature, claim to offer a noncontingent assessment of aesthetic value? Can the discussion of poetry by writers from other races and ethnicities lead to more enlightening discussions of the ways in which both canonical and noncanonical works can "employ complicated formal strategies to teach and delight"?[17] Should we accept the premise, common to many who work in the fields of feminism, multiculturalism, and cultural studies, that "assessing or cherishing literary merit is not our business in the new world order"?[18] Or should we attempt to find ways, in Eric Lott's formulation, in which "good art can actually further the ends of a politics cultural studies can respect"? According to Lott, aesthetic standards can be meaningfully applied not only to "high art," but to various forms of popular culture such as pop songs (Randy Newman's "Sail Away"), comedy routines (Richard Pryor), and music videos (Michael Jackson's "Black or White"). Such aesthetic evaluation of popular art forms not only leads to more subtle understandings of social and political content, but can lead to a "redistribution" of aesthetic pleasure in which the genuine aesthetic qualities of even the least privileged forms of expression can be taught and celebrated.[19]

Clearly, the issues for multicultural poetry are somewhat different from those in the study of "popular culture." Despite the ways in which some, like Moyers, would seek to establish a larger public for poetry through an appeal to its more "populist" elements—its universal accessibility, its personal or emotional power, and its value as community-based narrative or entertainment—most of the poets in Moyers's series would not consider their poems examples of "popular culture." For a traditional academic critic like Vendler, however, the gap between poetry as presented by Moyers's public television series and popular culture as presented through the same medium (for example, the airing of a public television special on the rock group REM, or the PBS series on the history of rock) is less significant than that which exists between all such "media events" and the arts at their most sublime. Vendler's disparagement of the poets in Moyers's series reflects a tendency to find worthwhile aesthetic complexity only in those works that offer a more rarefied form of pleasure, works that, in the terms of Pierre Bourdieu, are accessible only to those who have attained the cultural capital necessary to participate in the more sublimated aesthetic experiences they offer.

For Vendler, the purpose of such television programs as Moyers's should be to present "experts in imagination, language and literature," rather than narratives of human interest or celebrations of the human condition. Moyers's series is based on the premise that the more people who experience poetry—even if a less intellectually sophisticated form of poetry—the better. Vendler's critique is based on the opposite assumption: that to give people poetry under these circumstances, to "dumb it down" for an audience that is presumed to be unprepared for the difficulties of an Ashbery or a Bidart, or uninterested in gaining a better understanding of poetic art and tradition, is doing no one a favor. In fact, while Moyers's unstintingly "middlebrow" approach to poetry may reflect too low an opinion of the average public television viewer, Vendler's expectations of the mainstream media are almost certainly too high. Moyers's series is probably no better or worse in this respect than most cultural programming on television, which tends to sink toward the path of least intellectual resistance far more often than it reaches the kind of sublime insight or sophisticated analysis Vendler demands. It may be true audiences would expect to see evidence of "both gifts and training . . . in the production of violinists and lithographers," but how many television programs do we see that explore in any depth the technical or cultural aspects of art production or classical musicianship?[20]

Whatever lessons we may take from the Moyers series, we must see it as an example of the power available to the popular media in shaping the literary canon, a canon that may increasingly be determined not by poets and academic critics, but by media events and personalities. Every poet in this series will be seen and heard by far more people (six million, by the estimates of PBS, saw Moyers's previous series *The Power of the Word*) than will read or hear any other poet writing in America. The programs will be used in colleges and schools, and will influence the curriculum of teaching contemporary American poetry. Not only will more people watch this program than will buy all American poetry books combined in a given year; more will watch it than will experience the vast majority of popular performers as well. In strictly numerical terms, then, these poets will achieve instant canonical status in a way that few others can in a lifetime of writing and publishing. And while Sekou Sundiata may never be as well known to the general public as, say, Michael Jackson, he and the other poets in the series will attain a level of popular recognition available to few literary writers. Our notion of the canon may need to be reevaluated at a time when, to adapt Andy Warhol's phrase, even poets can have their fifteen minutes of fame.

Media fame is by definition ephemeral; the aesthetic text, on the other hand, is a multifaceted and lasting artifact that can transcend, while still recalling, its ethnic, racial, or ideological roots. Foregrounding the poet's identity (at least if identity is defined within the fairly narrow parameters of the current politics of multiculturalism) can be dangerous, leading either to obsolescence or to essentialism, if we do not also emphasize other aspects of the poet's craft. As Marjorie Perloff suggests, the privileging of "poetry by women of color over the poetry of white men" leads, in its most reductive form, to a romanticizing myth of the "Authentic Other" as by nature more exotic as a subject of study.[21] To anthropologize the study of poetry in the way Moyers's series does runs the danger of diverting our attention from the poetic text to the person who wrote it. It also makes the mistake of assuming (or at least implying) that the speaker or persona of the poem is in every case identical to (or even commensurate with) the biographical poet.

Ultimately, the importance of a poem can rest neither on its narrative content nor on the biographical position of the poet, however compelling that content or biography may be. In seeking to distinguish those works that are of purely transitory or topical importance from those that will have some lasting significance, the canon responds less to content—which is a clearly "contingent" value—than to form, which continues to exert a pressure on readers even when the content no longer appears radical or unfamiliar. In fact, the place where values are the most clearly contingent is *not* within the literary canon, which evolves relatively slowly and filters various perspectives over time, but within in the popular media, and especially the electronic media, where the dissemination of ideas and information is instantaneous and driven by the risks and rewards of capital.

This fact may lie behind much of Vendler's hostility toward the Moyers project. After all, a canon of poets she has lovingly and painstakingly promoted both from within the academy and from the pages of the *New York Times* and other publications has in one stroke of the mass media been supplanted by an alternative canon that, from her point of view, displays only dubious poetic achievements. No wonder she wishes to return our attention to a canon that has her own aesthetic imprimatur, rather than one sanctified only by a media personality with no literary credentials. The assumption made by Vendler in assessing Moyers's program is that there are others in the media who would or could do a better job of bringing poetry to a mass audience. Toward the end of her review, Vendler offers a series of suggestions for more advantageous approaches to poetry on television:

Let us ask—and show visually—what imaginative spin [poets] have put on phenomena in their poems, and why and how this imaginative transformation of reality occurs. Let us inquire—and illustrate with film clips—what aspects of language appeal to them for reworking and heightening. . . . Let us show what other arts—sculpture, jazz, marquetry, whatever—are important to them, with illustrations.

The Life of Canons and the Languages of Life 117

The structure of these sentences implies that Vendler herself might take an active role in such a project, although the "us" here might simply be a rhetorical call to the entire literary community or to the nation at large. But the problem remains that Vendler is an academic critic and educator and not a media personality, and that these two worlds remain, in American culture, very far apart. While it is certainly possible that Moyers could have presented poetry more interestingly and more effectively than he has, it could be argued that he should be praised for bringing poetry to the people in *any* form. As the *Poets and Writers* article makes clear, securing funding for the programs, despite Moyers's high-profile status, was not easy: Moyers and the producer of the series, David Grubin, were turned down by two dozen foundations and nearly abandoned the project before finding the necessary support. Regardless of what we may think of the final product, a large number of people will at least be exposed to poems that may send them out in search of more. In the future, perhaps Moyers will put together another program with more of Vendler's poets; or perhaps Vendler will produce another series of her own.[22]

In whatever case, it is clear that today the popular media, and especially television, have a greater capacity to destabilize the canon and to upset the expectations of the academic "keepers of the gate" than ever before. The question for poetry in the coming decades is, How will the mass media intersect with other social and cultural institutions to construct the poetic canon, or canons, of the twenty-first century? We should at the very least become suspicious, as Adrienne Rich suggests in her interview with Moyers, when capital and the mainstream media are willing to invest in the commodification of diversity. What resists this commodification may not be the narratives themselves—which operate according to exactly the kind of personal identity politics television viewers have become accustomed to by the barrage of talk shows and "infotainment" programs—but the ways in which those narratives achieve poetic form. What is certain is that exceptionally gifted poets will continue to emerge—both within the mainstream and from the margins—who will defy the power of any institutional framework, including the popular media, to contain or define them. We will continue to need critics able to evaluate the formal and linguistic strategies of poets, as well as to explain their positions within various institutional configurations. But the power of the mass media to construct aesthetic taste will put media entrepreneurs like Moyers, and not academic critics and grant committees, in positions of increasing responsibility for the process of canon formation within the field of American poetry.

The social composition of its audience is the primary context of any writing. Context determines (and is determined by) both the motives of the readers and their experience, their history, i.e. their particular set of possible codes. Context determines the actual, real-life composition of the literary product, without which communication of a message (formal, substantive, ideological) cannot occur.

—Ron Silliman, "The Political Economy of Poetry"

For whatever reasons, the generous impulse of poetry, the inclusive and embracing energies of poetry, had been left behind. It had been redefined as something that had to be studied, more an academic exercise than a vital part of our lives. And right now, at this moment, we are beginning to hear the first screams from people who have not been able to engage in the national dialogue. And the poets are the ones who, right now, are speaking from all these experiences, and a lot of the poems are screams of "I AM."

—Bob Holman

6. Poetic Screams of "I AM"
The Nuyorican Cafe and Spoken-Word Culture

The Nuyorican Poets Cafe is located in a section of New York's Lower East Side known as "Alphabet City," most famous in recent years as the site of altercations between homeless squatters and the New York City police. The blocks surrounding the cafe hardly suggest a typical venue for poetry readings: garbage-filled vacant lots punctuate rows of decaying tenements, and the signs of gentrification that mark the Tompkins Square area to the north have not yet reached this neighborhood. On entering the cafe, however, one is immediately embraced by a festive atmosphere: the narrow but surprisingly deep, high-ceilinged, brick-walled space exudes a warm, almost cozy feeling. The crowd itself is mostly young and includes an unusually diverse mix. Any given night might bring out aspiring teen-age poets, students from Barnard or NYU, and Beat-generation bards; the audience will include middle-class whites from Queens and Bensonhurst, Latinos from the Lower East Side, blacks from uptown, and visitors who have come to this mecca of slam poetry from Chicago, Los Angeles, Boston, or Dublin.

It's a hot midsummer night, and most of New York's literary community has escaped the city for cooler and greener pastures. While virtually all the city's reading series have been shut down for July and August, the Nuyorican is one of the few places where one can see and hear poetry performed on a regular basis throughout the summer. Tonight is Friday, "slam night" at the Nuyorican. If the Wednesday night "open slam" seems a more relaxed and impromptu get-together, Friday night has a carnival atmosphere, a feeling produced by the later starting time (10 P.M., as opposed to 9 P.M., for the "open"), the loud disco music and flashing lights, and the packed house. For this event, there will be five poets, each of whom will read twice, and five judges, chosen at random from the audience. The participants in the Friday night slam are poets who have either won a Wednesday night open, or who are known within the Nuyorican community. The judges are instructed to give scores from 1 to 10, down to two decimal places, from which the highest and lowest will be thrown out. In fact, scores such as 8.79 give a mock serious sense of precision to what is in many cases a fairly arbitrary scoring mechanism.

Lots are drawn to determine the order of the slam. The first performer is Gloria, who reads a lyrical, rhyming, somewhat surreal poem, "I Dreamed a River."[1] Gloria's poem, the most traditionally "literary" of the evening, is received with polite applause but little enthusiasm. It is followed by an erotic love poem by a Latina poet, Raquel; her poem is written in the idiom of the street, and it elicits more excitement from the crowd and higher scores from the judges. The third reader is Judy, an African American woman who reads a sentimental poem to her daughter. While her performance is less polished than those of the first two readers, the raw emotions of the poem appeal to the audience. Next comes Judith ("Bassi"), a tough and brassy Latina who reads an angry poem about the various men she has or hasn't slept with, punctuated with numerous expletives: Bassi's in-your-face style seems too aggressive even for the excitement-hungry crowd of the Nuyorican, and her scores fall below those of the other contestants. Finally the last reader, Lila, a white Jewish woman and first-time slammer, reads a controlled and persuasive narrative poem about working as an artist's model: it is generally well received, but scores below the more immediately accessible poems of Raquel and Judy.

After a break, the poets read their second round of poems, which stylistically follow the model of the first. Raquel is declared the winner, with Judy in second place. Lila and Gloria, arguably the most talented writers of the group, lack either the charismatic performance skills of Raquel or the raw directness of Judy, the two qualities that appear—at least in this instance—to be required of a successful slammer. Clearly, this is not a forum in which poems are recognized primarily for their verbal sophistication or artistry: for this audience, accessibility and emotion are most important.

Although the Friday night slam at the Nuyorican typifies several aspects of the slam phenomenon as it exists both in New York City and across the country, it by no means exhausts the possibilities for the slam format. In fact, the poetry slam has produced, in its first decade of existence, a relatively large community of poets and a remarkable variety of related cultural practices. From its humble origins in the late 1980s in the Green Mill Lounge of Chicago's Uptown neighborhood, the slam has grown into a nationwide practice with its own national organization (Poetry Slam, Inc.), its own newsletter (*Slam: The International Performance Poetry Newsletter*), its own set of rules and guidelines (now adjudicated at an annual national meeting), and slams held regularly in more than fifty cities, of which over thirty sent four-person teams to the most recent Annual U.S. Poetry Slam Championships. The slam has even become something of an international event, with slams held in England, Wales, Holland, Germany, Sweden, Finland, Australia, Israel, and Japan. In New York City alone, variations on the slam include the Erotic Slam, Hecklers' Slam, Low Ball Slam, Haiku Slam, Funny Poem Slam, Gay Pride Disco Slam, and Improv Slam; there are even "virtual slams" on the Internet. The anthology *Aloud: Voices from the Nuyorican Poets Cafe* (Henry Holt, 1994), edited by Miguel Algarin and Bob Holman, has proved to be one of the more successful poetry anthologies of recent years, selling sixteen thousand copies in its first year in print. The anthology contains more than a hundred poets associated with the Nuyorican, and the burgeoning ranks of younger slam or performance poets who were not included have already inspired calls for an updated edition. A few slammers—such as Paul Beatty, Dana Bryant, Reg E. Gaines, Lisa Buscani, Patricia Smith, and Maggie Estep—have already achieved national reputations based largely on the live performance of their poems. The "Free Your Mind" spoken-word tour, organized by MTVs Affiliate Promotions Department, has sent Estep, Reg E. Gaines, John S. Hall and other poet-performers on a nationwide tour of college campuses and other venues. Corporate sponsorship of slam teams has begun, with Mouth Almighty Records, a subsidiary of Mercury Records, sponsoring recent winners of the national championships.

The slam phenomenon has also led to the increased visibility of spoken-word poetry in general, which has prospered in the age of poetry/music crossovers. Poets like Bryant, Estep, Hall, Morris, and Henry Rollins have been involved with both kinds of performance. Reg E. Gaines has recorded two spoken-word albums and wrote the lyrics for the successful Broadway musical *Bring in Da Noise, Bring in Da Funk*. Estep's spoken-word recording, *No More Mr. Nice Girl*, has sold more than thirty thousand copies: a modest showing by the standards of the recording industry, but a clear bestseller by poetry standards. Slam poets, including Estep and Smith, have performed as part of the rock music festival Lollapalooza both during set changes and in a side-stage provocatively entitled "Revival Tent of the Rev. Samuel Mudd's Little Spoken-Word Armaggeddon." Slammers may not have the status of rock stars, but eight hundred people attended an *audition* in San Francisco for a road poet spot. Poets have appeared both on MTV's *Unplugged* series (where Estep's "The Stupid Jerk I'm Obsessed With" video was considered by many the highlight of the show) and in a half-hour segment of public television's *Alive from Off Center* entitled "Words in Your Face." Estep's video performance of "Hey Baby" even had the dubious honor of being aired on the *Beavis and Butthead* show, giving her work an exposure to an even younger audience.

In some cases, success in slamming has also led to publishing opportunities, a phenomenon that will no doubt continue as audiences for slam poets grow. Beatty's second book of poems, *Joker, Joker, Deuce*, was published by Penguin; his first novel is out and his second has reportedly sold for six figures. Hal Sirowitz's book *Mother Said* (Crown) has already sold eighteen thousand copies; Smith has three published books of poetry; Estep has published a novel and is completing a second. The slam phenomenon has been discussed in such publications as *Rolling Stone, High Times, Seventeen*, the *Village Voice*, the *New Yorker*, and the *New York Times*. Bob Holman, who has been variously called the "Guru," the "Czar," and the "Ringmaster" of spoken-word poetry, has made promotional appearances on such television programs as *Nightline, Good Morning America*, and the *Charlie Rose Show*. Slam poets have in some cases earned the status of local heroes and are seen as sources of civic pride. When the Cleveland team won the 1994 national slam, they were congratulated by the city council and the mayor, interviewed on a local talk show, and formally saluted by the county commissioner. In New Mexico, there is a statewide high school slam championship, and attempts are being made to sanction poetry slams as extracurricular events on the level of sports and debate.

Clearly, such popular and civic attention to poetry is unprecedented in recent American memory. It is too early to know exactly what the long-term impact of the slam and spoken-word phenomenon will be on poetic culture in America, but it is already clear that its influence will be decisive in several respects. The interpenetration of popular and literary elements that we find in the slam subculture will inevitably affect not only the production of poetry, but its audience as well. The demographics of poetry slams, as opposed to either mainstream academic poetry or experimental (Language) poetry, indicate its appeal among a younger, more racially diverse, less educated and less affluent audience. It is an audience that is potentially far larger than that for academic poetry. New York alone has hundreds of slam poets, and the number of people who attend spoken-word events in a given year at the Nuyorican, Biblio's, the Fez, Jackie 60, and other Manhattan venues is certainly in the thousands. When we multiply those figures by the number of cities with slams and various forms of open-mike and performance-oriented readings—from Portland, Maine, to Portland, Oregon—the audience is very large indeed by poetry standards, and growing rapidly. With the greater distribution network for spoken-word recordings provided by Tower Records and other chains, nonacademic audiences have ready access to spoken-word poetry in "published" as well as live form.

The greater emphasis on performance will also have an effect on the packaging and marketing of poetry in this country, but what will that effect be? Will the audiences who now attend slams begin buying books by other American poets? Will the slam continue to function as the primary form of poetic event within the spoken-word community, or will it give way to a more diverse constellation of formats, including mixed-media uses of music, dance, theater, video, and visual art?[2] Also unclear is the degree to which the new poetry will penetrate the popular marketplace of rap, rock music, and video. Will there be a "superstar" of slam poetry, a figure who will make the transition from the subcultural field of production to a more widespread cultural exposure? Will a spoken-word artist ever have a gold or platinum recording? Will we see increasing numbers of spoken-word performers on MTV, on CD recordings, and elsewhere in the mass media? These questions are all highly pertinent to a discussion of the slam, and more generally of a performance-oriented poetry, as a cultural practice, and they inform my own analysis of the slam subculture.

The poetry reading—as the most public site of poetry and the site of its oral performance rather than its written reception—is a crucial index of the way poetry is defined within a given culture at a given moment. First, the reading is an event that mediates between poetry as an oral and a written practice, thus calling attention to the aural/textual relationship that in part defines the poetic genre. Second, it is a ritual that mediates in the most direct way between poet and audience, thus establishing a social or interpersonal context for the poem. Finally, it is a forum that mediates between local communities of poets and the larger institutional structures of American poetry, thus acting as one of the few institutions that ensures a continued public for poetry. It is important to remember, however, that the poetry reading is itself a relatively recent development in this country. Only in the 1950s, with the highly successful reading tours of Dylan Thomas in the early part of the decade and the even greater popular success of the Beat readings later in the decade, did the poetry reading become a fixture of American poetic life and an important source of both income and publicity for poets. In San Francisco, and to a lesser extent in New York City, poets used the forum of the reading both to gain a larger popular audience and to distance their work from the formally constrained poems of the New Critical mode.

Michael Davidson has characterized the greater "performative impulse" that developed as an integral part of the San Francisco Renaissance of the 1950s.[3] In general terms, many aspects of the 1950s readings Davidson describes can also be seen as germane to the current spoken-word scene: the emphasis on performance and performativity, the social function of the audience as a community theater for the poem, the populist sense of the poem as direct communication, the de-emphasis of the written medium, and the importance of the physical presence of the poets themselves. Davidson describes one North Beach event, the weekly Blabbermouth Night held at a bar called "the Place," that anticipates more directly the slam itself. Like the slam, Blabbermouth Night was a mock poetry contest, founded by Jack Spicer, in which poets would engage in a kind of "spontaneous glossolalia" in front of the microphone, the "winner" receiving a free drink. While the North Beach bar and coffeehouse scene of fifties poets was clearly more "literary" than the current slam scene, it shared the sense of a community built around a regular event, "complete with hecklers, claques, and door prizes." San Francisco poets of the 1950s and 1960s also participated, much as do spoken-word poets today, in the nonliterary culture of the day, from Haight-Ashbury in the 1950s to concerts at the Avalan and the Filmore in the 1960s where Beat poets would warm up crowds for rock groups such as Jefferson Airplane and the Grateful Dead.[4]

The intersection of high and popular culture represented by the Beats anticipated the current trend toward a performance poetry that negotiates between a range of cultural discourses.[5] Some of the most salient aspects of slam or spoken-word poetry are the hybridization of cultural forms, the carnivalesque play with sociocultural categories, the emphasis on the body as an integral part of cultural semiosis, the analogy of the slam itself to a sports event with both individual and team competition, the emphasis on performance/performativity and entertainment/spectacle, the more explicitly violent and sexual content of much of the work, and the implicit parody of high cultural discourses. What may be less obvious to some readers—despite the apparent "high seriousness" of the poetic project as outlined by Holman, Miguel Algarin, and others—are the ways in which these poems can still be seen as participating in a realm of high, literary, or avant-garde cultural production. Skeptics may ask: this is fine as performance or entertainment, but in what sense is it "poetry"?

Just as not all MTV videos or all rap songs are identically situated with respect to generic definitions of popular culture, not all poets who participate in slams or who are active within spoken-word communities have the same relationship to traditional or culturally accepted definitions of "poetry." Even within the slam community, there exists a divide along the lines of high/low culture. In 1993 a slammer named Wolf Knight accused the organizers of the San Francisco National Slam of slanting the judging toward "the Chicago-NY-San Fran-Boston in crowd." Charging the slam bureaucracy (including Holman and slam organizer Gary Glazner) with cultural elitism, Knight vowed to "free poetry from the academic establishment and return it to the people."[6] Knight's comments may seem somewhat tendentious, given the apparent distance of all of this poetry from the "academic establishment," but they reflect the inherent tensions between slam's working-class origins and the slickness of more recent slammers, who often combine MTV-inspired performances and rap-influenced delivery. In the case of the Nuyorican, one might also contrast the cafe's origins as a center for a form of poetry strongly identified with a particular local and ethnic community (the Latinos, or Nuyoricans, of the Lower East Side) with its more recent manifestation as a center of media attention and a confluence of academic and nonacademic worlds: the slam can be read as either a clash or a fortunate fusion of avant-garde sensibilities and populist sympathies, of uptown rap and downtown poetry. For the most part, however, the slam scene has managed to remain relatively nonacademic in focus. As Nuyorican slam "host" Shutup Shelley puts it, the slam is a "black-market product" that has to compete—with far more modest resources—against the much larger economy of academic poetry and creative-writing programs.[7] In its most outrageous manifestations—like Verbal Abuse's annual "All-Star Poetry Burlesque," an evening including a striptease act and "red-light spoken word" from Empress Chi-Chi Valenti and other performers—the spoken-word scene seems as far from the genteel halls of academe as could possibly be imagined.[8]

One might wonder why it is necessary to engage the question of the slam's cultural status at all in a "postmodern" era when the boundaries between high art and popular culture have in the eyes of many commentators already been almost entirely erased. Indeed, as Jim Collins asks, "What value is there in making exclusionary distinctions about whether any text is popular culture?" We might simply say, with Geoffrey Nowell-Smith, that "the division, typical of the middle half of the century, between a popular culture which was increasingly industrialized, and a 'high' culture which clung to a preindustrial independence, has now broken down." Nevertheless, it is important to recognize, as does John Frow, that although "it is no longer possible to understand aesthetic culture as a unified and hierarchical system of value," we must continue to address the important problem "of how to describe contemporary relations of cultural value and authority, and their relation to social power." Rather than accepting either the postmodern elimination of cultural boundaries (as articulated by most contemporary writing within the fields of cultural studies, media studies, and communication studies) or the countervailing assumption that the boundaries are self-evident on aesthetic grounds (the position expressed by many within the academic and nonacademic communities concerned with traditional artistic fields), we need to ask what are the institutional gestures that define a cultural artifact with respect to the prevailing definitions of high culture and mass or popular culture. As Frow comments, "the regimes that make up the domain of 'high' culture consist of sets of interlocking institutions framing particular kinds of practice and producing certain axiological regularities." These institutions may in fact be very different in the case of mass or popular culture.[9]

Indeed, institutional contexts influence every point in the process of cultural production: prior to the creation or presentation of the cultural artifact (school curricula that reinforce certain aesthetic assumptions, writing programs and workshops, public and private funding), during the creation or presentation (performances, exhibitions, readings, venues for journal and book publication), and after the creation or presentation (critical reception, academic recuperation, analysis, canonization). Thus, when I invoke the terms "high culture" and "popular culture" I do so not in the name of an aesthetic dichotomy or a hierarchy of critical judgment, but with an awareness that the distinction between the two is predicated on a complex system of practices involving class, educational training, and other forms of social and cultural capital. Clearly, the neat and orderly boundary between practices ("high" and "low") or between audiences (highbrow, middlebrow, and lowbrow) has been problematized in a number of ways. Not only are different forms of taste, judgment, or "discrimi-natory ability" characteristic of different kinds of audiences (John Fiske), but we increasingly find sites and situations in which "the audiences of [different] cultural spheres overlap" (Jostein Gripsrud).[10] There are now "double-access" audiences as well as "single-access" audiences, audiences whose relationship to culture, rather than being overdetermined by class or education, is flexible and constantly evolving. As Kirk Varnedoe and Adam Gopnik write in the conclusion of *High and Low: Modern Art and Popular Culture*, "We live in a world . . . where Utamaro and *Doones-bury*, Elvis Presley and Jasper Johns, modern art in all its intensity and popular culture in all its pleasures sustain us nearly simultaneously, and each of us has to decide for ourselves what weight or measure to give to each of these things."[11] Even the long-accepted terms of the dichotomy as expressed here—between high culture as cultivated, intellectual, abstract, and formal and popular culture as visceral, formulaic, and unreflectively pleasurable—are beginning to erode, as we become increasingly aware of the important role of learning and discrimination in all forms of cultural production.[12] Popular culture has itself become more stratified and less easily definable (and dismissable) on aesthetic grounds, as forms of irony, pastiche, parody, and self-parody, as well as more sophisticated techniques of stylization and defamiliarization, are increasingly prevalent within such popular media as television, music, MTV, and Hollywood film.[13]

Yet despite the convincing argument that has been made in the case of several cultural genres for an aesthetic production that resists clear identi-fication as either "high" or "popular"—graffiti art and post-pop or meta-pop art; cartoon art, graphic novels, and experimental comics; under-ground, countercultural, or experimental rock; bebop and free jazz—such distinctions have not been broken down to the same extent within the field of poetry. Poetic practice in this country has been defined almost exclusively as either "high" culture—the current academic split being between a mainstream lyric (official high culture) and an experimental poetry (avant-garde high art)—or as a kind of "folk" culture, often with local or regional affiliations (cowboy poetry, street poetry). In the case of the poetry slam, however, and the spoken-word phenomenon more generally, we find a confusion of discursive modes and cultural positions that is different both from the appropriation of popular culture by academic or avant-garde poetry (as in the poems of, say, John Ashbery, Albert Goldbarth, or Charles Bernstein), and from the populist or proletarian poetry documented by Cary Nelson in *Repression and Recovery* (a tradition that persists, to some degree, in the work of a poet like Charles Bukowski and in much of the poetry one hears at open-mike readings).[14]

I would argue not only that slam poetry resists identification with either high or popular culture, but that it is a true hybrid of the two, inhabiting a cultural space that is simultaneously part of the aesthetic (literary) marketplace and part of a less aesthetically defined and more socially grounded popular marketplace. It is significant that the two "popular" genres with which spoken-word poetry has been most often compared—rap and MTV—are both themselves hybrid genres. Both exhibit a formal hybridization (sampling in the case of rap, pastiche/parody in the case of MTV), and both are historically hybridized from other more established genres (MTV from narrative film, advertising, and music performance; rap from various Afro-diasporic traditions and contemporary urban hip-hop culture as well as African American oral, poetic, and protest traditions).[15] Both rap and MTV generate a high degree of crossover appeal, and thus are able to reach a wide spectrum of people "from different racial or ethnic groups and social positions."[16] Both are complex practices that can be "read" on many levels, from the formal analysis of sampling and montage to the semiotics of cultural representation. Finally, both include a wide range of variant subgenres or modes of practice: in the case of rap, from the "gangsta rap" of NWA, Ice Cube, and Snoop Doggy Dogg, to the "playful Afrocentricity" of De La Soul, to the more literary rap of Arrested Development and Digable Planets, to the woman-centered rap of Queen Latifah and other female rappers; in MTV, from straight concert videos to highly stylized and self-conscious productions that adopt various "avant-garde" styles in order to subvert traditional forms of aesthetic discourse.[17]

The slam itself is as different from a conventional poetry reading as a punk-rock concert is from a classical string quartet. The most obvious structural difference between the slam and any other kind of reading is that the performances of poems are openly judged and scored. Poets read one poem at a time, with a maximum of three minutes for each reading.

Normally no props or musical instruments are allowed, but the slammers employ every other device at their disposal, from body language, to dress (from jeans and T-shirts to chic or sexy to the positively outré), to vocal modulations including screaming, whispering, chanting, singing, and rapping, to inventive uses of the microphone itself.

The slam has three key players. The first is the "host," a kind of master of ceremonies who not only picks the judges, explains the rules, and introduces the poet-contestants, but is also responsible for maintaining the pace and general liveliness of the event. Second are the poets, who try to read, recite, or perform their poems (preferably "off-paper") as dramatically as possible in order to obtain the highest scores from the judges and win the event. Finally, there is the audience, which both individually and collectively is an active participant rather than a passive spectator. Members of the audience not only judge the contest, but engage in a range of reactions to the performances (and to the judging), including applause (sometimes rivaling the yelps, whoops, and whistles of a sports event or rock concert), various forms of heckling (hisses, boos, cat-calls, and trading insults), and bantering with the "host." On a Wednesday night "open," most of the audience will be participants in one way or another: either as performers (as many as thirty a night), as judges, or as active rooters for their friends or for the kinds of poetry they like.

In fact, it is difficult to remain uninvolved or impartial at a slam: the element of spectacle draws the spectator into a ritualized world of audience participation as surely as *The Rocky Horror Picture Show* or, at the other end of the spectrum, a performance of *La Traviata* at the Met. The slam fuses successfully a "high cultural" literary event and the kind of urban nightlife we might find at a nightclub or rock concert. Unlike traditional poetry readings, which reify the "poet" as a distinct and lofty figure and the spectator as a silent and respectful listener, the slam creates a far more ambiguous interaction: everyone in the audience is simultaneously a potential poet, a "fan," and an "expert." Members of the audience not only "judge" the slam contestants (in a kind of parody of the judging of Olympic diving or figure skating); they may also be called upon to vote on such questions as whether to allow a late arrival to read. The slam is, then, despite the degree of discrimination implied by the judging, a highly democratic event. Although in one respect the slam format reinforces the distinction between artist and audience through the institutionalization of judgment, in another respect it flaunts that very institution by treating the entire affair, and the judging in particular, with a highly irreverent attitude. It is in fact customary to announce at the beginning of every slam that "the best poem always loses," thus on the one hand acknowledging the fallibility (or impossibility) of "judging" the success of an aesthetic artifact such as a poem, and on the other hand creating a real ambiguity about exactly what the event finally means. For some slammers, who take the event more seriously, receiving high scores and ultimately "winning" a slam (perhaps even going on to the semifinals, finals, or national slam) can be a matter of great importance, with serious economic consequences, including opportunities for publication or for a record or MTV deal.[18] For others, who recognize the self-parodic aspect of the event, it is simply a chance to have one's poetry heard in a public forum and to have some fun while doing it. The fact that the prize for winning is usually very nominal (ten dollars at the Nuyorican) further indicates its inverse relationship to more mainstream examples of such "contests," from the *Gong Show* and *Star Search* in the realm of mass culture to literary prizes or piano competitions in the realm of high culture. Yet the slam also has more serious ties to other cultural forms: from the medieval "word joust" to which it has been compared by various commentators, to other performative traditions such as the oratorical or declamatory traditions of Latino cultures, the rapping and call-and-response traditions of African American culture, and various traditions of spoken-word performance, stand-up comedy, and scat singing.[19] While some poems are clearly constructed according to more traditional aesthetic principles, others are geared to their value as entertainment, either as comedy or melodramatic narrative. Audience reactions vary according to the kind of poem and the type of performance; the slam can quickly shift from the noisy cheering of a professional wrestling match to a contemplative silence.

Another salient aspect of the slam is the sense of a community that grows up around the event. Many of the readers in a Wednesday night open are "regulars" who try out their poems week after week until they achieve greater success: one poet refers to himself as the "Grandmaster" of the slam, and others are clearly known to, and appreciated by, the audience. First-time slammers are called "virgins," and are loudly announced as such. The role of the "host" is an important part of the community experience: the host must introduce the poets and make them feel comfortable, while also entertaining the audience with a running commentary, or, as in the case of Wednesday night hostess Shutup Shelley, a kind of comedy routine. When Shelley hosts at the Nuyorican, she creates a generally supportive and nonjudgmental atmosphere; however, she will not hesitate to comment on a poet's reading. This usually involves words of encouragement—"Your poem rocks!" or "You've got a great mind!"—but occasionally greater skepticism, as when a poem seems overly "arty." Shelley's running commentary also serves to demystify the more "confessional" aspects of poetry. After one woman reads a poem about a rape, Shelley asks her, "Did that really happen to you?" Thus, the blurred line between poetic persona and real experience that serves as an enabling convention for much "workshop" poetry is broken down: poets are expected to be talking about their "real" lives, and if not, to own up to the fictional nature of the work.

The judging itself becomes self-parodically ritualistic, as a great deal is made of picking and introducing the judges, calculating and announcing the scores, and either applauding or booing the scoring. While the judging might at first appear as a crassly self-conscious way of "hyping" the spectacle, it later appears to be an effective means of creating audience involvement, especially in an environment where many of the spectators know very little about either traditional poetry or the etiquette of poetry readings. Despite the amount of ostensible attention paid to the scoring, it does ultimately play a secondary role to the poets themselves, many of whom have, if not much of a literary sense, at least a personal style that is projected, with more or less positive reception, to the audience. The most favorably received poems are often those with either a very personal or a markedly political content. Poems about relationships between the sexes, rape, AIDS, racism, homophobia, street violence, and anger toward the establishment tend to do well; poems with a more intellectual or aesthetic focus are less popular, sometimes eliciting such criticisms as "very literary" or "too intellectual." In general, the slam does reflect an anti-intellectual and antiacademic tendency; introverted poems, surreal language, or highly crafted lyrics can on occasion do well, but raw verbal energy is a safer bet. As Shutup Shelley announces, telling first-time readers to speak directly into the microphone, "the louder the better." The performance of poems is also very important, accounting for at least 50 percent of the score. A young African American named "Dark" manipulates the microphone to achieve various sound effects and turns his profile to the audience as he recites his poems; other poets, like Bassi, verbally assault the audience with their angrily shouted poems. Poets from different communities have radically different performance styles: African Americans tend to work out of hip-hop and protest traditions; Latinos out of a tradition of narrative storytelling and declamation; white poets out of confessional, Beat, or surreal traditions. Yet what is unusual about the Nuyorican setting is that all styles are appreciated and a surprising degree of interchange is possible between them.

The event at once celebrates the talents of the poets and demystifies the poetic "scene": one slammer, an older white man, is introduced as "a real poet who hangs out with Beat Poets like Gregory Corso." Shelley reminds another poet of the unlikelihood of any financial reward or fame: "You'll never be on MTV!" Of course, being on MTV is the ultimate goal of the slam poet, just as publication in *Poetry* or *American Poetry Review* is for the workshop poet. But at the same time, there is a realization that "success"—as measured by either book publication or a recording contract—is highly unlikely for most slammers. In fact, the event functions as much as an occasion for venting social and political frustrations and celebrating a mixed community of non-mainstream interest as it does as a forum for specifically "literary" activity. It is also a self-legitimizing, self-authorizing structure for young, often socially underprivileged writers. Rarely is poetry invoked as a written medium—texts of poems are viewed primarily as a means to oral performance—and rarely are canonical poets mentioned. The Nuyorican, along with other New York venues of performance, constitutes a poetic community that is virtually autonomous from either the world of American poetry at large or the literary canon. For many of these slammers, the model of the poem comes more from rap and other music lyrics, and from each other's oral performances, than from books of poetry.

The effect of poetry slams and spoken-word performance has been not only to revitalize the oral and performative aspects of poetry (and in doing so to reengage the audience as an active and integral context for the poem), but also to resituate the personal. Instead of the lyric "I" as constituted within the postconfessional workshop poem—a voice that relies on a common understanding of the bourgeois suburban subject, whose experience is often presented as a reflection of its assumed audience—we find a voice that is more popularly constructed, often adopting a slang idiom while de-emphasizing or parodying the "transcendent" or "sensitive" aspects of the lyric self and failing to provide the "revelatory" lyric moment. The poems, although they may share with the workshop lyric a more broadly defined sense of the personal, enact the personal as political, whether in gendered, racial, or class-based terms. Unlike the self-referentiality and avoidance of the political we find in most lyrics of the academic mainstream, these poems remain constantly aware of their own social and cultural positions. Slammers may be talking about themselves, but they are also talking in very direct and often subversive ways about a range of what Algarin calls "life's raw edges," from social and economic deprivation to urban violence, from racial injustice to sexual exploitation.[20]

For many of its supporters, the slam has proved the savior of American poetry, whose moribund state as of the early 1980s led many to speak of its demise. Within the spoken-word community, many will claim to have rediscovered a Whitmanesque or bardic authenticity of poetry that had been lost in the narrowness of academic practice. As Holman puts it in his own hyperbolic terms, "we are on the brink of a revolution that will bring poetry into the center of our lives for the first time since Plato kicked the poets out of the Republic."[21] The coverage of the slam in the non-academic media makes clear both the impact of the slam phenomenon on the national consciousness and its strongly populist roots. In *Common Boundary*, a New Age magazine devoted to "psychology, spirituality, and creativity," poetry slams are credited as "a key factor in the rebirth of poetry in this country" and an attempt "to put poetry back into the hands of the common person."[22] Slam and spoken-word poets have "reminded the nation that poetry has an oral as well as a written tradition." In *High Times*, a magazine devoted to the "alternative" music and drug culture, Linda Yablonsky celebrates the current generation of spoken-word poets as "the new rock stars," whose performances are "recharging the cultural batteries of urban nightlife in cities across the country." Comparing their popularity to that of cultural icons like Elvis Presley, James Brown, Aretha Franklin, Tim Leary, Mick Jagger, and David Bowie, she concludes: "Now, everyone wants to be a poet."[23] *Rolling Stone* predictably emphasizes the "rock & roll attitude" of slammers, and contrasts them with a parodied version of academic poetry: "They don't drone at you in front of a lectern or reel drunkenly like lost beatniks. They compete against each other in Gong Show-like slams where the audience rates the poems, or they come at you on MTV, where literature is packaged in 30-second sound bites."[24]

If slam poetry is distinguished from more traditional forms of poetry—and especially from the mainstream or workshop lyric—by its faster pace and its more aggressive relationship with the audience (its attempt, as Holman would have it, to put "words in your face"), it is also contrasted with other forms of popular entertainment. As Ken Tucker writes in the *New York Times:* "At a time when culture and entertainment seem overrun by computer-era technology and ironic self-consciousness, spoken-word performances radiate a sincerity, simplicity and directness that many listeners find refreshing."[25] Thus slams and spoken-word poetry are represented as a compromise between an overly intellectual, pretentious, or rarefied high culture and the cynical and overcommercialized productions of the pop-cultural simulacrum. They are an ideal forum for a generation of college-educated and highly sophisticated cultural consumers who have grown impatient with the terms by which the previous generation defined literary success and cultural respectability, but who have also moved beyond the kinds of pleasure afforded by the forms of popular culture as they exist in the mass marketplace.

My interest is not in providing an overall assessment of "Nuyorican" poetry, or more generally in evaluating the achievement of spoken-word or slam poets over the past few years. Instead, I will analyze the work of a few of these poets in as detailed and individualized a cultural framework as possible. In this way, I hope to avoid both the journalistic tendency to treat spoken-word poets as commodities in a pop-cultural marketplace and the tendency from within the poetry community to evaluate the cultural productions of spoken word in a narrowly textual or "literary" framework.[26] In fact, spoken-word and slam poetry needs to be analyzed according to a social and cultural semiotics that takes into account the poetic text (both written and oral) as well as the visual context provided by the text's performance and, in the case of videotaped or televised versions, by the choreographic and cinematographic representation (*mise-en-scène*) of the poem.

As Richard Middleton proposes in his analysis of popular music, performance practices can fruitfully be understood and evaluated not only according to formal and aesthetic criteria, but according to a range of other value systems that operate within a specific cultural framework.[27] Middleton provides the most systematic model I have found within the field of cultural studies of the range of modes of analysis that can usefully be applied to various kinds of cultural performance, including, I would argue, poetry slams, open-mike readings, or spoken-word recordings as well as popular music. Middleton's six categories of value are as follows: "positional values" (the way in which individual tastes and values intersect with group norms); "communicative values" (the way in which the poem "says something" that can be seen by its audience as understandable, interesting, appropriate, relevant, or adequate); "ritual values" (the way in which the poem or reading creates solidarity or constitutes a special world for both performer and audience); "technical values" (how successfully the poem makes reference to familiar codes, norms, and standards); "erotic values" (how the poem or performance involves, energizes, or structures the body); and "political values" (how the poem mobilizes explicit political content or orientation). In the course of any given slam, we can find each of these kinds of value emphasized within the performances of different poets and within the audience's responses to them. When members of the audience applaud a poet's performance or disagree with a judge's score, they are establishing positional values; when they heckle a poet or object to what they see as sexist language in a poem, they are asserting communicative values; when poets at the Nuyorican refer to their own "loisaida" status, they are expressing ritual values; when a poet picks up a strong rap rhythm or makes "jump cut" associations of images, she is displaying technical values; when a poet reads a graphic poem about sex with his girlfriend, or moves his body in rhythmic accompaniment to the poem, he is engaging erotic values; when poets read poems about AIDS, about the limited opportunities of black schoolchildren in New York City, or about racial hypocrisy in South Africa, they are manifesting political values. While not all of these levels may be equally apparent in a given poem or performance, most successful spoken-word and slam poetry depends on at least some of these values.

The most successful poets within the spoken-word community are those who have been able to develop an identifiable personal style or persona, while incorporating a range of influences from both popular and literary culture. In the case of Hal Sirowitz, a poet in his late forties from Queens who has been a member of the New York national slam team and a performer on MTV and at Lollapalooza, the characteristic style and persona are most apparent in his "Mother Said" poems.[28] These poems typically begin with an opening refrain along the lines of the following from "Deformed Finger":

> Don't stick your finger in the ketchup bottle,
> Mother said. It might get stuck, &
> then you'll have to wait for your father
> to get home and pull it out.

Sirowitz clearly plays off a familiar tradition of Jewish humor, combining the stand-up comedy shtick based on the trope of the "Jewish mother" with the tradition of the cautionary tale. In Sirowitz's poems, the use of totally deadpan exaggeration takes the recited narratives beyond the genre of stand-up comedy and into the realm of psychological and metaphysical absurdity. By the end of the poem, the finger is not only deformed (having been violently pulled out by the boy's father), but it becomes the pretext for his later rejection by a girlfriend (and, by extension, for all subsequent disasters in the poet's life). As in all of these poems, the trivial and often repressed facts of daily domestic life (sticking fingers in the ketchup bottle, putting arms out the car window, finding brown stains on underwear) become in the voice of Sirowitz's "mother" the occasion for a paranoiac speculation on the disastrous consequences to follow.

Sirowitz achieves his effect through a wonderful sense of comic timing and a verbal compression that makes every word count. As the poem "One Thing Leads to Another" suggests, there is always a somewhat perverse but inescapable logic at work:

> And when
> you leave the house & get a wife,
> she won't be related to you, except
> by marriage, so she won't be as tolerant
> as I am. You don't want her to do separate washes,
> one for her clothes, another for yours,
> because that'll get her into the habit of doing
> other things separately, like eating. And
> once she realizes how much more enjoyable it is
> not to eat with you, & not have to hear you
> chomp on your hamburger, she might try not to
> live with you too, which means divorce.

Rather than a story that leads to a single punch line, we find a series of slight twists in the linear logic (playing with the cautionary adage "one thing leads to another"), each building on the comic effect of the others. As successful as Sirowitz's poems are on the page, they gain appreciably from oral performance. In the recording of Sirowitz reading his poem "Chopped-Off Arm" at the 1993 National Poetry Slam in San Francisco, Sirowitz's slow, monotone delivery and Jewish Queens accent capture perfectly the voice of the ever-suffering "Jewish mother," lending an air of authenticity and poignancy to an absurdly comic narrative. The interaction with the audience is important as well. Sirowitz has total command of an audience that not only laughs at the poem's funnier moments, but also chants the "Mother said" refrain along with him:

> Don't stick your arm out of the window,
> Mother said. Another car can sneak up behind
> us, and chop it off. Then your father

will have to stop, stick the severed piece
in the trunk, & drive you to the hospital.
It's not like the part of your telescope
that snaps back on. A doctor will have to sew it.
You won't be able to wear short sleeves in the summer.

Here we find a poem that depends on positional, communicative, and ritual values in addition to technical or aesthetic ones. Yet the evocative images of the poem and the unexpected turns in its logic make it aesthetically compelling as well. What Sirowitz has achieved in these poems is a hybridization of a popular form (stand-up comedy) with a literary form (the short narrative poem or dramatic monologue), creating something that is recognized as his own brand of spoken-word performance.

Maggie Estep, as the title of her recording *No More Mr. Nice Girl* indicates, adopts the very different persona, the neurotic, streetwise, sexually empowered, angry, grittily sophisticated, postfeminist urban female.[29] As she puts it in the opening line of "I'm Not a Normal Girl": "I'm not a normal girl, I'm an angry sweaty girl, so bite me!" Though she may suffer the trials of everyday life in the city—including pushy drug dealers and harassing males—and though she may be an "emotional idiot" who becomes obsessed with "stupid jerks," Estep's persona leads a fantasy life as "Sex Goddess of the Western Hemisphere" (a woman too busy "taking care of important sex goddess business" to actually engage in sex) and "Ingeborg, Mistress of the Night" (a sci-fi "avenging angel of the underworld" who rises out of toilets to bite the buttocks of "Aryan Nation skinheads" with her comic-book fangs). Like Sirowitz's poems, Estep's work is clearly informed by the genre of comic monologue, but rather than the deadpan irony of Sirowitz's performances (each a minimalist vignette), we find a breathless explosion of language inflected by popular culture and delivered with manic intensity. Both poets employ a poetic of hyperbole; but where for Sirowitz the seemingly insignificant moment becomes life's potentially epochal moment, for Estep the sense of larger-than-life expansiveness is always present. If Sirowitz is the passive victim, always silenced by his overbearing mother's hypothetical stories (his "own" voice, significantly, is never heard), Estep is, as she herself puts it, a woman "blowing her own horn endlessly." Rejecting the "self-deprecating" attitude of "date-rape poems, et al.," Estep celebrates her power through a Whitmanesque persona, one that allows her to be a "sex goddess" one night and a politician (who runs on a platform of stained panties) the next:

It'll be a revolution,
a brand new twist on evolution, yeah!
And I'll fix up the economy,
create jillions of jobs in the panty stain removal industry,
retired bondage queens in spiky boots
walking the creases out of people's
caked-with-slime panties,
and all of America will be chanting:
Thank you, Not Normal Girl
Thank you, Not Normal Girl
Thank you, Not Normal Girl.

The outrageous kinkiness of Estep's spoken-word pieces is in stark contrast to Sirowitz's flatly understated diction. Both poets, however, work in a mode that is decidedly (and I believe self-consciously) antilyrical. For Sirowitz, the rejection of lyricism is manifested in the flatness of diction, the refusal of apparent emotion or sentimentality, and, despite the highly personal and autobiographical nature of his poems, the denial of a moment of revelation or transcendence.[30] For Estep, the rejection can be seen in a defiantly antilyrical stance toward the world and a cynical relationship with the narcissistic self-involvement of the personal as it is reflected both in the "talk show" mentality of the media culture and in the "confessional" lyric. "Fuck me, I'm all screwed up, so fuck me!" she begins one piece. In another, "I'm an Emotional Idiot," she creates a schizophrenic monologue that flips back and forth between an emotionally dependent speaker who demands increasing commitment from her partner and a woman trying desperately to rid herself of an overly attentive man:

I'm an emotional idiot
so get away from me.
I mean, come here.

Wait, no,
that's *too* close,
give me some space
it's a big country,
there's plenty of room,
don't sit so close to me.

Hey, where are you?
I haven't seen you in days.

Whadya, having an affair?
Who is she?
Come on,
aren't I enough for you?

Estep's intensely narcissistic poems are ironic to the point of self-parody, as she is able to laugh at the excesses both of the slam culture and of her own participation in it ("I gotta go on the Charlie Rose Show / and MTV and become a parody / of myself"). In "The Stupid Jerk I'm Obsessed With," we can take neither her persona nor her unrequited love with much seriousness. This is hardly Sylvia Plath's tormented and suicidal speaker, but a mock-tragic persona who, after "stick[ing] her head in the oven," plans to "overdose on nutmeg and aspirin or sit in the bathtub / reading *The Executioner's Song*." Since many of her poems deal with sex (or in this case sexual dependency), Estep establishes a connection to her audience through reference to erotic values, but she also makes effective use of positional values (especially through the use of a frustrated and ironic persona to whom many—especially young urban women—can relate) and communicative values, commenting on such issues as drugs, sexual exploitation (both at the personal and the societal level), sexism, and female empowerment.

Estep can also indulge in flights of quasi-surreal imagination, as when she attempts in "Paradise Lost" to explain to an insistent crack dealer that her needs cannot be satisfied by drugs:

I want to wipe the glare
I want windex and windows open on the blasting blue sky
I want the sky
I want Jimi Hendrix, Johnny Cash
I want some cold hard cash
I want to wring the wet towel of my soul dry as dry
I want Safeway, safe sex, a bombed-out cinema multiplex, OK?

As is clear in this excerpt, Estep's spoken-word idiom is packed with references to popular and consumer culture. Where Sirowitz's world is devoid of cultural markers (except for those intrinsic to a universalized sense of Jewish culture), Estep's is a world in which everything is thrown into the cultural mix, from Latino hairdressers, phone porn packaged for "late night 900 number ads," and the corner grocery store to Estep's own pantheon of cultural heroes, which includes on seemingly equal terms Baudelaire, Miles Davis, and John Belushi. Though Estep's attitude of cultural irreverence is more 1990s postmodern pastiche than 1970s punk feminism, one can find echoes in her work of Patti Smith's gritty surrealism, and her conscious debts are more to music and music lyrics than to poetry.[31] Estep is also a no-holds-barred satirist, taking on everything from "pointless intellectual discussions" to "New Age Ritualistic Enema Cures," from "unmitigated bimbos" to pro-lifers to gangster rappers.

As with Sirowitz, the spoken performance is crucial to a full experience of Estep's poems. Her spoken-word compositions bear a close family resemblance to rock lyrics, reflecting Estep's background as a both a singer and songwriter. Her album is itself a generic mix, containing some spoken-word pieces (with musical accompaniment), some sung spoken word, and one straightforward rock song. This mixture creates a generic confusion. What do we call these pieces: poems, songs, or something in between? Even when she speaks her poems, the rhythms and overall delivery are clearly influenced by the musical backgrounds supplied by her band, I Love Everybody. Yet while Estep herself is skeptical of her status as a "poet," others seem to be less particular:

> I have to admit, I really don't think I am a poet. I just wrote shorter and shorter prose pieces and other people called them poems. You will have noticed, my work is not exactly traditionally poetic and I love clunky and simple language, run-on sentences, etc. . . . I'm really a prose writer masquerading as a poet and it's getting harder and harder to make [my writings] seem like poems. But, other people do keep calling them poems. I go to the comedy club open mike sometimes to read new stuff and they call me "the Poet."[32]

In fact, there is no single label that does justice to the range of cultural practices that define Estep's work: stand-up comedienne, performance artist, monologuist, spoken-word artist, lyricist. Although she numbers among her literary influences Henry Miller, William Burroughs, Jean Genet, and Celine ("a bunch of degenerate white guys"), she has no pretensions about the high seriousness of her poetic ambitions, which she dismisses with characteristic irreverence: "I sort of wrote my first poem so that I could use the word 'cheese' a lot."

The term that has generally been applied to Estep and those few like her who have successfully made the transition from poetry slams to the popular media is "MTV poet," or in the case of Estep, "MTV Poet Laureate." Clearly, there is a good deal of tongue-in-cheek humor in these characterizations (perhaps even a degree of self-parody on the part of the spoken-word community), but there is also some hubris and a not inconsiderable amount of promotional savvy. To a generation far more familiar with the fast-paced visual medium of MTV than with poetry readings or with literature in any form, the label "MTV poetry" makes a good deal of sense, as do forums such as Lollapalooza. Ever since Henry Rollins began using his status as a rock musician to promote his image as a spoken-word artist (giving three-hour concerts of monologues in lieu of songs), the equation of poetry and popular performance has been a familiar one to those in tune with developments in popular culture.

But what does it mean, exactly, to be an "MTV poet"? First, it suggests a more populist form of poetry, one less interested in complex literary tropes than in the kind of high-impact language and narratives that will appeal to a younger audience. Linda Yablonsky's *High Times* article on spoken word, for example, while it begins with the more literary lineage of slam poetry (the Beats), ends with a succession of quotes that imply a more popular, or populist, agenda. Dana Bryant tells us that performance poets are making poetry more "user-friendly" ("bringing poetry down to the people"); Estep likens poetry to "the way we talk"; and Matthew Courtney ("a prime promoter of poetry unfettered by serious literary treatment") concludes with the ultimate statement of populist relativism: "We all got a poem in us. Everything's poetry. Don't let anybody tell you different."[33] While there is a measure of truth in each of these representations of the spoken-word movement, they also serve an overly monolithic treatment of a cultural form that has a highly complex derivation and a wide range of stylistic and cultural orientations. And while the distinction between high and low culture is clearly outmoded in most academic discussions of postmodernity, this is clearly not the case in nonacademic journalistic writing, where, in the "alternative" popular media, at any rate, the dichotomy is preserved, and the triumph of the popular over intellectual or "high" forms of culture is celebrated.

The second characteristic of "MTV poetry" is its performative aspect. Though spoken-word and slam poems can work well on the page, they are intended to be heard by and achieve their greatest effect before a live audience, or at least an audience that is watching television or listening to a recording. Thus, for spoken word, a poet's "personality" is as important as his or her words. As Estep puts it: "Poets' personalities are just as key as are bands.'" This may not be altogether surprising to those who were raised on a diet of Burroughs, Kerouac, and Ginsberg, but it certainly flies in the face of the New Critical theories of poetic "impersonality" that have dominated thinking about poetry in the academy, and it even goes far beyond the kind of "confessionalist" impulse that governs most current poetic writing. Clearly, the concern of spoken word with packaging a personality through language and oral performance differs from workshop poetry's concern with "voice" or "persona" as a kind of distanced and aesthetically mediated version of the poetic "self."

Clearly, the emphasis on personality makes spoken-word poets more analogous to rock or pop stars than to other writers: these poets are far more likely to be compared with Bob Dylan or Patti Smith than with T. S. Eliot or Anne Sexton. This identification in turn brings about a much greater emphasis on the visual: poetry performance is a highly visual medium as well as an oral one, and the poet's physical appearance, her "look" or his good looks, has become important. In the coverage of spoken-word poets within the popular press, the "sexiness" of their image is emphasized, rather than their artistic or intellectual attributes. Estep, for example, is described by Yablonsky as a "full-lipped, raven-haired cutie," and Dana Bryant as "tall, black, and beautiful"; both Edwin Torres and Matthew Courtney are portrayed as fashionably post-Beat hipsters sporting goatees.[34] This is, after all, an arena where image counts for as much as substance, where everything from body language to clothes makes an important statement. Estep herself clearly recognizes this fact: "Stuff like 'The Stupid Jerk I'm Obsessed With' would have gotten a lot less mileage if performed by, say, a 350 pound diesel dyke with acne. I have no illusions about any of that. I got where I got with a combination of catchy writing and photogenic looks."[35] The importance of such physical presentation—second nature to any form of "popular" culture—is in marked opposition to the iconography of mainstream academic poetry, where a poet's physical demeanor is rarely alluded to.

Finally, the visibility of slam and spoken-word poetry on MTV and in the mass media in general has increased poets' desire for some kind of fame or commercial success.[36] Even if only a handful of poets can actually make a living off spoken-word poetry and performance, the model of those few poets—Estep herself, Paul Beatty, Reg E. Gaines, and Tracie Morris, for example—who have achieved something like commercial success through their work makes it a more appealing option to others. In any case, the presence of spoken word provides another alternative for poetic self-fashioning, a different career path from either the academic poet with a position teaching in a creative-writing program or the bohemian poet waiting tables or working in a bookstore.

How far these developments in performance-oriented poetry will take American poetic culture in the late 1990s and beyond is still very unclear. Estep, who at thirty-two is as much a veteran of the spoken-word "revolution" as anyone, is already turning to other pursuits: a "fictional autobiography" (*Diary of an Emotional Idiot*) and a novel (*Pivot of the Universe*), as well as another recording. Most of the work being read at slams is too overtly political for her taste: she considers her own work to be political "only from the stance of the personal as political," and defines herself as a "Do Me Feminist" who rejects the "over the top PC" agenda of many women slammers.

While Sirowitz and Estep represent the more general sense of a revitalized spoken-word or performance culture, one particular form of spoken word, the "rap-meets-poetry" phenomenon, has attracted more attention than any other. The hip-hop poetry phenomenon runs the gamut from rappers who perform poems (Michael Franti on *The United States of Poetry* or KRS-1 on *Words in Your Face*) to poets who count rap and hip-hop among a variety of influences; it includes a generation of African American poets, such as Paul Beatty, a highly regarded poet in his mid-thirties who won the Nuyorican's first annual Grand Slam in 1990 and appeared on *MTV Unplugged* before landing a contract for his first book. Tracie Morris is a talented contemporary of Beatty and another slam champion; Reg E. Gaines was the first to take the new spoken-word style to disc in his 1994 CD *Please Don't Take My Air Jordans*. These poets represent a generation for whom the raw political style of Nikki Giovanni, Amiri Baraka, and Sonia Sanchez fuses easily with the urban hip-hop culture of the past decade to create a politically aggressive form of performance poem. Articles in popular magazines such as *Rolling Stone* and *High Times* have celebrated this new synthesis, but some critics from the African American community, like Henry Louis Gates and Amiri Baraka, have expressed reservations about the impulse to collapse two cultural practices with very different histories and formal procedures into one.[37] If Gates is cautious about the interaction of rap and performance poetry, Amiri Baraka is more openly critical of slam poetry's attempt to sell a spoken-word imitation of rap as poetry. According to Baraka, mixing rap and poetry will only "make the poetry a carnival," exposing it to the same kind of "commercial showiness" that has affected the culture of rap music.[38]

To some extent, this kind of commercialization has already taken place within the slam subculture. The organizers of the 1994 slam, held in Asheville, North Carolina, promoted the event as a poetry festival or "slamfest," complete with T-shirts and book and tape sales. Performances on MTV, with the rock circus Lollapolooza, and on well-publicized spoken-word "tours," such as the twenty-city MTV-sponsored "Free Your Mind" tour, clearly create a highly commercial environment for poetry. It is an environment that is threatening to many within the poetry culture, who either find it demeaning to poets or fear that it will undermine poetry's perceived aesthetic autonomy.[39]

Even for poets whose careers were launched by the slam, like Paul Beatty, the slam format and the concomitant identification with spoken word as a primarily performance-based and rap-inspired medium can prove limiting. Beatty worries that the cultural and racial stereotyping implied by the labels "street poet," "slam poet," or "spoken-word performance poet" could prevent readers from taking his written poems seriously: "It's very important for me as a black person to establish that the word is a written presentation. If you really want to break new ground, then it definitely has to be done in writing."[40] Beatty's work exemplifies the culturally hybrid quality of much slam poetry, moving between the more "literary" aspirations suggested by the written form of his poems (which Ginsberg has compared to "microchips bursting with information") and the more "popular" or "street" idiom that punctuates his compositions. As Algarin implies in the title of his introduction to the *Aloud* anthology, spoken word is "the sidewalk of high art," a form of poetry where strikingly different cultural registers mix in new combinations. Beatty exemplifies this mix-and-match approach to poetry, a poetry that contains the same kinds of urban energies as sidewalk art or graffiti art: in fact, Quincy Troupe compares Beatty's poetry to the work of graffiti painter Jean-Michel Basquiat. As Therese Svoboda suggests, Beatty's works invoke "Whitman, sixties' revolutionary rap, call and response, the 'Beats,' [and] jazz." At the same time, his poems also manage to quote Shakespeare and to cite a range of cultural references from Immanuel Kant to Michael Jordan.[41]

Like Estep, who is followed by "MTV poet" wherever she goes, Beatty has been irrevocably identified with the label "hip-hop poet": he has been called "the bard of hiphop" (*Newsweek*) and "the hinge between hip hop and poetry on the page" (*Aloud*). Yet Beatty explicitly rejects the identification of his poetry with "popular" forms such as rap or stand-up comedy, and he is wary of the ephemeral nature of a subculture that places its emphasis on the glamour of the performance (and the accessibility of the message) rather than on the greater density and permanence that can be achieved in the written poetic text:

> I don't want to do poetry and music, a popular culture thing, you know, "Put a beat back there and the shit'll sound clean and yeah, yeah, yeah. . . ." The Last Poets were OK, there's some shit in there, but the thing for me with poetry is you got to deal with it. That's the part I don't like with some of the poetry that's happening now. . . . It's so easy to sit there and agree with, like, stand-up comedy.[42]

Those with some knowledge of Beatty's work and of the larger context in which he is writing have managed to avoid such labeling, finding new ways of identifying the particular synthesis he represents. According to Jessica Hagedorn, Beatty's poetry "moves to fierce urban rhythms, both cool and hot," generating "a rush of intense visual images and electric word music."[43] Certainly Beatty, along with Estep, has had the most success of any of the poets of their generation to emerge from the slam environment. Beatty's success in the slam, performance, and video format has produced a substantial interest in his written texts as well. His first book, printed in a run of a thousand copies by the Nuyorican Poets Cafe Press in 1991, sold out in five months; more recently, he was one of only a handful of contemporary poets to be published by Penguin's poetry series. Beatty's most successful poems are those that deal in unexpected or mythic ways with the icons of black urban culture, as the following examples from *Joker, Joker, Deuce* illustrate. In "A Three-Point Shot from Andromeda," basketball players shooting and slam dunking on an urban playground become space travelers ("black gods flying on neighborhood rep"). In an elegantly crafted comparison, the "rain-rusted orange" rim of the basketball net becomes the rings of Saturn, as the bullet-punctured backboard becomes the star-filled sky and the players themselves are transformed into the constellations as they soar toward the hoop. Other poems often make a more direct commentary on race and racial inequality. In "Tap Tap on Africa," Beatty focuses on race and racism by imagining the world as a "Rubik's cube":

> a game of plastic plate tectonics
> where the object
>   is continental segregation
>
> the challenge is to put each color on a different side
>
>   the greens over here
>   the yellows
>   over there
>   blues next to the red knuckleheads
>   and the whites on top

Yet despite the frequently political tone of his poetry, Beatty is no apologist for simple solutions such as Afrocentrism, which, as he suggests at the end of the poem, "solves the problem / by spray paintin the whole thing black." By juxtaposing the pseudoscientific solution proposed by white culture (emphasized through the metaphorical use of the mathematically complex but ultimately useless Rubik's cube) with the more violent but equally false solution offered by the radical Afrocentric community (emphasized by the evocation of spray-painted graffiti as the at once creative and destructive impulse within the urban ghetto), Beatty comments on the seemingly unbridgeable gap between the two cultures.

In "Darryl Strawberry Asleep in a Field of Dreams," Beatty once again casts a cynical eye on cultural constructions that reinforce racist messages. Here he comments on the Hollywood film *Field of Dreams*, which featured the attempt of a white Iowa farmer to reconstitute the (white) major-league baseball teams of the 1910s in his cornfield:

> and not only was the ball white
>
> shoeless joe jackson was white
>   his uni was white
>   all the dead white players was white
>   takin batting practice in white home uniforms
>   under white iowa clouds

While "white boys" may believe "this is the best movie theyve ever seen," young black players like Darryl Strawberry (whose persistent drug problem has tarnished the luster of his tremendous talents and allowed him to be dismissed as another casualty of race and culture in this country) and young black fans like Beatty himself are excluded from such a vision. Beatty describes his own reaction to the film, hoping for a rain-out of the white game so that players from the Negro leagues, such as Cool Papa Bell and Josh Gibson, can play instead. But in the world of the movie, one that reflects a real-world racial divide in which "black people smiled and fell in single file / to pay to watch mel ott run through Fences," we see not the great players of African American history, but "white doctors who played / only an inning and a half in the show," who "pray for a tinker everlasting chance to groove the o–2 sinker." Beatty plays ironically both with the film's premise (the Iowa cornfield becomes a literal ballplayers' "heaven") and with its most repeated line: "If you build it, they will come." The poem concludes with its most subversive lines, as Beatty condemns not only the hypocritically self-indulgent and racially insensitive values portrayed in the film—a film about a sport played, at the professional level, primarily by black men, yet targeted primarily at white audiences—but more generally the hypocritical representations of the American dream that pervade popular culture:

and put the suicide squeeze on my mother's mother
whose color
is the same
as a night game infield

        . . . and the people will come

to see that black fathers to be
    with scars on their knees
        from shinbones split in half
            and knocked off kneecaps
practice the tap dunks they will pump on their daughters n sons

        . . . and the people will come. . . .

is this heaven
    no its iowa

is this heaven
    no its harlem

is this heaven
    no its bedrock

is this heaven
    no its cabrini green

do they got a team
aint sure they got dreams
damn sure aint got a field
or crops that yield
is that the sign for steal
i approach the third base coach
and ask is all movies for real

Beatty uses the field of the page to represent the field of dreams evoked by the title, shifting the formal layout of the poem on the page as he shifts discursive or tonal registers. While the poem would no doubt be even more effective as a performance piece—in which the use of rhyme, cadence, and speech could be more fully emphasized—it is already powerful as a written poem, especially if read in the context of the Nuyorican culture. It might not be taking the analogy too far to suggest that it also works as a commentary on the position of young black poets—especially those who lack the credentials of an academic background—who are in a similar position to that of black ballplayers in a segregated society. Like Darryl Strawberry, young black poets may be sleeping only because no one has offered them a dream or a level playing field.

Clearly, Beatty has used the forum of the slam to boost his own poetic career, yet his desire to avoid being labeled as a "rap poet," "street poet," or "spoken-word poet" indicates a predicament he shares with other young performance-oriented poets: they hope to use the mass media and a more popular identification of spoken word to reach a larger audience, while still gaining the respect and cultural legitimacy given the serious literary artist. This two-directional ambition, and the degree of cultural ambivalence it suggests, is crucial to an understanding of this poetry and its subculture.[44] The ambivalence can be seen both in the poems themselves and in the way they are packaged, sold, and received. When the trade press Henry Holt published *Aloud,* it decided on the subtitle *Voices from the Nuyorican Poets Cafe,* thus avoiding the words "poem" or "poetry." While this may have been a successful marketing device, it is certainly one aimed at a nonliterary audience. Even Holman, one of the strongest boosters for a more populist poetry, regrets the press's decision on exactly the grounds of cultural identification; by refusing to openly advertise its texts as serious literature, the book too easily concedes the field to other forms of poetic writing.[45]

I would certainly not want to defend on aesthetic grounds all of the poems contained in *Aloud,* or all of the poems read at slams and open-mike events throughout the country, but I do believe it is important to remember that the division between the standards to be applied to a written text (traditional literature) and the standards to be applied to an oral text (dramatic performance) is counterproductive for understanding this poetry. What the spoken-word phenomenon has convincingly demonstrated is that the published anthology is no longer the privileged forum for presenting the work of these poets, as it is for mainstream academic poets. Instead, the written text is only one of *several* media through which the poetry of Nuyorican and other spoken-word poets can reach the public, including live performance (slams, open-mike readings, spoken-word tours), audio recordings, MTV, and films like *Words in Your Face* and *The United States of Poetry.*

Many questions remain to be answered. Will the current state of multicultural tolerance and interracial dialogue represented by the Nuyorican and larger slam community continue to flourish, or will the ever-growing community of spoken-word and performance poetry splinter into smaller and more fractional communities organized along racial, ethnic, gendered, ideological, or stylistic lines?[46] Will the slam community continue to define itself in opposition to other poetry communities, including both the mainstream academic community and the avant-garde or experimental community? What possibilities will there be for increasing interchange and hybridization between these different communities? Will slams serve as alternatives to traditional poetry readings on college and university campuses? Will performance poetry become part of the creative-writing curriculum?[47] Will more slam poets earn MFAs, and more academically trained poets turn their talents to performance or recording rather than publishing? Will we see an increase in linguistic and formal experimentation—even variants of Language poetry—within the slam format? These various questions will serve as a backdrop for future discussions of the spoken-word or slam culture. There is no doubt, however, that the way in which we define American poetry in the coming decades will be significantly influenced by what the poetry slam and the spoken-word subculture in general have achieved in a relatively brief span of time.

7. Poetry on Television?

The United States of Poetry
as Video-Poetry Revolution

When I first met Bob Holman in the summer of 1995, he had recently completed work on *The United States of Poetry,* a five-part PBS television series documenting the breadth and energy of contemporary American poetry, and he was in the process of becoming one of the most influential figures in American poetic culture. The series of half-hour programs to be broadcast the following winter were unlike anything that had been done with poetry before. First, *The United States of Poetry* would demonstrate that the presentation of poetry in the mass media need not be confined to a traditional format: on the contrary, cutting-edge video techniques could be used to present, perhaps even to enhance, the experience of the poem. Second, the series would help legitimate and bring to a more general audience what had been a fast-growing trend in poetry since the late 1980s: the oral or performative mode of poetry made popular in coffeehouses, open-mike readings, and poetry slams. Finally, the project would break new ground by aligning the poetry culture with the very different cultural spheres of film production and MTV. According to Holman's account, *The United States of Poetry (USOP)* captured a new spirit in American poetry. Poetry had come off the page and onto the airwaves; it had come out of the stuffy halls of academe and into the cafe, the bar, and the street. Poetry could be popular without being commercial or unimaginative; experimental without being arcane; serious without being pretentious, dull, or self-righteous; funny without being crass or superficial. The revolution in poetry made possible by the new technologies in video and audio recording, CD-ROM and the Internet, would help return poetry to its origins as an oral, performative, and interactive practice, while at the same time allowing poetry to reach a much larger audience than it had in print.

Holman came to the project of *USOP* with credentials in avant-garde literary production that spanned at least two decades. Starting with his work at the St. Marks Poetry Project, where he coordinated the Monday night poetry/performance series—a predecessor of the Nuyorican slam— he has continued to pursue various projects with remarkable energy and conviction. He directed plays by Tristan Tzara and Antonin Artaud at the Poet's Theater; he hosted "The Double Talk Show" with Pedro Pietri at the Life Cafe (a forum for such countercultural poets as Quincy Troupe, Jessica Hagedorn, and Amiri Baraka); he joined with Miguel Algarin in reopening the Nuyorican Poets Cafe, where he hosted weekly poetry slams and organized national slam teams; he co-edited the anthology *Aloud: Voices from the Nuyorican Poets Cafe;* he co-founded a spoken-word record label (formerly Nuyo Records and now Mouth Almighty Records, a subsidiary of Mercury Records); and he helped organize and run the active Rap Meets Poetry reading series.

Although Holman's organizational and entrepreneurial efforts went relatively unnoticed by a wider audience throughout the 1970s and 1980s, the immense success of the poetry slam has helped to propel his rise to prominence in the 1990s. If the slam was anathema to most of what the mainstream academic culture believed poetry to be, it proved far more attractive to Americans under forty than the kind of elegantly crafted, quietly pitched, and thematically reticent verse published by the vast majority of academic journals and presses. Seizing on the enormous potential of the slam both as a forum for alternative poetries—especially those with a minority or multicultural focus—and as an entertaining form of ritualized spoken-word performance, Holman and Algarin made the slam a central event at the newly reopened Nuyorican Poets Cafe, which soon became a regional center and a national mecca for performance-based poetry.

The second new forum for poetry—a forum whose potential would only begin to be tapped after the slam brought performance poetry to national attention—was that of video and television. Unlike the slam, videotaped or filmed poetry did not provide a live experience, nor could it achieve the unique sense of immediacy and excitement created by a slam. It did, however, provide tremendous possibilities for transmitting poetry in new ways to new audiences. While poetry films had been part of the poetry scene for some time, most notably in the 1985 *Poetry in Motion*, produced by Ron Mann, they had received virtually no mainstream exposure, partly because of low budgets and resultingly low production values, but also because the poetry video seemed to most people, until very recently, a decidedly marginal form. In 1987, having overcome his own reservations about the appropriateness of using television to present poetry, Holman began working with Danny O'Neil, a television producer for the New York PBS affiliate WNYC, to put together a series of "Poetry Spots," short videos of poets such as John Ashbery, Amiri Baraka, Dennis Cooper, and Paul Beatty, which could serve as a buffer around programs that did not fill their half-hour slots. The spots proved even more successful than Holman or his producers had imagined, and they earned three local Emmys during their six broadcast seasons. Now, instead of the perceived enemy of poetry, television "was to become an ally, a means of transmission, a collaborator."[1]

In 1990, through a serendipitous encounter, a young film producer named Joshua Blum began attending slams at the Nuyorican. Impressed by the oral and visual impact of the slam, Blum approached Holman about making a television film based on the event, and Holman, not surprisingly, agreed. Holman and Blum brought together many of the most prominent New York performance poets for a test shooting, but filming the slam as such proved to be something of a disappointment, since much of the energy of the live slam was lost when it was captured on film. Nevertheless, Blum and Holman persevered, putting together a demo film, *Smokin' Word*, which combined some of the footage from the slam itself with other poems performed in a studio setting. With performance poet Matthew Courtney serving as "host," the film featured such spoken-word artists as Maggie Estep, Paul Beatty, Jennifer Blowdryer, Pedro Pietri, Eric Begosian, and Holman himself.

Holman and Blum next approached MTV with a proposal to make a video based on the demo, but their idea was rejected (although MTV soon began producing its own poetry videos in the *Unplugged* series, using much the same format and several of the same poets). Public television's *Alive from Off-Center* series took on the project, and Holman and Blum teamed up with Mark Pellington, an award-winning MTV filmmaker, to produce their first broadcast-quality film, *Words in Your Face*. This half-hour PBS program featured a wider range of poets and styles, and it employed more innovative film and production techniques, such as cutting written and spoken text into the individual poets' spots. The film also pointed toward a more overtly political subtext, and toward the gritty urban scene that would become a trademark of the Nuyorican style. A poem by Sekou Sundiata was followed by a cut to footage of the Rodney King beating; the rapper KRS-1 performed the didactic racial litany "We Must Learn"; Willie Perdomo recited the chilling "Nigger-Reecan Blues." Other poems ranged from the humorous (Matthew Courtney's "Honey I'm Home," or Deacon Lunchbox chainsawing a book), to the multicultural mixing of mambo (John Leguizamo), rasta (Mutabaruka), and African folk music (Thomas Pinnock). At the same time, various written texts punctuated the performances, posing provocative questions about the relationship of language to systems of power and meaning—"When was the last time someone said something that made you believe?" "What do words mean?" "White Equals Right?"—or commenting on the necessity to recognize the power of language: "Read between the lines," "Words are dangerous," "Words can kill people."

Innovative as it was, *Words in Your Face* was only a step toward the far more ambitious goal of *The United States of Poetry*, a poetry series that would include poets from all over the country. After two years of planning, writing proposals, and unsuccessfully seeking grants from various sources, Holman, Blum, and Pellington applied to ITVS (Independent Television Service), a funder of non-mainstream television projects. With the majority of the funding for the project coming from ITVS, the filmmakers and their crew set off on a twelve-week, 13,000-mile bus tour around the country, filming some eighty poets along the way. *USOP* would differ from Holman and Blum's earlier collaborations in that—while it still featured poetry of the urban, spoken-word variety—it also included very different kinds of poets, including three Nobel prizewinners (Derek Walcott, Czeslaw Milosz, and Joseph Brodsky), the current poet laureate (Rita Dove), a former president (Jimmy Carter), musicians Lou Reed, Michael Franti, and Leonard Cohen, actor Johnny Depp, drag-performer Lypsinka, and various cowboy poets, Beat poets, and regional poets. The poets range in age from seven to eighty-seven, and they represent racial, ethnic, and linguistic backgrounds from Tlingit-speaking Nora Marks Dauenhauer to Caribbean dub–poet Everton Sylvester to bilingual Latino poet Javier Pina to Hawaiian-pidgin poet Lois-Ann Yamanaka to American Sign Language–poet Peter Cook. Significantly, the film also presents a spectrum of poets from the most familiar and celebrated (Dove, Ginsberg, Walcott, Brodsky) to the most marginal and obscure. In fact, *USOP* is quite determined in its stated mission of not only showcasing more familiar poets but of discovering or uncovering new ones, of "unveil[ing] a new nation." Here we find Dan Powers, a poet from Nashville with only two chapbooks to his credit; Nerissa Diaz, an eleven-year-old Latina schoolgirl; Sheryl Noethe, a dedicated but relatively undiscovered poet who teaches poetry to head trauma survivors in Missoula, Montana; and Besmilr Brigham, a septuagenarian poet from New Mexico whose only book of poems was published in 1971.

The United States of Poetry also differs from previous attempts to put poetry on television, especially the poetry series hosted by Bill Moyers. Significantly, Holman's introduction to the book based on the series never mentions Moyers, the oversight implying that The United States of Poetry is the first television series based on poetry.[2] But Holman's willful forgetting of Moyers's PBS series cannot hide the fact that The Language of Life and Moyers's other programs represented for Holman, Blum, and Pellington the antithesis of what poetry on TV should be, epitomizing a format to be avoided at all costs. Moyers's productions are largely static, consisting of head shots of the poet reading followed by shots of the audience reacting. Frequent shots of the rapt audience suggest a reverential attitude toward poets and poems; the listener is less interactive with the poet's performance than passively attentive to it. Finally, the poets at the podium generally convey little personality, which is allowed to surface more clearly only in the more "casual" interview segments.

The format of the Blum/Holman/Pellington film, on the other hand, allows for an entirely different kind of creativity. Poets helped choreograph their own segments, took more active roles in choosing the visual images to accompany their poems, and in some cases even selected the musical background. The intended audience is clearly different as well. USOP is aimed not only at the middle-aged, white, middle-class audience targeted by the Moyers films, but at a younger and less socioeconomically stable sector of the population, one that has been increasingly distanced from poetry. Where the Moyers series uses television as a means to the end of presenting and interpreting poetry, Holman uses The United States of Poetry to pose the question "How can you translate poetry to television"?[3] Thus USOP is particularly concerned with the medium itself, or rather with the interaction of two very different media—poetry and television—that provide very different aesthetic and representational possibilities. Pellington's innovative filmmaking techniques (adopted from the more "postmodern" cinematic vocabulary of MTV production), and his often striking use of cinematography and visual effects, work to foreground the visual medium of television to a far greater extent than does the conventional format of the Moyers programs, while the musical background and overall use of sound in the films adds yet another crucial dimension. All of these elements, along with the choreography of the poets' own performances, interact in significant ways with the poetic text itself, creating an aesthetic layering that in its totality attempts to capture the thematic and stylistic texture of the poem.

In analyzing *The United States of Poetry* as an aesthetic and cultural artifact, I am interested primarily in exploring two questions. First, how does *The United States of Poetry* use the aural and visual media to translate poetry into television, and to enhance the various thematic, stylistic, symbolic, and performative possibilities of the poems themselves? And second, how does Holman use the new media to construct a particular vision of American poetry that differs from previous attempts to put poetry on television? Although one of these questions is primarily formal or aesthetic in nature, and the other primarily sociocultural, they are closely related concerns. Unlike the decidedly mainstream and middlebrow spin of the Moyers series, this is a film with attitude: an attitude conveyed both by the technical production of the series and by the choice of poets. Holman's "canon" of American poetry is very different from that of Moyers, despite a mix of poets that on the surface appears equally "multicultural." It is difficult to imagine Moyers dealing with the irreverent iconoclasm, the raw, confrontational, "in your face" quality of many of the poets on *USOP.* While Moyers accepts and even encourages a certain degree of marginality as long as it remains within the borders of mainstream American propriety, he would be hard-pressed to deal with several of the issues presented in Holman's series: homosexuality and cross-dressing, homelessness and prostitution, racial anger and urban despair.

This difference in attitude is also reflected in the choices made by Holman and Blum in putting the project together. Not only do many of the poems contain either overtly political messages or more subtle political subtexts, but the overall conception of the series suggests that it takes certain ideological positions, in contrast to the tactfully depoliticized nature of the Moyers programs. Taken as a whole, the series is not particularly subversive, and in fact celebrates many aspects of American life, but it clearly reflects a degree of anger and disillusionment with the status quo of American culture, and on a more local level, with American poetic and literary culture. And despite Blum and Holman's claims to have included every group of poets, it is fairly clear from even a cursory glance at the contents of the series that mainstream academic poetry (which numerically accounts for most of the published poetry in the United States) receives relatively little airtime. In fact, Holman's introduction to the book based on the series is fairly straightforward in its dismissal of the academic mode. After having spent nearly two pages extolling the virtues of poetry slams, the Nuyorican Poets Cafe, cowboy poetry, American Sign Language poetry, the Naropa Institute, electronic poetry, and Language poetry, Holman finally turns to academic poetry:

> And what of the Academy? Surely, in the five hundred universities and colleges across the country, there are degree-granting writing programs that appreciate the flame of a new poetry. Many of the poets in *The United States of Poetry* teach, and the harder one tries to find the Academy, the more it disappears into a shroud of dust.[4]

Holman's carefully chosen words disguise what one must assume to be stronger feelings about the academy and its mainstream, conventional, or workshop mode.[5] In fact, while it may be the case that many of the poets in *USOP* are teachers of one kind or another, the number who hold regular positions in academic creative-writing programs would not make a long list. Most of the poets in the series who do have academic affiliations are either minority writers or foreign-born Nobel Prize winners. For example, the only poet in *The United States of Poetry* who is also included in Helen Vendler's quintessentially academic anthology, *The Harvard Book of Contemporary American Poetry*, is Rita Dove, whose symbolic capital as the first African American poet laureate transcends even such stylistic and ideological divisions as those separating Holman from Vendler. Holman even avoids, where possible, the more high-profile poets in the multicultural community (often also those with academic affiliation), featuring, for example, the lesser-known Henry Real Bird, Nora Marks Daunhauer, and Jim Northrop rather than more familiar Native American poets such as Joy Harjo, Linda Hogan, Louise Erdrich, or Adrian Louis.

The most obvious omission from the series, whether intentional or not, are the poets most clearly associated with the academic creative-writing culture, or what Charles Bernstein calls the "official verse network": the white, educated, middle-class, heterosexual, mainstream poets familiar from poetry journals like *American Poetry Review* and anthologies like *The Morrow Anthology of Younger Poets*. Given the fact that they represent the largest single population of publishing poets in America, their exclusion at times makes it seem as if the program should be titled *The United States of Marginalized Poetry*. Also arguably underrepresented are poets of the experimental type most often associated with Language poetry, though the presence of Carla Harryman and Larry Eigner in the series at least gives a nod in the direction of a linguistically innovative poetic. While making some gesture toward including the full range of American poetries, the film clearly emphasizes certain kinds of poetry more than others—in particular those that either reflect a multicultural orientation or lend themselves to performative styles. For this reason, it is less successful as a representative sampling of American poetry, and more successful as an amalgam of several recent trends in poetic writing and performance.

Numerically, at least, the most representative group appears to be poets who are in one way or another indebted to rap or hip-hop, with its streetwise vernacular, rhythmical cadences, and aggressive political attitude. According to Holman's introduction to the book based on the series, rap is "at the center of a new definition of poetry," or at least of a particular brand of nonacademic urban multicultural poetry.[6] If Gil Scott-Heron and the Last Poets were the first to popularize spoken-word performance in the early 1970s, their jazz-inspired performances prepared the ground for the hip-hop poetry of Michael Franti, Paul Beatty, Tracie Morris, and Ismail Azim El (Invisible Man). If we broaden the scope to the influence of African American musical and cultural forms such as jazz and scat, we can also include in this category Quincy Troupe, Michelle Clinton, Wanda Coleman, Ruth Forman, and Amiri Baraka.

Another strain of highly political poetry, a poetry that depends on the performance ability of the poet as much as the words themselves, can be identified under the rather loose rubric of "street poetry." Featured in *The United States of Poetry* we find Miguel Algarin, one of the founders of the original Nuyorican Poets Cafe in the mid-1970s and a long-time advocate of urban poetry. We also find Pedro Pietri, "a fixture of the streets of Nueva York"; the streetwise Brooklyn poet Peter Spiro; Robert Chambers, a former homeless man and activist for the homeless of Los Angeles; the "renowned street poet" Sparrow; Luis Alfaro, a gay Chicano poet from the Los Angeles barrio; Lord Buckley, the performer/comic who died in 1960; and Willie Perdomo, whose street lyric "Papo's Ars Poetica" ends with the lines "I'm home in / the street of / this poem where / I'm stuck." The urban street takes on a wider significance in the series as a whole when we consider the videos of Everton Sylvester, Ruth Forman, Dennis

Cooper, Genny Lim, Ismail Azim El, Maggie Estep, and Emily XYZ, each of whom uses different aspects of the street to comment on the American experience.

A final defining mode of the series is a tradition of avant-garde performance. We find Alfaro, reciting his poem while stripping down to a black negligee; Estep, moving in and out of the camera frame and kicking the camera with her boot; Wanda Coleman, performing her poem as a parody of the Home Shopping Network; John Wright, dressed in a cook's uniform as he stirs up a "Boulder Valley Surprise" of radioactive waste; Matt Cook, sitting on the curb outside a 7–Eleven telling why "James Joyce was stupid"; John S. Hall, drinking a martini in evening dress while describing aberrant sexual acts; Emily XYZ, giving an energized recital of her multilayered performance piece with the actress Myers Bartlett; Allen Ginsberg, sitting cross-legged in his pajamas while reciting his poem "Personals Ad"; or Lypsinka giving a campy performance of Elizabeth Barrett Browning's sonnet "How Do I Love Thee? Let Me Count the Ways." Each of these poets shares a desire to resist the identification poetry has received within the academic mainstream. Their poems display the range of current practices and in their ensemble represent a playful or irreverent reaction to the stultifying modes of conventional narrative and lyric poetry most commonly found in the academic workshop environment.

Since I cannot address in detail *USOP* in its entirety, my analysis concentrates on the most overtly political program of the series, ironically entitled "The American Dream," and attempts a closer reading of a few of the poems and their televisual frames. To my mind, it is this program that presents the most striking contrast with previous attempts to put poetry on television, including those of Moyers. The at once didactic and subversive intent of "The American Dream" is made clear in Holman's introduction to the text version. After invoking the "great argument" over whether a poem is "inherently political" or whether a poem with political intent "cease[s] to be a poem," Holman answers his own rhetorical question in no uncertain terms: "In The American Dream, language becomes a weapon, a stiletto of meaning to pierce the nonsensical rhetoric of politics, to unmask the cynical grasp of advertising." Here, poetry is depicted as a means of empowerment for the underprivileged and underrepresented. Poetry should be considered, "not as a literary conceit, but as an actual tool for building a new society, a tool for a new patriotism [for] the redefinition of our nation." [7]

The program begins with one of the most basic American icons, the Statue of Liberty, but it soon becomes clear that the image of "Miss Liberty" will be appropriated in a highly unconventional way. Rather than a triumphant beacon welcoming immigrants to the New World, the statue becomes—in Thylias Moss's brief but provocative poem "Green Light and Gamma Ways"—an image of the immigrant herself, a surreal emblem of minority identity:

> She is a minority too, color
> of ridiculous Martian fable
> and not a man.

Here we find what will become a dominant strategy throughout the program and the series as a whole: the use of an icon with an established cultural or political history in order to create a parody or reversal of its expected symbolic meaning. The opening shot is the traditional postcard image of the Statue of Liberty, basking in the glow of sunrise with boats passing in the harbor. As the poem begins, however, the image of the statue's face fades out and is replaced with shots of Moss's African American face. In the final image of the segment, a hand reaches in to grasp a toy model of the statue, thus further undercutting the statue's status as a universal icon of national ideology, one that in its conventional representation is outside the reach of the very people it was intended to celebrate. The poem's ironic reversal of the statue's iconic significance is made more pronounced by a man's voice in the background, reciting disconnected pieces of the American "pledge of allegiance": "Indivisible . . . pledge allegiance . . . one nation . . . one nation."

Moss's playful but trenchant irony sets up the next two poems, both heavy-hitting political texts: Leonard Cohen's "Democracy" and Amiri Baraka's "The X Is Black."[8] The two poems complement each other's political messages, and by the end of Baraka's poem there should be no doubt in the viewer's mind not only that poetry can be political, but that *The United States of Poetry* has a well-defined ideological position. The concept of "democracy"—and its cynical abuses by the ruling forces of middle-class white America—appears to be the thread connecting the two poems. Cohen, seated at a desk in a darkened space, reads his poem in a near monotone, accompanied by an ominous background score that becomes an aural analogue for the powerful visual imagery of the video. Cohen's darkened silhouette is set against an illuminated background that alternates between the American flag and a flag-shaped bar code; when his face appears, his eyes are hidden by dark sunglasses. These images suggest a motif of military intelligence or espionage—perhaps a CIA operative—although the blackened silhouette against the bar code might also connote the erasure of individual identity within the military-industrial-corporate hegemony of late capitalism.

Like Moss's poem, "Democracy" takes a fundamental American principle and turns it on its head, showing an ideological cliché (liberty, democracy) to be only a false promise. Cohen's rhymed lines and almost singsong rhythms are particularly effective in oral performance, picking up the multiple ironies of the language. The poem's principle refrain, "Democracy is coming to the U.S.A.," suggests that like China and other less-than-democratic nations (significantly, Tiananmen Square is mentioned in the first stanza), the contemporary United States is far from having achieved true democracy:

> From the wars against disorder,
> from the sirens night and day;
> from the fires of the homeless,
> from the ashes of the gay:
> Democracy is coming to the U.S.A.

The United States, Cohen suggests, may have different problems from China, but they are no less severe. The rhyme of "gay" with "U.S.A." emphasizes the discrepancy between the various stark images of American life presented in the poem—crime, homelessness, AIDS, alcohol and drugs, and environmental pollution—and the falsely hopeful and ultimately empty ideology of "democracy." Democracy may be "coming to American first," but it is coming for all the wrong reasons:

> It's here they got the range
> and the machinery for change
> and it's here they got the spiritual thirst.
> It's here the family's broken
> and it's here the lonely say
> that the heart has got to open
> in a fundamental way:
> Democracy is coming to the U.S.A.

Here the meanings of words show a kind of ideological slippage: the "range" could be the cattle range of the mythic American West, but it is also a range to be used for shooting, bombing, or nuclear testing.

Similarly, the "fundamental way" refers both to Muslim fundamentalism (echoing an earlier line that refers to women kneeling to pray on "the desert here and desert far away") and the fundamentalist Christian right (also picking up resonances of "the American way" and "America first"). Overall, Cohen's poem is a tour-de-force of aural-visual synthesis, in which both music and visual imagery contribute powerfully to the poem without overwhelming its verbal message. Not surprisingly, given Cohen's considerable experience as both a musical performer and a poet, "Democracy" is one of the most successful spots in the program and in the entire series.

Baraka's poem, subtitled "Spike Lie" and in part a commentary on Spike Lee's film *Malcolm X,* also addresses the question of democracy, and also uses the familiar and politically charged icon of the American flag with subversive intent. Baraka's conceit, however, is quite a different one. In the image of an "X" burning a hole in the flag, we find an inverted image of Ku Klux Klan members burning crosses on African American yards, houses, and churches. This X, Baraka tells us in no uncertain terms, "is that place where we live / the Afro American / Nation." Baraka uses the visual iconography of the American flag in a particularly effective way to show "that place / empty of democracy," where African Americans live:

> If the flag
>> catch afire
>> & an X burn in
>> the only stripes is
>> on our back
>> the only star
>> blown free
>> in the northern sky
>> no red but our
>> blood, no white
>> but slavers and Klux in robes
>> no blue
>> but our songs

While Baraka's poem may lack the complex linguistic subtlety of Cohen's "Democracy," its use of the flag as a highly loaded symbol of American ideology (one often appropriated by the political right) is a powerful reminder of social and racial inequality. Here again the visual imagery strongly supports the ironic message: the segment begins with a black X, which fills the entire screen, and ends with a white X, which burns.

The interrelated thematic concerns of the first three poems of "The American Dream" already suggest that *The United States of Poetry* is designed to work on a level larger than that of the individual poem. At its best, the series achieves a collage-like structure, bringing the often disparate visions of different poets into harmony or at least a meaningful juxtaposition, a whole that can be more powerful than the sum of its parts. At other times, however, we are struck by the unevenness of the material, and the problematic nature of the attempt to present a truly democratic spectrum of poetry becomes apparent. The fourth poem, "Face to Face," by eleven-year-old Nerissa Diaz, contributes little to our appreciation of American poetry and virtually nothing to the consideration of poetry as a political medium. Here, unlike in the first three poems, the visual imagery fails to enhance the poem's trite ideas: shots of a school interior and close-ups of the girl's face are as flat and unimaginative as the poem itself.

Perhaps the inclusion of Diaz's poem can be justified as a bridge between the more cynical poems of Moss, Cohen, and Baraka and the gently pastoral poem of cowboy poet Vess Quinlan.⁹ The quiet lyricism of Quinlan's poem "Sold Out," which concerns the need of an older rancher to sell his horses, is exemplified by the final lines:

> We don't speak of causes or reasons,
> Don't speak at all;
> We just stand there
> Leaning on the weathered poles,
> While shadows consume the pasture.

While Quinlan's poem can easily be read as a commentary on the American dream—perhaps as a narrative of the disappearance of a certain kind of life in the West—its political message is left relatively ambiguous. The "shadows" that "consume the pasture"—a symbolic rendering of the unspoken "causes or reasons" for the sale—might represent, as the poem's title suggests, the effects of big business on the independent rancher, the uncaring attitude of the banks, or perhaps simply the encroachment of modern life on a simpler and no longer viable existence. In one of the more overt uses of visual symbolism of the entire series, however, the film-makers overdetermine the poem's meaning by cutting from the pastoral image of late-afternoon sun on the corralled horses to that of a huge green cement dinosaur with the American flag waving behind it. The image is a potent one, linking both with the flags of Cohen's and Baraka's poems, and with the Statue of Liberty of Moss's "Green Light and Gamma Ways":

now the reclaimed green icon of Miss Liberty is transformed into the crass commercialism of the dinosaur, an inverted symbol of an American dream gone somehow wrong. Not only is the independent rancher in the poem a cultural anachronism, the image suggests, but so is the American dream as we knew it.

The next two poems underscore this sense of the American dream gone wrong in very different ways. Genny Lim's "Winter Place" presents the urban scene of San Francisco, a landscape that exemplifies all the contradictions of contemporary American life. Here "MTV couples glide frozenly" past the unseen "wounds of North Beach," seeing only their own "store-bought reflections" in "ray-banned eyes," while the "corporate buffalo roams" through the "teeming waterhole" of "winos . . . refugees, bag can ladies and panhandlers." Lim's poem returns us to the darkly ironic vision of Cohen, as in the lines that end the filmed version:

> It ain't so bad
> the Indians once said as
> they traded their land for horses
> as they traded their land for firewater
> It ain't so bad

The American dream may be a reality for the privileged few, Lim suggests with savage irony, but only at the expense of those forgotten people on whose land and lives it was achieved: Native Americans, Chinese "Coolies," "Eye-talians," and all the other "fugitives" who have contributed to the American melting pot.

John Wright's poem "Boulder Valley Surprise" is a more humorous interpretation of what can go terribly wrong with the best-laid plans for America. In a parody of a television cooking show, Wright spells out a literal recipe for disaster. The poem traces the changes in the Rocky Mountain ecosystem over both prehistoric and historic time, culminating in the accelerated destruction of the natural landscape:

> then, with a large spatula
> smooth out even layers of concrete
> on any possible surface
> saute in carbon monoxide
> bake with electromagnetic waves until saturated
> in a large sealed container
> cook plutonium until doomsday

garnish with shopping malls, tanning salons
virtual reality arcades and crystal emporia
set blender on puree
bring to a boil
run from the kitchen

The deadpan humor of Wright's poem benefits greatly from its video interpretation as a postmodern performance piece. Wright, wearing a chef's cap and apron, delivers the poem in a monotone while mechanically stirring. At the same time, universal symbols for automobiles, money, television, guns, poison, and atomic energy are flashed onto the screen; these icons lend an eerie sense of Cold War America to the piece, contributing to the poem's implicit critique of the "progress" of American civilization. Wright's poem, along with those of Jim Northrop and Wanda Coleman later in the program, demonstrate that humor and satire can be effectively used in political poetry, something seldom seen in mainstream American verse, where political statement is almost always accompanied by an earnest or self-righteous tone.

Wright's poem is followed by a series of works by poets from various racial and ethnic minorities. Ruth Forman's poem "Stoplight Politics" addresses class tensions as exemplified by two young women within the African American community. Jim Northrop's "Shrinking Away" recounts with biting satire the story of a Native American Vietnam veteran's unsuccessful sessions with a psychiatrist. Luis Alfaro's "Orphan of Atzlan" describes the doubly marginal situation of the "Queer Chicano" in Los Angeles. Wanda Coleman's "Talk About the Money" uses a parody of the Home Shopping Network to critique the American obsession with financial gain. Javier Pina's "Bilingual in a Cardboard Box" uses both Spanish and English to expose the contradictions between the American dream of wealth and happiness and the reality for many Latinos of poverty, prejudice, frustration, and loneliness. And Robert Chambers's "Tumbling," a raw-energy howl of urban despair, translates into language the experience of the homeless, "tumbling through the Safety Net of the American Economy."

Chambers's poem represents the end of the downward trajectory of "The American Dream," a program that, in stark contrast to Moyers's vision of poetry as an uplifting answer to America's problems, presents a poetry filled with pain and anger against the status quo of American society. The program ends with the slightly more hopeful vision of Lawrence Ferlinghetti's "I Am Waiting," a poem whose tonal ambiguity leaves open-ended the questions raised about The American Dream. As Holman suggests, "the poets will not answer the questions, but ask them," and the questionable status of Ferlinghetti's utopian vision at the end of the poem ("and I am awaiting / perpetually and forever / a renaissance of wonder") puts the ball back in the readers' court.[10] The message with which we are left appears to be that it is up to the audience, not the poet, "to really discover America," thus confirming Holman's vision of a more interactive poetry.

The poems Holman, Blum, and Pellington selected for "The American Dream" may not be universally appealing, but they are effective as pieces of a startling mosaic of contemporary American life. This is an America not often seen in the mainstream media, and certainly not seen in American poetry, whether it be *The Language of Life*, poetry anthologies, or mainstream literary magazines. Some viewers would no doubt consider the program's message excessively cynical, an impression that is heightened by the material interpolated between the poems themselves. In addition to the image of the green dinosaur, we find words and images liberally scattered through the program, from the sardonic word-images of Barbara Kruger to images of Mount Rushmore; from shots of the Capitol and the "good life" of the 1950s and 1960s to lines of poetry from Langston Hughes ("America never was America to me") and Robinson Jeffers ("No bitterness: our ancestors did it"). Finally, there is the refrain, which constitutes an ironic verbal motif for the program: "What is the American Dream? You mean like family, home, apple pie, baseball? Life is good."[11] Taken in their entirety, these visual and verbal markers provide a frame for the fourteen poems, helping to guide the viewer toward the overall message: the American Dream as we once believed in it is a bankrupt fantasy, the product of manipulative portrayals by advertisers and conservative politicians.

Clearly the intent of the program, and of the series as a whole, is to shock the viewer out of the complacency not only of television viewing, but of poetry reading. As Holman and Blum put it in the book version of *USOP*, readers of poetry must be charged "with a new activism."[12] This is no doubt a worthwhile mission, if somewhat overambitious for a two-and-a-half-hour series. The question, however, is whether the format of *USOP* really encourages viewers to overcome "the passivity that TV has seemed to engender," or whether, like the MTV format on which it is largely based, it is perpetuating just such passivity. By providing such an unrelenting commentary on the poems heard, both in the visual production of the poetic segments themselves and in the interpolated words and images, are Holman, Blum, and Pellington giving the viewer enough space to think for himself, to hear, understand, and appreciate the poems on their own terms? As Howard Rosenberg suggests in his generally positive review of *USOP* in the *New York Times*, it is unclear exactly what the audience is getting more of, poetry or high-concept television production: "Does the razzle-dazzle of production overshadow or nullify the poetry being celebrated? Do the visuals in 'USOP' support the poetry or vice versa? Are we seeing with the eyes of the poets or with the eyes of the producers? Are we sharing the imagination of the bard or the program maker?"[13]

These are all legitimate questions about such a new and experimental hybrid format, and they are the questions that have dominated discussions of the series within the poetry culture. Despite the obvious power of the series, it is not entirely clear "just how fully or deeply . . . we can hear the poetry when the pictures and music are so commanding."[14] Television is, after all, a predominately visual medium, and on a first viewing it is clearly the visual images, and not the words themselves, that will make the greatest impact. Anecdotal evidence for this tendency has been suggested by Joe Amato, who relates how at least one student in the undergraduate class to which he showed the film was so entranced by the visuals and music that she stopped listening to the words entirely.[15] Despite Holman's claim in my interview with him that *"The United States of Poetry* is not interested in 'interpreting' the poems," the series implicitly provides several layers of meaning. Poems are not simply presented as if on the pages of an anthology; instead, like songs on MTV, they are surrounded by a range of semiotic markers that convey particular interpretations, an extratextual frame that may in some cases prove more compelling than the words themselves. Further, we must ask how the repeated strategy of using visual icons to undercut traditional American values, ideologies, and representations problematizes the claim of an unmediated airing of the poem. Does it work against the multiplicity of poetic voices it is meant to enhance?

These questions raise other concerns about the choices made in producing *The United States of Poetry.* For example, does it really do justice to the poetry to present fourteen poems in under thirty minutes, or does it merely create the kind of easily consumable and overproduced postmodern artifact most commonly associated with MTV? As E. Ann Kaplan has accurately observed in the case of MTV,

The channel hypnotizes more than others because it consists of a series of extremely short (four minutes or less) texts that maintain us in an excited state of expectation. . . . We are trapped by the constant hope that the next video will finally satisfy and, lured by the seductive promise of immediate plenitude, we keep endlessly consuming the short texts. . . . The "decentering" experience of viewing produced by the constant alternation of texts is exacerbated on MTV because its *longest* text is the four-minute video.[16]

While I hesitate to equate the experience of *The United States of Poetry* with that of typical MTV programming, there are clear similarities between them. The sense of "decenteredness" described by Kaplan is clearly a part of the effect achieved by *USOP,* as indicated not only by the extremely short exposure to any given poet (seldom longer than two or three minutes per poem), but also by the frequent use of jump-cutting, fast-motion filming, and other techniques that serve to accelerate the pace of the program still further, thereby creating the kind of hypnotic state Kaplan describes. As if the effort to absorb a poem every two minutes were not enough, the audience is also bombarded with various other texts and images, including brief quotations by various poets as well as "found poems," such as a soldiers' drill, cheerleaders' chants, a square dance call, and a jump-rope rhyme. When added together, the total number of "poems" presented in a given half-hour segment may be as high as twenty, thus giving an average of about ninety seconds for each poetic experience. Clearly, the pace of the series is based more on the format of the slam or open-mike reading, when thirty poets might share the stage on a given night, than on the conventional poetry reading; it is not intended to provide the same experience as a Moyers program highlighting one or two poets in an hour-long presentation. Yet one wonders whether the pace is *too* rapid, even in this postmodern age of infomercials and fast-action video games. The average viewer not familiar with the work of these poets will have trouble even remembering their names by the end of the program, let alone any detailed sense of the poems themselves.

In fact, in some troubling ways, *The United States of Poetry* risks being more interested in poetry as entertainment than in poetry as literary text. This sense is corroborated by the quote from W. C. Williams that is repeated as a kind of mantra at the beginning of each program: "If it ain't a pleasure, it ain't a poem." Yet despite the folksy wisdom of Williams's aphorism, it is not simply immediate gratification, but a deeper form of appreciation, that most accurately defines the experience of poetry. *USOP* makes little concession to the need for adequate time to absorb the poetry, seeming to revel in the speed with which it can move from image to image, from poem to poem. Such a premium on speed has led to other editorial decisions as well: many of the poems have been condensed from the printed version, presumably to allow them to fit within the allotted time slots. In the case of a poem like Ferlinghetti's "I Am Waiting," we hear only about 15 lines of a 125-line poem, and there is no indication in the reading of the poem that these are in fact excerpts, or poetic "sound bites," rather than the poem in its entirety. Not only does such cutting suggest (perhaps falsely) that those responsible have little concern for the integrity of the text—surely a 15-line poem is very different, both formally and rhetorically, from a 125-line poem—but it also suggests a condescending attitude toward the viewer, who is presumed not to know, or not to care, whether poems are being read in their entirety or in excerpted form. Surely it would not strain the attention span of the average viewer to hear more than fifteen lines, but if the constraints of time necessitate shorter spots, why not present shorter poems in their complete form rather than give piecemeal versions of longer works? What is even more puzzling is the cuts made in a relatively short poem like Quinlan's "Sold Out," where lines are simply left out or changed for no apparent reason.

Such attention to textual fidelity may appear trivial to some—who would no doubt argue that it is the *experience* of poetry, and not the textually faithful presentation of each poem, that is celebrated in *USOP*—but this attention reveals the greatest limitation of what is in most ways a well-conceived and well-executed project. In general, there is a tendency to treat poems more as scripts for oral performance than as carefully crafted written texts; for the most part, the series focuses more on creating a concentrated oral and visual impact than in exploring issues of poetic language and textuality.[17] As Amato has suggested, the series may ultimately have "less to do with poetry than with a particular kind of spectacle," a media spectacle, in Guy Debord's terms, more commonly associated with late-capitalist advertising and consumerism than with poetry.[18]

Nevertheless, Holman and his collaborators must be given credit for bringing to the television screen a landmark project, a video-anthology of American poetry that makes a defining if rather idiosyncratic statement about the place of poetry in the 1990s. With little support from the PBS network, which, according to Holman, "disowned the series" after it was made, the team of Holman, Blum, and Pellington accomplished something genuinely new and innovative in American television.[19] The series is certainly the most progressive use of the film/video media to present poetry to any kind of mass audience, and whether or not it succeeds in presenting, as Holman suggests, "a way to read a poem on TV," it does provide a number of memorable moments, some of them involving poets little known to a general audience. Among the high points of the series are Lois-Ann Yamanaka's Hawaiian-pidgin narrative "Boss of the Food"; Emily XYZ and Myers Bartlett's breathless rendition of "Slot Machine"; John S. Hall's perfectly pitched performance of the campy "My Lover"; Sparrow's irreverently tender poem about dropping things on the streets of New York City ("A Testimonial"); Tracie Morris's tour-de-force hip-hop performance of "Project Princess"; Dennis Cooper's haunting "Two Whores"; Besmilr Brigham's fragile "Tell Our Daughters"; and Larry Eigner's moving "What Time Is."

The United States of Poetry represents only one of many possible ways of putting poetry on television, but it is clearly a step in the right direction. It is not an attempt to present or establish a poetic canon; instead, it is an attempt to portray an eclectic and sometimes surprising array of poetic and performative talent, to present a road map to the various poetries being produced in the United States in the mid-1990s. Greeted with none of the literary fanfare surrounding the airing of Moyers's *The Language of Life,* it has nonetheless captured far more successfully than the Moyers series the multiform energies of contemporary American poetry, and it has exploited more effectively the possibilities for using the media to expand the poetic audience. It remains to be seen which of these approaches will serve as the model for future attempts to present poetry in the popular media. It is clear, however, that to talk about poetry today is also to talk about the use of the media, about how poetry is represented (whether in print, audio recording, television, or cyberspace), and about how different formats mediate the poetic object in new and significant ways.

Conclusion

Toward a Poetics and a Poetic Culture

for the Next Century

In the past three decades, American poetic culture has undergone a profound transformation that has affected almost every aspect of its existence. In publishing, the most evident change of the contemporary era has been a radical decentralization of publishing venues, as the number of independent and university presses publishing poetry has risen dramatically and the number of trade presses publishing contemporary poetry has correspondingly fallen. Micropresses and little magazines now far outstrip the trade presses and nationally circulated magazines in both readership and influence.[1] In terms of institutional infrastructure, the poetry culture has transformed itself by constructing an extensive system of academic creative-writing programs, supported by corollary systems of literary centers, granting institutions, contests and awards, conferences and workshops, writers' colonies, academic presses, and academically affiliated journals. Finally, in its relation to popular culture and the media, American poetry has abandoned its rarefied position as the print genre epitomizing high literary culture, and has increasingly defined itself as a dialogic cultural mode exploiting forms of popular media from public television to MTV, from sound recordings to CD-ROM.

These changes in the institutional, economic, demographic, and cultural orientation of American poetry have been accompanied by equally important changes in the dominant forms of poetic practice. In the 1950s, various countercultural poetries—later to be grouped by Donald Allen under the rubric "New American Poetry"—evolved against the backdrop of New Critical formalism and the quasi-formalist academic lyric represented by the poems in Hall, Pack, and Simpson's *New Poets of England and America*. Through the 1960s and '70s, as I have argued, this split not only continued to define American poetic culture, but became further reified by increasingly rigid institutional structures. Certain kinds of poetry came to be identified with a network of academic creative writing, as the Iowa Writers' Workshop and a burgeoning system of other writing programs based on its model ensured an ever-greater population of poets trained in the creation of short free-verse postconfessional domestic lyrics. Other kinds of poetry, especially the open-field or "projective" poems associated with the Beats and Black Mountain and the verbally experimental poems of the New York school, would be identified with alternative scenes such as New York's St. Mark's Poetry Project (officially founded in 1966, but with roots in the experimental poetry scene of the late 1950s and early 1960s), the Naropa Institute's Jack Kerouac School of Disembodied Poetics, and the more widely disseminated nonacademic poetry community of the San Francisco Bay Area.

By the 1980s, American poetic culture had reached the moment described by Jed Rasula at the end of his book *The American Poetry Wax Museum,* a moment of apparent stasis in which the poetry world could be configured into four easily discernible if highly unequal "zones":

(1) [T]he Associated Writing Programs, consisting of some three hundred institutionalized venues of creative writing instruction; (2) the New Formalism, with a small but visible number of adherents, whose goals are supported by a combination of small presses, large trade publishers, and a few highbrow quarterlies; (3) language poetry, with a well-established alternative press network, and a considerable critical reputation; and (4) various coalitions of interest-oriented or community-based poets (which obviously renders this fourth zone more heterogeneous and fluid than the others).[2]

In the mid-1990s, while these defining features continue to apply to a large degree, a single anatomy of the poetic landscape such as that Rasula provides has become far more problematic.[3] In the most abrupt change in North American poetic culture since the 1950s, the resurgence of poetry as an oral, public, and performative medium has led to a vibrant nonacademic scene that challenges the prevailing rubrics delineated by Rasula. At the same time, as we have seen in the final chapters of this book, the influence of the popular media on poetic production and reception has had a rapid and profound impact on issues ranging from canonicity to poetic language and form. Defining the dominant modes of poetry in our era has itself become more than ever before an open question, the answer to which depends a great deal on what criteria we use for measuring poetic dominance, success, or importance.

If we were to measure poetic dominance by popularity and book sales— as we would do if poetry were measured by the same criteria as forms of popular culture—the most successful poets of the past twenty-five years have been Rod McKuen, Lawrence Ferlinghetti, Allen Ginsberg, Charles Bukowski, and Maya Angelou. If we measured it by the kind of professional eminence resulting in membership on the various boards and committees of the poetry establishment, the ascendant poets of our era would include Daniel Hoffman, Mona van Duyn, Donald Hall, Anthony Hecht, W. S. Merwin, Robert Pinsky, Maxine Kumin, and Louise Gluck. If we measured it by positions in highly ranked academic departments of creative writing, the list of the most influential poets in America would include Jorie Graham, Robert Hass, Edward Hirsch, Richard Howard, Charles Wright, Michael Ryan, and Norman Dubie. If we measured it by their status as poet-scholars and poet-critics, the list of the most distinguished poets would include Allen Grossman, John Hollander, Mary Kinzie, Stephen Yenser, Heather McHugh, Alan Shapiro, Susan Howe, Nathaniel Mackey, Barrett Watten, Bob Perelman, and John Taggart. If we measured it by inclusion in the most widely used classroom anthology, *The Norton Anthology of Modern Poetry*, the most prominent poets of our age would include June Jordan, Michael Harper, Cathy Song, James Tate, Carolyn Forche, and Gjertrud Schnackenberg. If we measured it by critical reception in the academy, the most important poets would include John Ashbery, Adrienne Rich, Robert Creeley, and A. R. Ammons. If we measured it by the ability to win prestigious prizes such as the Pulitzer, the Bollingen, the MacArthur, or the National Book Award, the list of successful poets would include Mark Strand, Charles Simic, Irving Feldman, Donald Justice, Mary Oliver, Philip Levine, James Tate, and Yusef Komunyakaa. If we measured it by the ability to sustain an important avant-garde practice, the list would include poets such as Jackson Mac Low, Clark Coolidge, Charles Bernstein, Michael Palmer, Barbara Guest, and Lyn Hejinian. If we measured it by the ability to reach alternative or multicultural communities, the list would include Sherman Alexie, Linda

Hogan, Jimmy Santiago Baca, Marilyn Hacker, Jessica Hagedorn, Genny Lim, Miguel Algarin, Quincy Troupe, and Amiri Baraka. If we measured it by the amount of exposure in the popular media, the list would include Bob Holman, Sekou Sundiata, Maggie Estep, Tracie Morris, and Wanda Coleman.

Any of these criteria, as well as others that I have no doubt neglected to mention, will generate a list of writers who by some standard or other can be, and will be, considered "major poets." But the partisan battles over such ascendancy are ultimately of less interest than attempts to account for the overall trends in American poetry and the poetic culture that informs it. What direction will poetry take in the decades to come? Most ages think themselves pivotal, and ours is no exception. In very different ways, commentators as diverse as Bill Moyers, Bob Holman, Charles Bernstein, and Adrienne Rich have all made claims for the crucial importance of poetry at this moment in history, for its uniquely transformative power as a form of social and aesthetic discourse. As I hope this book has demonstrated, I am in large part in agreement with these claims, especially when they are made in the spirit of inclusion and exploration. Yet the exact nature of the changes American poetry is currently undergoing is harder to determine.

As a tentative conclusion to this study, then, I will not offer a polemical argument about the state of contemporary poetry. Nor will I offer a set of prescriptions for how to cure poetry—in an "age of prose," or more to the point, in an age of MTV and poetry slams—how to restore poetry to its traditional sense of formal "rigor," or how to preserve a particular cultural definition of what poetry has (traditionally) been or should (ideally) be. Instead, I will offer my best assessment—based on my own fairly close observation of contemporary poetic culture over the past decade—of the most significant directions poetic practice is likely to take in the near future. In tracing what has happened to Rasula's anatomy of the state of poetry since 1990, I will attempt to situate some of the trends that are most likely to shape the trajectory of North American poetry over the coming decades.

Of the four primary "zones" of American poetry described by Rasula, New Formalism appears to have had the least longevity. In fact, since it reached its height of notoriety and influence in the late 1980s, New Formalism has virtually disappeared from critical debate. The apex of New Formalism's literary fashion corresponded with a burst of critical and editorial activity, including articles by Dana Gioia and Brad Leithauser in the *Hudson Review* and the *New Criterion,* respectively (both in 1987), anthologies of "formal" verse published in 1986 and 1988, and critical studies by Timothy Steele and Wyatt Prunty, both published in 1990 but presumably undertaken in the mid- to late 1980s.[4] In 1991, toward the end of New Formalism's strongest period of influence, the academic critic Joseph Conte still describes a symmetrical opposition between New Formalism and Language poetry. While he finds New Formalism to be a "retrogressive" approach and Language poetry to be a "progressive and inventive approach to poetic form," he nonetheless characterizes them as "two factions" of American poetry, each of which has "courted both notoriety and serious critical attention."[5] From the present vantage point, however, Conte's estimate of the New Formalism's historical importance may have been overstated in relation to that of Language writing. While few critical studies of New Formalism or anthologies of neoformalist poets have appeared in the past few years, articles on Language poetry, collections of their work, and books of essays devoted to the contemporary avant-garde continue to appear with increasing regularity.

This difference may be explained by the fact that New Formalism, despite a few outspoken advocates, never fully achieved the communitarian, sociological, or ideological dimensions of a fully articulated poetic movement in the way Language poetry did. While Language poetry emerged in the 1980s as a "relatively cohesive cultural and publishing network with a proven ability to establish international reputations," New Formalism continued to function more as a splinter group of mainstream academic poetry than as a truly alternative poetic.[6] In fact, while New Formalist and the closely affiliated "new narrative" poetry is represented by a small press, Story Line, and maintains a relatively strong presence in the pages of the *Hudson Review,* it has never managed to propagate a range of little magazines and publishers to rival the network of alternative presses and journals serving Language poets and affiliated writers over the past decade.[7] Further, while New Formalism has remained a parochial phenomenon, Language poetry has spread into a movement with significant international dimensions: poets in Canada, Great Britain, Australia, and New Zealand participate in the same large-scale poetic project as U.S. Language poets, while affiliated poetic movements are active in France, Italy, Germany, Russia, and China.

As I have argued throughout this book, the academic workshop mode of the "official verse culture" and the Language mode of the experimentalist subculture remain the two most influential styles of poetry, the former clearly dominant in economic, institutional, and numerical terms, the latter increasingly dominant in terms of academic critical reception. But in the decade since the original anthologies dedicated to these two modes were published, their practitioners have aged. The "younger" mainstream academic poets anthologized in Smith and Bottoms's *Morrow Anthology of Younger Poets* and Myers and Weingarten's *New American Poets of the Eighties,* as well as the experimental Language poets in Douglas Messerli's *Language Poetries* and Ron Silliman's *In the American Tree,* are advancing toward middle age, the average age now more than fifty. Thus in both cases there is at present a significant generational divide between those old enough to have been Morrow poets or to have participated in the original manifestation of the Language movement (roughly poets age forty-five or older) and those who have emerged in the period since the mid-1980s. In the case of both communities, it would appear that the younger genera- tion — those now in their thirties and early forties — have for the most part fared less well than their predecessors, having missed the defining mo- ments in the respective traditions. If the second-generation Language poets (a group that has alternatively been labeled "post-Language," "emerging avant-garde," "New Coast," or simply "G2") have been unable to achieve either the kind of radical innovations in poetic theory and practice of the original Language group or the kind of notoriety that greeted the Lan- guage poets in the 1980s, younger poets of the mainstream academic cul- ture have seemingly failed to create *any* kind of generational identity for themselves.

If the two groupings of poets appear demographically similar — both reflecting the differences between a "baby boom" generation that came of age in the 1960s and a "post-boomer" generation that reached its maturity in the politically placid period of the late 1970s and 1980s — the genera- tional and communitarian dynamics at work within the two zones are quite different. This difference may in part arise from the fundamental sociocultural difference between a network that is built around an aca- demic workshop model of teacher and student (approximating the mas- ter/disciple relationship in traditional forms of art), and a primarily non- academic and countercultural model in which issues of hierarchy, power, and authority are more frequently and openly contested, and in which lin- guistic and social critique is not only tolerated by encouraged. In a culture like that of mainstream academic poetry, there is every incentive to play the role of the dutiful son or daughter by quietly accepting one's prizes and publishing one's books, without disturbing the status quo. In a cul- ture like that surrounding Language poetry, on the other hand — where there is little at stake in economic terms (few if any jobs for young experimental poets, few prizes to be won), and a higher premium on cultural and intellectual capital—there is every reason to stake out one's theoretical and poetic territory by challenging one's elders. Thus while the success and visibility of younger mainstream poets is still measured largely by their résumés of degrees, awards, and prizes, that of younger Language-oriented poets is measured, at least in part, by their active participation in the critical debates surrounding contemporary poetics.

What this difference means in terms of a meaningful distinction between the two subcultures is that whereas Language poetry has continued to function as a community, even across the generational divide, the poetic mainstream functions less as a poetic community (as it still at least to some degree did in the days when Iowa's centralizing influence was much greater than it is today) than as a vast network of interlocking institutions. As a result, it is difficult to find any kind of concerted project being carried out by younger poets writing in the mainstream tradition. Thus far, no anthology has appeared that documents the development of the current generation of young academic poets in the way *Morrow* and other similar collections like *New American Poets of the Eighties* and William Heyen's *The Generation of 2000* did a decade or so ago. Those poets under forty-five who have achieved the most accolades within the academic mainstream—such as Mark Doty, Sophie Cabot Black, and Karl Kirchwey—seem to represent no common direction other than a continuation of the free-verse or pseudo-formal lyric of their predecessors. While new themes may occasionally emerge in these poems—such as Doty's meditation on AIDS—there appears to be little in the way of a significant shift in practice from the predominant modes of the past thirty years. And since few of these younger poets write criticism or even reviews, it would be difficult to assess their project even if they had one. They may speak articulately or even eloquently about specific poems, as they do in the "Contributors' Notes and Comments" section of *Best American Poetry* volumes, but there is little indication of a historically located sense of their own poetic.

Doty is an interesting case to examine, since he is among the most highly acclaimed poets of his generation (at forty-five, he is generationally at the upper limit of what we might still consider "younger poets"), and a poet whose rapid rise to success appears to herald the emergence of a new generation of prizewinners. Doty has published four books of poems, the last, *Atlantis,* with the trade press HarperCollins. He has also won an astonishing number of grants and awards in the last few years: in addition to a Whiting (1994), a Guggenheim (1994), and grants from the NEA, the Ingram Merrill Foundation, the Massachusetts Artists Foundation, and the Vermont Council on the Arts, he has won the Los Angeles Times Books Award and the National Book Critics Circle Award (both for his third book, *My Alexandria*), was a finalist for the National Book Award, and was selected by Philip Levine for the National Poetry Series. Doty has also made his way quickly up the academic ladder, teaching at Sarah Lawrence College and Vermont College before landing his current tenured position at the University of Utah.

Clearly, Doty writes the kind of poems that those in the mainstream poetic and reviewing community wish to encourage. His last two books have been prominently reviewed (in the *Yale Review*, *New England Review*, *Parnassus*, *TLS*, and the *New York Review of Books*), and have even more than the usual adulatory blurbs from some of the most prestigious American poets: Levine, Richard Howard, and Mary Oliver. Levine claims, with some hyperbole, that Doty is "the poet to complete the century of William Carlos Williams and Wallace Stevens," and that he is "a maker of big, risky, fearless poems." Howard reads *Atlantis* as an exemplary model of the "American Sublime" (one wonders whether Harold Bloom would agree), and compares him, somewhat less hyperbolically than Levine, to Amy Clampitt. Oliver calls the book "ferocious, luminous, and important," calling attention to Doty's celebration of "the striking and graceful forms of the physical world."[8] Doty's poems appear to fall into two rather distinct categories: narrative or "confessional" poems, which often deal with AIDS, and especially with the illness and death of his companion Wally Roberts; and more descriptive poems, which deal with nature or with physical details of the urban environment. Many of the latter type are reminiscent of Clampitt or her predecessor Elizabeth Bishop in their use of specific details to tell a story or meditate on some aspect of life. Too often, however, these poems lack the hard-edged concision and wry tone of Bishop, veering instead into excessive sentimentality or bathetic philosophizing.

An example of these tendencies can be seen in a passage from the poem "Long Point Light," in *Atlantis*. Having described the lighthouse indicated by the poem's title, a building whose symbolic function in the poem is made abundantly clear ("our last outpost in the huge / indetermination of sea"), the poem's speaker declares in a maudlin moment of spiritual reflection:

It seems cheerful enough,
    in the strengthening sunlight,
        fixed point accompanying our walk

along the shore. Sometimes I think
    it's the where-we-will-be,
        only not yet, like some visible outcropping

    of the afterlife.

"Long Point Light" also exhibits another tendency of Doty's poetry
that is shared by many of his contemporaries: the use of pseudo-formal
verse patterns that imitate the visual aspect of formal poetry but with
no real formal structure. Here the line lengths appear entirely arbitrary,
ranging from four to twelve syllables, yet the stepped-line tercets do not
correspond to any discernible formal principle such as Williams's triadic
foot.[9] The frequently enjambed line breaks, which seem to be motivated
by typography rather than meaning or rhythm, add little to the stanzaic
form, which comes to seem more an affectation than an effective stylistic
device.[10]

    In another version of the nature poem, "Difference," included in the
1994 *Best American Poetry* volume, Doty displays a clear connection not
only to Bishop, but to Williams and Marianne Moore as well. Compare
the opening lines of the poem—

                The jellyfish
                float in the bay shallows
                like schools of clouds,

                a dozen identical—is it right
                to call them creatures,
                these elaborate sacks

                of nothing?

with the well-known opening of Marianne Moore's 1921 poem:

                        The Fish

                wade
                through black jade.

    And with William Carlos Williams's almost equally famous poem of
1935:

The Yachts

contend in a sea which the land partly encloses
shielding them from the too-heavy blows
of an ungoverned ocean when it chooses

Whether Doty's poem is a self-conscious allusion to these two predecessor poems or merely an unintended imitation of them is not clear,
though the fact that he fails to mention any such tribute in his commentary (claiming, in fact, that the poem "seemed to write itself") suggests
the latter. Yet the resemblances are so obvious as to be almost embarrassing. The ocean landscape, the rhetorical question with which he begins,
the comparison of the living "creature" with an object from the nonliving
world, and even the rhythmic device of the first two lines (though without
the formal disruption of using the title as part of the first line), all suggest a poem that not only could have been written a half-century ago, but
was written, in only slightly different forms, by the American modernists.
Even the primary theme of the poem—that "words can only be metaphors for what they represent" and that language is "as slippery, undulant
and unreliable as the uncapturable world it attempts to fix"—seems trite
and familiar. A reading of the poetry of Ashbery, or even of Stevens, would
offer a more subtle interpretation of this argument.

Admittedly, Doty is only an isolated example and not representative of
a generation, just as Stephen Dobyns is not entirely representative of his
slightly older generation of "workshop" poets. But if I were to venture a
comparison of the two poets, I would say that, rather than any kind of ad-
vance in poetic practice beyond the casual free-verse narrative exemplified
by Dobyns, Doty's work represents a retreat into an even more traditional
form of lyric. His lyric is based less on the controlled manipulation of
voice than on a form of aestheticism that manifests itself in the pseudo-
formal impulse of the poems (exhibiting neither the merits of formalism
nor those of free verse); in the search for a form of beauty, transcendence,
redemption, or celebration that can seem sentimental or artificial; and in
the overwrought poeticism of much of the language. For many younger
poets, the kind of lyric embodied by Doty's poems represents a dead
end, leaving a generation of poets up the creek wondering what has happened to the mainstream. As Leonard Schwartz suggests, most younger
poets of the last two and a half decades have not only "advanced without the comforting banner of a poetic movement to wave," but have had
to do "without the sense of a shared community to lend solidity to their

projects." For this reason alone, they look either to a more theoretically and ideologically engaged avant-garde such as Language writing, or to a more socially interactive scene such as that of spoken word, or of the kind of multicultural poetries that, in Adrienne Rich's terms, "embody the dialectics of 'otherness' in language itself."[11] My own sense, from talking to MFA students on the two campuses where I have taught, is that the poetic mainstream as it has been defined over the past twenty or thirty years no longer provides a sufficient model of either poetic writing or poetic community. Yet many younger poets remain unsure about the alternatives to the kind of poetry supported by academic creative-writing programs.

The most visible alternative to the academic mainstream over the past two decades has clearly been Language poetry, the only context for American poetic writing of the past thirty years that has constituted both a viable movement and a recognizable community.[12] But for many younger poets, including those most strongly committed to the kind of linguistic and ideological project undertaken by the Language poets, the excessively doctrinaire rhetoric of the original Language group and its seemingly exclusionary emphasis on difficulty, opacity, and abstraction, render it a "hegemonic mode of experimental formalism" rather than an approachable model for poetic practice.[13] What Mark Wallace has described as the "post-Language crisis" is a very real problem for many young poets who wish to participate in the emerging avant-garde. The "cohesive, group-oriented publishing network of the language writers" has made it difficult for many younger poets not already part of that network to find support and publishing venues for the poetry.[14] Further, the far larger and more geographically dispersed network of contemporary avant-garde poets makes it very difficult to replicate the strongly cohesive and communitarian sense of the original Language writers, or their "strikingly clear" vision of themselves and their project. Finally, the emerging generation of the avant-garde has been unwilling to take the extreme positions adopted by Language poets in the late 1970s and 1980s, positions that required rejecting most forms of poetry that did not conform to avant-gardist criteria, and accepting certain ideological stances toward literature, language, and capitalist society.

As Wallace suggests, the net result of these various factors is that the poets of the emerging avant-garde have "a much less clear theoretical similarity than the language writers," and therefore appear to some readers "a directionless group."[15] This impression is given not only by the wide range of poetic and political positions represented by anthologies of emerging avant-garde writing such as *Writing from the New Coast* and *A Poetics of*

Criticism—a diversity of views and approaches that can potentially be seen as a failure to develop a meaningful poetics or politics—but also by a tendency to be wary of direct statements. As Robert Bertholf writes in the preface to *Writing from the New Coast,* this generation prefers to work by a method of fable or parable rather than by direct polemic or argumentation, thus generating "a language structure that is "disengaged [and] abstracted," working by "inference, not by direct reference."[16] Perhaps it is this same reticence that has prevented most of the younger avant-garde poets from writing the kinds of sustained critical and theoretical essays that characterized the Language poets and that in large part brought them to the prominence they now enjoy.

Even more troubling is the tendency toward defensiveness, sometimes to the point of sounding reactionary, that marks the attitude of many younger poets of the experimental camp. This defensive posture may stem from the inability of younger poets to accomplish what their own promotional rhetoric claims as their goal: namely, to "cut loose from the writing of the 1970s and 1980s" and to "build new structures for . . . formulating human desires in language."[17] They thus either attack Language poetry or refuse to acknowledge the significance of its influence. In the 1970s, when the various poets who would come to constitute the Language group began to formulate their ideas and practices, they opposed themselves to a moribund avant-garde culture consisting primarily of a relatively exhausted form of the New American Poetry of the 1950s and early 1960s. Not only was the poetic practice of the Language poets strongly demarcated from that of avant-garde poets of the previous generation—such as Charles Olson, Robert Creeley, Robert Duncan, Gary Snyder, Jack Spicer, Frank O'Hara, and John Ashbery—but the strength of their theoretical writings and the commitment of their ideological positions confirmed that independence and enabled them to establish a radically new poetry. The original Language poets, while rejecting aspects of their predecessors' project, could display a degree of critical generosity toward the previous generation that is lacking in most current projects. In his introduction to *Writing from the New Coast,* an anthology whose contributors could mostly be described as post–Language writers, Steve Evans barely evokes Language writing, despite including several Language writers in his list of major poets in the "oppositional tradition" of which the anthology is part.[18] And in *A Poetics of Criticism,* the introduction written by editors Juliana Spahr, Mark Wallace, Kristin Prevallet, and Pam Rehm fails even to mention the context of Language writing in which it is clearly and importantly located.

On the other hand, poets like Lew Daly and John Noto take the more confrontational approach, launching direct attacks on Language writing, and especially on what they see as its programmatic reliance on critical theory. As Wallace argues, these poets may deserve a degree of respect for "their willingness to take on directly the identity crisis haunting emerging avant garde writers."[19] But at the same time their arguments fundamentally misrepresent much of the Language project, thus doing a disservice both to the Language poets and to their own generation of emerging writers — a generation that, by implication, appears incapable of understanding and constructively engaging with the work of their predecessors.

But the shift in position represented by poets like Daly (who favors a poetry more in keeping with the spiritual philosophy of Levinas than with the theory of Derrida and Althusser), Noto (who advocates a "New Synthesis" of biological, technological and lyrical forces), and others, such as Charles Borkhuis (who proposes a synthesis of surrealist and Language-based writing), is also symptomatic of a larger trend in the poetry culture toward increasingly hybrid and nonaffiliated modes of poetry. More than ever, presses and magazines are crossing the borders to include poets from different camps. Wesleyan University Press has been a leader in publishing a wide range of poets, from an experimentalist like Susan Howe to more traditional poets like James Dickey and Mark Rudman; journals like *Grand Street*, the *Chicago Review, Iowa Review*, and *Agni Review* increasingly offer a wider spectrum of poets. Poets themselves are capable of establishing more flexible affiliations, both in the range of sources and influences from which they draw and in the venues they seek for their publishing. Donald Revell, whose recent books have been published by Wesleyan, places poems in journals ranging from the experimentalist *Tyuonyi* and *Sulfur* to the more mainstream *Boulevard* and *Pequod*. Forrest Gander, another Wesleyan poet, has built a career on publishing in even more disparate magazines, from *Sulfur* and *O-blek* to the seemingly antithetical *Southern Review* and *Partisan Review*.

Such split alliances would have been rare a decade or two ago, but now appear increasingly common. The recent anthology *Primary Trouble*, published by Talisman House and edited by Leonard Schwartz, Joseph Donahue, and Edward Foster, contains a number of poets who are either very loosely affiliated with particular schools of writing, or who resist such efforts at categorization altogether. In his introduction, Schwartz rejects such labels as "avant-garde," "experimental," and "antiacademic" as "inconclusive." Instead, he traces the lineage of the majority of the poets included to three major sources: the New American Poetry, especially comprising poetry engaging "mythic material"; the New York school; and Language poetry. Schwartz is particularly careful, however, to avoid associating his poets too closely with Language practice, arguing that poets "may be affiliated in part with the L=A=N=G=U=A=G=E project without . . . sharing in that school's agenda for poetic hegemony."[20]

The younger poets included in *Primary Trouble* certainly provide more hope for the future of American poetry than mainstream academic poets like Doty. But although many of the younger poets in the anthology—including Gander and Revell, as well as Andrew Shelling, Virginia Hooper, Laura Moriarty, Stephen Sartarelli, Elizabeth Robinson, Claire Needell, Andrew Joron, and Drew Gardner—are engaged in innovative poetic projects, the overall account of their poetry in the anthology's introduction leaves us wishing for a clearer sense of direction:

> While the anthology is in no way thematic, there *is* a common interest here in a certain vocabulary, a certain set of possibilities toward which these texts have tended and been chosen. To call this interest "the sacred" would be too officious. To speak of it as "the spiritual" would be amorphous, too easily misconstrued in terms of belief and not imagination. . . . To call it a new eroticism would also be reductive.[21]

Amid the careful equivocation of "a certain" and "have tended," we find out more about what the poetry is *not* than about what it is. The various terms and phrases that have been used to describe the turn in recent "experimental" or "avant-garde" writing—a greater sense of spirituality or transcendence, a new eroticism, a poetry focused on the "self" rather than on abstract issues of "language," a poetry that can retain its political commitment without abandoning clarity and even lyricism— all suggest a retreat from the avant-gardist legacy of both Language writing and experimental modernism. Such a retrenchment may be inevitable in the aftermath of Language poetry's difficulty, just as a similar retrenchment followed the most extreme forms of poetic innovation in the modernist period. Nevertheless, the kind of critical looseness engendered by Schwartz and others who attempt to represent the new poetry illustrates the lack of a strong critical and poetic direction, as opposed to the harder-edged polemic of poets like Watten, Andrews, and Bernstein, or of anthologists like Silliman and Messerli. The publisher of *Primary Trouble,* Talisman House, advertises the anthology as "pivotal to our understanding of directions in American poetry," comparing its importance to that of

Donald Allen's *The New American Poetry*. Unfortunately, however, neither the book's introduction nor its contents confirm such claims. While the anthology may be of interest to those few readers who can appreciate the often subtle distinctions made between different groups within the experimental wing of American poetry, it does little to provide a direction for the future of American avant-garde writing. In fact, the anthology will in all likelihood be less influential than either Ron Silliman's *In the American Tree* or Douglas Messerli's *Language Poetries*, which have been, as Hank Lazer suggests, "the two most important anthologies of contemporary American poetry" since Allen's benchmark collection.[22] Given the growth in numbers of "experimental" poets over the past thirty-five years, and even over the past decade, it would be impossible to claim the kind of inclusiveness, or even representativeness, of Allen's groundbreaking collection. But beyond that inevitable demographic reality, *Primary Trouble* seems arbitrary in its selection of some poets over others: why, for example, include Moriarty—the only poet under forty-five in the anthology who is strongly associated with Language or post–Language writing—rather than equally deserving contemporaries such as Juliana Spahr, Peter Gizzi, and Elizabeth Willis? The anthology seems unable to articulate a vision of just what makes this poetry significant and how it differs from other forms of contemporary lyric.

Overall, the most vibrant area of American poetry may be that represented in another recent anthology, Walter K. Lew's *Premonitions: The Kaya Anthology of New Asian North American Poetry*. Lew's collection of experimental multicultural poetry represents a significant departure from earlier collections of Asian American poetry, such as Joseph Bruchac's *Breaking Silence: An Anthology of Contemporary Asian-American Poets* (1983) and Garrett Hongo's *The Open Boat: Poems from Asian America* (1993). Unlike those anthologies, Lew's collection goes beyond "conventional models of verse" to encompass the "many ways in which language is drastically reshaped into fresh articulations, ranging from video collage and highly compressed prose poems to cyberpunk critiques of ethnic mimicry."[23] There is some overlap between the poets in *Premonitions* and those in *The Open Boat*—a central core including John Yau, Arthur Sze, Lawson Fusao Inada, Russell Leong, Jessica Hagedorn, Agha Shahid Ali, Marilyn Chin, David Mura, and Vince Gotera grounds both collections. But Lew's anthology pushes more vigorously in the direction of experimental or avant-garde practice, while Hongo's leans heavily in the direction of a mainstream academic lyric with an Asian or multicultural inflection.

Premonitions is for the most part very successful in its project, one that must be seen as particularly radical given the traditional resistance of multicultural or identity-based literature to any formal and linguistic innovation that threatens to complicate its predominantly thematic concerns. Lew presents a wide range of experimental and politically engaged poetry, much of it by poets unknown to a general audience. Although we find some of the more familiar names, we also find a number of lesser-known and younger poets who will set the future course for Asian American poetry, and more generally for multicultural poetry, in the decades to come.[24] Refreshingly, in an age when poets in anthologies seem to be ever more mature (mid-career poets defined as "younger," and older poets defined as "mid-career"), over half the poets in *Premonitions* are under forty. They include poets like Myung Mi Kim and Tan Lin, whose closest stylistic affiliations are with Language poetry; R. Zamora Linmark, Barry Masuda, and Lois-Ann Yamanaka, who create complex cultural ironies through the use of Hawaiian pidgin; Gloria Toyun Park, who works between video and poetry; Ann Kong, Brian Kim Stefans, and Jean Yoon, who experiment in a variety of innovative formats; and Amitava Kumar, a performance artist, photographer, and writer whose poems range from biting parables like "History" and "Iraqi Restaurants" (reminiscent of the epigrammatic poems of Ed Dorn's *Abhorrences*) to the sweeping cultural and political poem "Mistaken Identity."

Taken as a whole, *Premonitions* offers one of the most encouraging signs that there is a future for poetry in North America. The combination of the linguistic and formal energies of the avant-garde or experimental tradition with the transcultural and interpersonal energies of an expanded racial and ethnic context seems to be generating a more radical and more innovative practice than either one is capable of creating and sustaining in isolation. While a recent conference devoted to experimental poetry, "Assembling Alternatives," remained predominantly uniracial, there are indications that the multicultural canon may breathe new life into the experimental avant-garde just as the avant-garde injects a new vitality into multiculturalism.[25]

If the 1970s and 1980s were the era of "opening the canon," the 1990s will probably be seen as the decade in which the cultural parameters of poetry have been more profoundly redefined than at any time since the 1950s. The trend toward more performance-oriented poetries that has been addressed at some length in this book is one instance of such redefinition, and one that will no doubt continue for some time to come, given both the relative youth of the poets engaged in the spoken-word, performance, and slam scene, and the ability of poets to reach potentially far larger audiences via recordings and television. The interest in performance and spoken-word recording is not confined to the kinds of "street" or post-Beat poetry one might encounter at a typical slam. In fact, there is a clear trend toward performativity in the more experimental or Language-based community as well, as evidenced by the number of highly performative readings at the "Assembling Alternatives" conference, and by the number of recordings of avant-garde work that have been released in recent years.[26] Another important shifting of parameters involves the increasing use of electronic media to present poetry on-line or in CD-ROM (and hypertextually enhanced) format.[27] These developments will help to keep alive traditions of poetic innovation that do not rely on the dominant institutions of American literary culture—the trade presses that pour thousands of dollars into the advertising budgets of award-winning books, mainstream magazines like the *New Yorker* that can afford to lose millions of dollars a year, or large foundations like the Lila Wallace/Readers Digest Fund that, as Charles Bernstein has observed, are more strongly committed "to the administration of culture than to the support of poetry." As Bernstein writes, "a new literature requires new institutions, and these institutions are as much a part of its aesthetic as the literary works that they weave into the social fabric."[28]

Such literary institutions may well evolve, in the coming decades, at sites and within communities not associated either with the academic creative-writing network or with mainstream trade and academic publishing. These sites and communities may include electronic journals, publishers, and Web sites; various forms of readings, slams, and performance; and the many zines and micropresses associated with innovative, experimental, and radical poetries. If poetry is once again to assume the kind of social, cultural, and aesthetic role it has had in the past, it must struggle to overcome the forces of intellectual apathy and cultural conservatism that have acted as a dead weight on American poetic practice over the past several decades. Rather than politicize and polemicize differences between mainstream and multicultural, between establishment and avant-garde, between official and alternative, let us celebrate (and reward financially with awards and grants) those who have made pathbreaking contributions in all domains of American poetry: from Amiri Baraka to Jackson Mac Low, from Bob Holman to Susan Howe, from John Taggart to Lyn Hejinian, from Miguel Algarin to Rae Armontrout, from Douglas Messerli to Jerome Rothenberg, from David Antin to Leslie Scalapino, from Lorenzo Thomas to June Jordan, from Wanda Coleman to Erika

Hunt.[29] Only when we recognize American poetry as a macrocommunity with shared interests and agendas, not simply a field of competing subcultures and institutions, can we move beyond "opposing poetries"—to borrow Hank Lazer's term—and face our *common* enemy: the impoverished cultural spirit of American life.

Notes

Introduction

1. The most comprehensive studies in the sociology of American literature—those of William Charvat, Nina Baym, Michael Denning, and Cathy Davidson, for example—have dealt primarily with the "popular" forms of the nineteenth century, especially the novel.

2. Robert von Hallberg's *American Poetry and Culture, 1945–1980* (Cambridge: Harvard University Press, 1985) does explore various cultural contexts within which post–World War II American poetry can be read, including such issues as audience and the canon, politics, popular culture, and tropes of suburbanization, travel, and tourism. However, von Hallberg is more interested in the way popular culture appears as a thematic presence in poetry than in the way poetry participates in or resists an economically or socially inflected system of cultural practice.

3. The relationship between poetry and the growing field of "cultural studies" is still a problematic and contested one. See, for example, Carrie Noland's "Rimbaud and Patti Smith: Style as Social Deviance," *Critical Inquiry* 21, no. 3 (1995). Within the field of contemporary poetry criticism, the most significant recent departures from the formalist high-cultural mode include Ron Silliman's *The New Sentence* (New York: Roof Books, 1987); Walter Kalaidjian's *Languages of Liberation: The Social Text in Contemporary American Poetry* (New York: Columbia University Press, 1989); George Hartley's *Textual Politics and the Language Poets* (Bloomington: University of Indiana Press, 1989); Rachel Blau DuPlessis's *The Pink Guitar: Writing as Feminist Practice* (New York: Routledge, 1990); Marjorie Perloff's *Radical Artifice: Writing Poetry in the Age of Media* (Chicago: University of Chicago Press, 1991); Charles Bernstein's *A Poetics* (Cambridge: Harvard University Press, 1992; Maria Damon's *At the Dark End of the Street: Margins in Vanguard American Poetry* (Minneapolis: University of Minnesota Press, 1993); Alan Golding's *From Outlaw to Classic: Canons in American Poetry* (Madison: University of Wisconsin Press, 1995); Jed Rasula's *The American Poetry Wax Museum: Reality Effects, 1940–1990* (Urbana: National Council of Teachers of English, 1995); Hank Lazer's *Opposing Poetries*, 2 vols. (Evanston: Northwestern University Press, 1996); Bob Perelman's *The Marginalization of Poetry: Language Writing and Literary History* (Princeton: Princeton University Press, 1996); Bruce Andrews's *Paradise and Method: Poetics and Praxis* (Evanston: Northwestern University Press, 1996); and Michael Davidson's *Ghostlier Demarcations: Modern Poetry and the Material Word* (Berkeley: University of California Press, 1997).

4. Theodor Adorno, "Lyric Poetry and Society," *Telos* 20 (1974): 157.

5. Calvin Bedient, "The Retreat from Poetic Modernism," *Modernism/Modernity* 1, no. 3 (1994): 221.

6. See Silliman, "The Political Economy of Poetry," in *New Sentence*, 28–29.

7. Stephen Fredman, *The Grounding of American Poetry: Charles Olson and the Emersonian Tradition* (New York: Cambridge University Press, 1993), 69–70.

8. Theodore Adorno, "Culture and Administration," in *The Culture Industry: Selected Essays on Mass Culture* (New York: Routledge, 1990), 94.

9. The Internet is providing a new and as yet relatively unexplored means of community building. The "poetics list" administered by Charles Bernstein and centered at SUNY Buffalo has more than four hundred subscribers from the United States and around the world. The "list" provides a valuable forum for the exchange of information, and for discussion and debate among the "experimental" poetic community; exchanges on the list are also archived for future reference, thus creating a unique form of virtual institutional memory.

10. I am thinking here in particular of anthologies published by such presses as New Directions and Sun & Moon. Both of these are independent presses that can in a sense be seen as part of the "community" of poets they publish. James Laughlin, until recently the publisher of New Directions, was a longtime champion of the literary avant-garde, and Douglas Messerli of Sun & Moon is himself a poet with active connections to Language poetry and the associated literary avant-garde. Nevertheless, such presses are still institutions that can, depending on their infusion of capital into the literary marketplace and their success in penetrating the literary field, have a significant impact on the kinds of poetry that get written and published.

11. Ron Silliman, "Canons and Institutions: New Hope for the Disappeared," in *The Politics of Poetic Form: Poetry and Public Policy,* ed. Charles Bernstein (New York: Roof, 1990), 157.

12. Ibid., 156.

13. Take, for example, the following assertion in the introduction to the multicultural *Heath Anthology of American Literature* (Lexington, Mass.: D. C. Heath, 1990): "The most profound change that has occurred during the past twenty years is . . . that literature can no longer be divided into 'mainstream' and 'marginal'" (1785). This misleadingly suggests not only that venues for the publication of forms of writing hitherto deemed unacceptable to the mainstream have suddenly appeared, but even more surprisingly that *readers* have suddenly decided to accept a far wider spectrum of writing, including writing that is openly political, confrontational, or experimental. Such an assertion is certainly not true in the case of avant-garde writers such as the Language poets, but it is also not entirely true in the case of the writings of other "marginal" groups. It is particularly surprising to find such an assertion in the pages of the left-oriented Heath anthology, which might be expected to remind its readers that the kinds of struggles for legitimacy represented by "marginal" literature duplicate similar struggles in the larger political and social arena, struggles having to do with class as well as race, gender, and ethnicity. For a balanced discussion of these issues, see Jeffrey Nealon's chap-

ter "Politics, Poetics, and Institutions: 'Language' Poetry," in his *Double Reading: Postmodernism after Deconstruction* (Ithaca: Cornell University Press, 1993). For a more partisan discussion, see Rasula, *American Poetry Wax Museum.*

14. Also see Wai Chee Dimock and Michael T. Gilmore, eds. *Rethinking Class: Literary Studies and Social Formations* (New York: Columbia University Press, 1994).

15. Some of the most interesting examples of scholarship in this field include Janice Radway's work on the construction of a "middlebrow" canon in the Book-of-the-Month Club and a "popular" canon in the romance novel, Richard Ohmann's work on canon formation in contemporary American fiction, and Alan Golding's work on the use of poetry anthologies in constructing a more restrictive canon of American poetry. For a discussion of canonical issues as they relate to specific authors, see Michael Bérubé's comparison of the reception of Thomas Pynchon and Melvin Tolson, in *Marginal Forces/Cultural Centers: Tolson, Pynchon, and the Politics of the Canon* (Ithaca: Cornell University Press, 1992).

16. Cary Nelson, *Repression and Recovery: Modern American Poetry and the Politics of Cultural Memory, 1910–1945* (Madison: University of Wisconsin Press, 1989), 264–65.

17. Or, to quote Terry Eagleton in a paraphrase of the same argument, Shakespeare "is great literature because the institution constitutes him as such" (*Literary Theory: An Introduction* [Minneapolis: University of Minnesota Press, 1983], 202).

18. Nelson, *Repression and Recovery,* 67–69.

19. Ibid., 260.

20. Helen Vendler, *The Music of What Happens: Poems, Poets, Critics* (Cambridge: Harvard University Press, 1988), 39.

21. Golding, *From Outlaw to Classic,* 51.

22. See Barbara Herrnstein Smith, "Contingencies of Value," *Critical Inquiry* 10 (1983): 22.

23. McClatchy proposes a poetic canon, the same one that can be found in his *Vintage Anthology of Contemporary American Poetry* (New York: Random House, 1990), composed of an all-white, predominately male, East Coast, academically sanctioned group of poets. In fact, McClatchy's rhetoric involves a romanticization of the canon itself and of its legitimizing function as a conveyer of permanent aesthetic truths: his criteria for poetic excellence include "generous thematic range," "amplitude of vision," "the rigor of the sublime," and "the language of the old masters" (20). For McClatchy, poetry must above all be in dialogue with "conventions": these, presumably, will keep it "rigorous" and "disciplined" and keep out the undesirable poets who do not measure up to such an aesthetic. Those who display any obvious interest in politics, society, or radical experimentation are by definition excluded from any canon McClatchy will construct.

24. Damon, *Dark End of the Street,* 239–40.

25. Ibid., ix, x.

26. Ibid., 161. Damon's argument raises important questions about the canon, but it begs others. It is unclear, for example, to what extent a writer like Gertrude Stein should be considered "marginal" or part of a "shadow canon." The fact that she was Jewish and a lesbian does not erase the fact that she was a central figure in American expatriate literary culture. When writers like Stein are read as canonically marginal, one wonders, what is left of the "real" canon against which Stein supposedly works?

27. These studies include Robert Pinsky's *The Situation of Poetry* (Princeton: Princeton University Press, 1976), and more recently J. D. McClatchy's *White Paper: On Contemporary American Poetry* (New York: Columbia University Press, 1989), Jonathan Holden's *The Fate of American Poetry* (Athens: Georgia University Press, 1991), Dana Gioia's *Can Poetry Matter?* (St. Paul: Graywolf, 1992), and Vernon Shetley's *After the Death of Poetry: Poet and Audience in Contemporary America* (Durham: Duke University Press, 1993).

28. McClatchy is interested primarily in midcentury Ivy Leaguers, and Holden in contemporary "workshop" poetry; Shetley presents a relatively mainstream but somewhat more challenging canon, which he locates in the tradition of Elizabeth Bishop, James Merrill, and John Ashbery; Gioia has a loosely New Formalist agenda. All of these poet-critics shy away from poetry that poses a serious challenge to the status quo of mainstream poetry.

29. Shetley cites Bishop, Merrill, and Ashbery as models of what current poets should aspire to achieve in their work. It is interesting to note that Gioia and McClatchy, as well as Shetley treat the solidly canonical and relatively uncontroversial Elizabeth Bishop as a poetic exemplar for the contemporary age. One has to wonder whether her status, at least for nonfeminist male critics, has become that of a token woman poet who, despite her biographical lesbianism, is still safely bound within the decorum of seemingly nongendered white genteel tradition. McClatchy writes of her "austere grandeur," Shetley of her "silences" (a gender-coded way of distinguishing her from Merrill's "work" and Ashbery's "difficulty"), and Gioia of her "reticence" and "reassuring" presence.

30. Gioia, *Can Poetry Matter?* 37.

31. Hank Lazer, *Opposing Poetries. Volume One: Issues and Institutions* (Evanston: Northwestern University Press, 1996), 56.

32. McClatchy, *White Paper*, 5, 20; Lazer, *Opposing Poetries*, 57.

33. One of the best responses to accounts such as McClatchy's and Shetley's is a book like Perloff's *Radical Artifice*, which not only engages the new in provocative and insightful ways, but demonstrates the ways in which contemporary poetry can be read in broader contexts. In comparing the language of talk shows to that of speech-based poetry, for example, or reading the poetic image in the context of the advertising image, Perloff has demonstrated that the cultural field known as "poetry" is not hermetically sealed off from the rest of society: in fact, mass culture can and should be read as an important intertext for postmodern poetry. Perloff

refuses to engage in the same terms of critical debate that have dominated the discussion of contemporary poetry in recent years, either as an apologist for the contemporary scene, or as a Cassandra proclaiming the demise of poetry in America.

Chapter One

1. Donald Hall, "Poetry and Ambition," in *Poetry and Ambition: Essays, 1982–1988* (Ann Arbor: University of Michigan Press, 1988).

2. Greg Kuzma, "The Catastrophe of Creative Writing," *Poetry* 148, no. 6 (1986); Joseph Epstein, "Who Killed Poetry?" *Commentary* 86, no. 2 (1988): 13–20; Charles Bernstein, "The Academy in Peril: William Carlos Williams Meets the MLA," in *Content's Dream: Essays, 1975–1984* (Los Angeles: Sun & Moon, 1986).

3. Robert Peters, "The Present State of Poetry," part 4: "The Mammoth Cloth Beast of Poetry," *New York Quarterly* 30 (summer 1986): 113–20.

4. Jed Rasula, "Literary Effects in the Wad: Handling the Fiction, Nursing the Wounds," *Sulfur* 24 (1989): 77–78.

5. Dana Gioia, *Can Poetry Matter?*

6. Joseph Brodsky, "An Immodest Proposal: Why American Poetry Belongs in the Supermarket," *New Republic*, 11 November 1991, 31.

7. The 1996 Poetry Publication Showcase, an annual event inaugurated by New York's Poet's House in 1992, included 1,225 books of poetry published over a sixteen-month period in 1994 and 1995 by 404 presses. Jane Preston, assistant director of Poet's House and curator of the showcase, estimates that this represents "about 80% of the total"; but this figure is based only on a "gut feeling" (private correspondence with author, 5 June 1996). Charles Bernstein has told me that he is skeptical of this total, and estimates that the total number of micropress books and chapbooks may be double that included in the Poet's House exhibit. My own sense is that the number of presses and books of poetry is in all probability far greater than that represented by Poet's House and listed in their annual *Directory of American Poetry Books*. Many of the presses listed in Len Fulton's *Directory of Poetry Publishers*, 10th edition, were not included in the Poet's House list; beyond that, there are a number of additional presses that publish poetry that are not listed by either directory.

8. See Mary Biggs, *A Gift that Cannot Be Refused: The Writing and Publishing of Contemporary American Poetry* (New York: Greenwood, 1990).

9. See the statistics on book reviewing in Jed Rasula, "Part of Nature, Part of—'US'? The Role of Critics and the Emperor's New Clothes in American Poetry," *Sulfur* 9 (1984).

10. In its annual list of over four hundred "Notable Books" for 1992, for example, the *Times* listed only seven books of poetry, of which only three were by living American poets. By 1997, that number had declined even further, to five books, one of which was the posthumous *Collected Poems* of Amy Clampitt.

The other four were Jorie Graham's *The Errancy*, Jane Kenyon's *Otherwise: New and Selected Poems*, Robert Hass's *Sun under Wood*, and Maxine Kumin's *Selected Poems, 1960–1990*. The coverage of poetry in the daily *New York Times* is almost nonexistent: for example, not a single one of the 251 daily literary reviews in 1993 dealt with contemporary poetry.

11. Books *about* poets, such as biographies, are reviewed with greater frequency than books *by* poets. Apparently the editors feel that most readers are more interested in the lives of poets than in poetry itself.

12. Epstein, "Who Killed Poetry," 20.

13. Gioia, *Can Poetry Matter?* 2.

14. Lance Dean, review of *Can Poetry Matter? American Literature* 66 (1994): 193. Perhaps the most telling criticism offered by Dean is that the antiacademic stance and "plain-sense" tone of the essays, combined with the dismissal of both academic poetry criticism and academic poetry, "replicates the very schism [Gioia] decries."

15. Calvin Bendient, "The Retreat from Poetic Modernism," *Modernism/ Modernity* 1, no. 3 (1994): 223.

16. Marjorie Perloff, "Poetry Doesn't Matter," *American Book Review* 15, no. 5 (1993): 7. As Jed Rasula indicates, Gioia fails to distinguish between different kinds of poets who teach in the academy, thus collapsing every "academic" poet into a caricature of the "MFA careerist" trapped in the "publish-or-perish cycle of academia" (*American Poetry Wax Museum*, 418). In fact, there is a significant difference between the position of a poet-critic like John Hollander, a workshop poet in a mainstream creative-writing program, and an experimental Language poet teaching in the university.

17. Gioia, *Can Poetry Matter?* 256.

18. See Carrie Noland's account of the "decline of poetry studies within the academy" in "Poetry at Stake: Blaise Cendrars, Cultural Studies, and the Future of Poetry in the Literature Classroom," *PLMA* 112, no. 1 (1997). According to Noland, "poetry appears to be the genre whose traditional status within the humanities curriculum is most seriously threatened."

19. Both of the journals publish reviews written almost exclusively by white male establishment poets, although the reviewers for the *Hudson Review* display a more New Formalist bias than the predominantly mainstream *Poetry*. Both also review a disproportionate number of books from trade presses, especially Norton and Knopf, and rarely cover books from more "alternative" small presses such as those that publish formally innovative poetry or work by poets of color. Regular reviewers for *Poetry* have included David Barber, Calvin Bedient, Henry Taylor, Robert Shaw, David Baker, Ben Howard, Robert Shaw, Bruce Murphy, and Sandra Gilbert; for the *Hudson Review*, the list of reviewers includes R. S. Gwynn, David Mason, Mark Jarman, Robert McDowell, and Thomas Disch. Taken as a group, this stable of reviewers would hardly seem to represent the high-

est level of intellectual and artistic accomplishment in contemporary American poetry. See also Marjorie Perloff's analysis of the "abysmal state of poetry reviewing" in "What We Talk about When We Talk about Poetry," *PNReview* 23, no. 5 (1997): 18.

20. Rasula, "Literary Effects," 77–78.

21. See the entries for the various publishers in *1995 Poet's Market*.

22. To quote Adrienne Rich: "Hacker's energetic vision and active solicitation policy literally changed the formerly dessicated magazine. Despite vocal protests by writers, publishers, and others, she was fired by the trustees of Kenyon College." See Adrienne Rich and David Lehman, eds. *The Best American Poetry, 1996* (New York: Simon and Schuster, 1996, 18.

23. Gioia, *Can Poetry Matter?* 7; Alan Golding, "Language-Bashing Again," 93; Lazer, *Opposing Poetries,* 55–56.

24. Bérubé, *Marginal Forces/Cultural Centers, 49–50.*

25. In fact, a recent publication of the MLA, *Redrawing the Boundaries: The Transformation of English and American Literary Studies* (1992), edited by Stephen Greenblatt and Giles Gunn, contains two chapters dealing with the field of "composition studies" but none dealing with creative writing. The teaching and theory of creative writing are consistently excluded from academic discussions of "literary studies."

26. Barrett Watten, from an interview with Andrew Ross, in "Reinventing Community: A Symposium on/with Language Poets"; originally published in the *Minnesota Review* and reprinted in *Aerial* 8 (1995): 198.

27. Sandra Gilbert, "Feminist Criticism in the University," in *Criticism and the University,* ed. Gerald Graff and Reginald Gibbons (Evanston: Northwestern University Press, 1985), 121; Patrick Parrinder, *The Failure of Theory: Essays on Criticism and Contemporary Fiction,* (Totowa, N.J.: Barns and Noble, 1987), 13; Marjorie Perloff, *Poetic License: Essays on Modernist and Postmodernist Lyric* (Evanston: Northwestern University Press, 1990), 21. Perloff cites as representative the collection *Lyric Poetry: Beyond the New Criticism,* ed. Chaviva Hosek and Patricia Parker (Ithaca: Cornell University Press, 1985). Of the poets discussed in the book, only Stevens and Auden are from the modern period, and none are from the contemporary era.

28. Jonathan Culler, *Framing the Sign: Criticism and Its Institutions* (Norman: University of Oklahoma Press, 1987), 49.

29. Ibid.

Chapter Two

1. McClatchy, *White Paper,* 8–10.

2. During the 1970s and 1980s, while the total number of master's degrees in

English declined from over 10,000 to under 6,000 and PhDs in English literature fell from over 1,900 to under 900, enrollments in graduate creative-writing
programs increased dramatically, to the point where creative writing became the
second largest field for graduate degrees in English, surpassing the combined field
of speech and rhetoric. See the *Digest of Education Statistics*, 1994 edition, published by the U.S. Department of Education Office of Educational Research and
Improvement. If we look only at the "terminal" degrees for creative writers and
academic scholars, the ratio of MFAs to PhDs has shifted even more dramatically
in the direction of creative writing degrees: as PhDs in literature have fallen, the
number of programs offering MFAs has undergone a fourfold increase (from fifteen in 1975 to more than sixty today).

3. Kate Adams, for example, argues that creative-writing programs have effectively narrowed "the range of the American poetic voice." Adams cites the example of the mainstream academic anthology *New American Poetry of the 1980s*
(Boston: Godine, 1991), edited by Roger Myers and Jack Weingarten, in which
sixty-one of the sixty-five poets hold graduate degrees in creative writing, and of
which thirty-five (over half) have been produced by a single institution: the University of Iowa. Sixty-three of the poets included are college or university teachers,
and twenty-two have been either directors of writing programs or editors of journals. According to Adams, the academic writing program, and in particular the
graduate program, functions as an exclusive institution that cuts poetry off from
audiences outside the university rather than encouraging the greater accessibility
of poetry. "[T]he graduate school as an institutionalized intellectual marketplace"
prevents the free exchange from poet to audience by emphasizing a highly specialized form of writing that is consumed primarily by other members of creative-
writing academia ("Academe's Dominance of Poetic Culture Narrows the Range
of American Poetry," *Chronicle of Higher Education*, 18 May 1988, 48).

4. See George Garrett, "The Future of Creative Writing Programs," in *Creative
Writing in America*, ed. Joseph Moxley (Urbana: National Council of Teachers of
English, 1989).

5. See Stephen Wilbers, *The Iowa Writers' Workshop* (Iowa City: University of
Iowa Press, 1980), 98.

6. It should be noted, however, that the Iowa program, which was founded
in 1931 and officially named the "Writers' Workshop" in 1939, was well established by the early 1950s. By 1958, one-third of the American poets included in
the Meridien anthology *The New Poets of England and America*, edited by Donald
Hall, Robert Pack, and Louis Simpson, were Iowa students or graduates, and by
1965 the Writers' Workshop had grown to an enrollment of 250 students, many
of whom went on to found, direct, and teach in other writing programs.

7. Although the absolute dominance of the Iowa program may have waned
somewhat from its high point in the 1950s and 1960s, the "Iowa Writers' Workshop" still has far more influence and stature than any other program. In the

period 1970 to 1980 alone, Iowa graduates were awarded by the poetry culture more than the graduates of all other programs combined: they won the Yale Series of Younger Poets Award for a first book no less than four times (Peter Klappert, Michael Ryan, Maura Stanton, and Leslie Ullman) and were also voted the Lamont Selection for a second book four times (Stephen Dobyns, Peter Everwine, Larry Levis, and Michael van Welleghan). During the period 1967 to 1978, Iowa produced Dobyns, Klappert, Ryan, Stanton, Levis, Ullman, Norman Dubie, Albert Goldbarth, David St. John, Rita Dove, and Jorie Graham, a roster of many of the most prominent names in mainstream American poetry today. While other MFA programs such as Arizona, Montana, Utah, Columbia, Cornell, Houston, Alabama, and the University of California, Irvine, have achieved "second-tier" status, none has yet come close to challenging Iowa as the preeminent program.

8. Harrison White and Cynthia White, *Canvases and Careers: Institutional Change in the French Painting World* (New York: Wiley, 1965), 1.

9. Charles Altieri, *Self and Sensibility in Contemporary American Poetry* (New York: Cambridge University Press, 1984), 205.

10. White and White, *Canvases and Careers*, 2.

11. Thomas Disch, "The Castle of Indolence," reprinted in *The Castle of Indolence: On Poetry, Poets, and Poetasters* (New York: Ricador, 1995), 14.

12. Holden, *Fate of American Poetry*, 11.

13. Ibid., 11.

14. Pierre Bourdieu, *The Field of Cultural Production: Essays on Art and Literature*, ed. Randal Johnson (New York: Columbia University Press, 1993), 51.

15. This is not to deny that poets have always had an important role as legitimators or shapers of the canon; that role, however, was traditionally played outside the kind of *institutional* structure supplied by the university. The traditional function of the poet writing criticism—whether in the form of essays, reviews, lectures, or letters—seems to me substantially different from the current emphasis on tasks such as running creative-writing programs, organizing university-sponsored reading series, and serving on prize committees.

16. Bourdieu, *Field of Cultural Production*, 124.

17. Tanner, "How to Be an Artist in the Anthill of Academe," *AWP Chronicle*, March/April 1991, 8–9.

18. Silliman quoted in Andrew Ross, "Reinventing Community," 44.

19. Tanner, "How to Be an Artist," 11.

20. *AWP Newsletter*, September/October 1987.

21. Chris Semansky, "Discourse, Institution, and Profession: A Profile of Creative and Critical Practices" (PhD diss., SUNY Stony Brook, 1993), 77–78.

22. Eve Shelnutt, "Notes from a Cell: Creative Writing Programs in Isolation," in *Creative Writing in America*, ed. Joseph Moxley (Urbana: National Council of Teachers of English, 1989), 13.

23. Ibid., 7.

24. Peter Stitt, "Writers, Theorists, and the Department of English," *AWP Newsletter*, September/October 1987, 3. The title of Stitt's piece once again suggests that critics and theorists are not also "writers," a commonly expressed bias among "creative" writers.

25. Marjorie Perloff, "Theory and/in the Creative Writing Classroom," *AWP Newsletter*, November/December 1987, 4.

26. Shelnutt, "Notes from a Cell," 9, 11.

27. Ibid., 23.

28. Poets on both sides have had experience with the creative-writing academy: Gioia left an academic track to study business at Stanford and work for General Foods, and two of the most prominent Language poets, Barrett Watten and Bob Perelman, were students at the Iowa Workshop in the early 1970s before moving in the direction of a radically experimental practice. Both Watten and Perelman went on to earn PhDs in literature and criticism, and while both of them hold tenure-track positions in universities, neither of them teaches "creative writing."

29. George Garrett, "The Future of Creative-Writing Programs," 59.

30. See David Smith, *Local Assays: On Contemporary American Poetry* (Urbana: University of Illinois Press, 1985), 217, 221. The specific historical origins of academic creative writing have been more accurately traced by Semansky.

31. Ibid., 225.

32. Ibid., 218, 217, 224.

33. The "charismatic ideology," through which the author is viewed as the "first and last source of the value of his work," attempts to conceal any consideration for the means by which a work is produced, the institutional authority that allows its production, or the role of the "cultural businessman" (editor, publisher, etc.) in promoting, disseminating, or consecrating that work (Bourdieu, *Field of Cultural Production*, 70).

Chapter Three

1. Andreas Huyssen, *After the Great Divide: Modernism, Mass Culture, Postmodernism* (Bloomington: Indiana University Press, 1986), ix. See Marjorie Perloff's discussion in chapter 1 of *Radical Artifice*. Perloff characterizes the postmodern critique of the avant-garde as follows: "The thesis that the contemporary avant-garde is no more than a recycled version of Dada revolt, that it can do no more than spin, so to speak, its Duchampian wheels, returning again and again to the 'scene of provocation' of the early century but devoid of that scene of inherently political motive, has been a commonplace of postmodern theorizing" (9). Perloff does not herself share these views, and her entire book is, in an important sense, a defense of the contemporary poetic avant-garde.

2. Some of Language poetry's detractors have posed this question very directly.

See, for example, the forum, "Political Poetry and the Formalist Avant-Gardes," published in *City Lights Review* 1 (1987). Adam Cornford, while acknowledging that "the only formalist avant-garde in American poetry today is the 'language-centered writers' or language poets" (134), dismisses Language poetry's claim to have any meaningful political effect on its readers; the post-1945 avant-gardes, including Language writing, are "emptied now of the ambiguously radical energy possessed by their forebears" (132). James Brook is even more unequivocal in characterizing the Language poets' claim to an avant-garde status as "ridiculous" (143).

3. Bernstein, *Content's Dream*, 247.

4. Silliman, *New Sentence*, 31.

5. Michael Greer, "Ideology and Theory in Recent Experimental Writing; or, The Naming of 'Language Poetry,'" *Boundary 2*, no. 16 (1989): 337. For Greer, Language writing "loses any political or aesthetic significance it may have had in its own right as this binary historical map is drawn, and it becomes merely a way of provoking or irritating some fictional 'mainstream'" (340). Nealon concurs with Greer, arguing that the "determining binary map" that is drawn between mainstream poetry and Language poetry makes the "fragmented text of language poetry suddenly become easily readable—the location of the work and the intention behind it having been ascertained" (Nealon, *Double Reading*, 151). I agree that such binarisms run the risk of totalizing and reifying a very complex set of relations; however, I would not be as quick as Greer and Nealon to deny the value of any oppositional framework for Language poetry. Like the historical (modernist) avant-garde from which it is descended, Language poetry necessarily defines itself—and is in turn defined by those critics sympathetic to its project—as a counterhegemonic political, aesthetic, and social practice. To some degree, what Nealon calls the critical "domestication" of Language writing exists in the process of bringing any avant-garde into the cultural consciousness; in the case of Language writing, such critical attention has been a necessary phase in the evolution of experimental, innovative, or "postmodern" American poetry beyond the small coterie of little magazines and micropresses where it began two decades ago. It is disingenuous to suggest, as Nealon does, that "[l]iterary criticism reduces the complexity of language poetry to an accessible and commodifiable code or intention, just as workshop poetry reduces the complexity of poetic experience to the consumability of an epiphany" (152). This is a false analogy, first of all because it compares the effect of criticism to that of poetry, and second because it suggests that Language poetry has in fact become as accessible to most readers as "workshop poetry." Since this is clearly not the case (as Nealon later in his essay appears to recognize), I can only assume he means to deconstruct only the most facile analyses of Language poetry, not all such analyses.

6. See Jed Rasula's discussion of these anthologies in *American Poetry Wax Museum*, as well as Alan Golding's discussion in *From Outlaw to Classic*. The terms of this opposition are also largely agreed upon by the poets themselves.

Jonathan Holden, for example, an unambiguous advocate of the mainstream, writes of a "mainstream of American poetry [that] has continued to be, whether narrative or meditative, in a Realist mode that is essentially egalitarian, university-based, middle-class, and written in free verse" ("American Poetry," 273). This mainstream, according to Holden, occupies a middle ground between the new Right—"a small but disproportionately influential and wealthy elite sympathetic to such modes as the New Formalism"—and the new Left represented by Language poetry—"a small but well-entrenched, disaffected set . . . of 'critic/poets.'" Language poets are equally clear in defining the mainstream, or "official verse culture," as what Ron Silliman calls "the anti-theoretical college workshop tradition" ("Canons and Institutions," 164).

7. The influence of gender on the respective cultural positions of Hejinian and Dobyns may be significant, but it is certainly not the determining factor in shaping their poetic careers. Many male poets have followed career paths similar to Hejinian's, and many female poets have had careers more like Dobyns'.

8. Ross, "Reinventing Community," 27.

9. I adopt the term "precanonical" from Richard Ohmann's work on canonicity in contemporary fiction. In "The Shaping of a Canon: U.S. Fiction, 1960–1975," *Critical Inquiry* 10 (1983), Ohmann designates as "precanonical" a group of authors who have not yet attained full canonical status, but who have nonetheless achieved a high degree of prominence within the literary community.

10. *The Balthus Poems* (1982) is 45 pages long and contains 32 poems; *Black Dog, Red Dog* (1984) is 84 pages and 38 poems; *Cemetery Night* (1987) is 99 pages and 47 poems; *Body Traffic* (1990) is 137 pages and 75 poems.

11. Rasula, "Part of Nature," 155–56.

12. Altieri, *Self and Sensibility*, 73.

13. The publisher of Sun & Moon Press, Douglas Messerli, has informed me that the print runs average about two thousand copies; thus, Hejinian's book has sold more than eight thousand copies.

14. I define as "mainstream" publications those that are indexed in *Book Review Index*.

15. Lyn Hejinian, "If Written Is Writing," in *The L=A=N=G=U=A=G=E Book*, ed. Bruce Andrews and Charles Bernstein (Carbondale: Southern Illinois University Press, 1984), 29.

16. Lyn Hejinian, "The Rejection of Closure," in *Writing/Talks*, ed. Bob Perelman (Carbondale: Southern Illinois University Press, 1985), 281.

17. David R. Jarraway, "*My Life* through the Eighties: The Exemplary L=A=N=G=U=A=G=E of Lyn Hejinian," *Contemporary Literature* 33 (1992): 320.

18. Perloff, *Radical Artifice*, 164.

19. Bernstein, quoted in Hilary Clark, "The Mnemonics of Autobiography: Lyn Hejinian's *My Life*," *Biography* 14 (1991): 317.

20. Ibid., 239.

21. For a more general discussion of the intersection of poetry and politics in Language writing, see George Hartley's *Textual Politics and the Language Poets* (Bloomington: University of Indiana Press, 1989).

22. Clark, "Mnemonics of Autobiography," 237.

23. Lyn Hejinian, "Strangeness," *Poetics Journal* 8 (1989): 38.

24. Mark Jarman, "Journals of the Soul," *Hudson Review* 46 (1993): 416.

25. Thomas Lux, review of *Cemetery Nights* in *Western Humanities Review* 42 (1988): 176; Robert Shaw, review of *Cemetery Nights, Poetry* 150 (1987): 238; Ben Howard, "World and Spirit, Body and Soul," *Poetry* 158 (1991): 347; Dick Allen, "Shrinkages and Expansions," *Hudson Review* 40 (1987): 511.

26. This is not to suggest that we need adopt a single evaluative standard for American poetry. Nonetheless, such widely disparate conclusions about the same poems may indicate a degree of randomness and a lack of consistently applied standards in contemporary reviewing practices.

27. Janice Radway, "The Book of the Month Club and the General Reader: On the Uses of 'Serious' Fiction," in *Literature and Social Practice,* ed. Phillipe Desan, Priscilla Parkhurst Ferguson, and Wendy Griswold (Chicago: University of Chicago Press, 1989), 155.

28. Walter Kalaidjian, *American Culture between the Wars: Revisionary Modernism and Postmodern Critique* (New York: Columbia University Press, 1993), 193.

29. Andrew Ross, "The New Sentence and the Commodity Form: Recent American Writing," in *Marxism and the Interpretation of Culture,* ed. Cary Nelson and Lawrence Grossberg (Urbana: University of Illinois Press, 1988), 364.

30. Ibid., 365.

31. Ibid.

32. Hal Foster, "What's New about the Neo-Avant-Garde?" *October* 70 (1994): 20–22.

33. Ibid., 31. Although books by Charles Bernstein and Susan Howe have been published by Harvard University Press and Wesleyan University Press, they are very much the exception to the experience of the avant-garde or Language community in general. In fact, the vast majority of poets associated with experimental writing continue to occupy a decidedly marginal status with respect to the literary and academic establishment. Language poetry has its champions (Marjorie Perloff the most prominent among them), but there remains a strong resistance to their work both within the "official verse culture" and within the more general literary-academic culture. For a fuller discussion of the place occupied by Language poetry with respect to poetry's canonizing institutions, see Alan Golding's chapter " 'Provisionally Complicit Resistance': Language Writing and the Institution(s) of Poetry," in *From Outlaw to Classic.* Golding makes a convincing case for Language poetry's resistant and antiassimilationist stance, despite its "provisional complicity" with "the canon-making institutions that it would reshape" (170).

34. Donna Haraway, for example, adopts the futuristic metaphor of "cyborg

poetry" to describe Language writing, which she views as a heteroglossic means of achieving a radical cultural politics, "a kind of cultural restriction enzyme to cut the code" of increasingly technological and alienating language-systems (*Simians, Cyborgs, and Women: The Reinvention of Nature* [New York: Routledge, 1991], 245).

35. Ross, "New Sentence," 372.

Chapter Four

1. See Ohmann, "The Shaping of a Canon." There is in fact significant overlap between these anthologies of "younger" poets and more general mainstream anthologies such as those published by Harvard, Vintage, and Norton. Rita Dove, Louise Gluck, Albert Goldbarth, Jorie Graham, Robert Pinsky, and Dave Smith are all included in the Harvard anthology. The Norton anthology contains Dove, Gluck, Graham, Smith, and Pinsky, and Norman Dubie. Vintage includes Dove, Gluck, Graham, Pinsky, Smith, Robert Hass, and Edward Hirsch.

2. These include Syracuse (Dobyns), Virginia (Dove), Arizona State (Dubie), Wichita State (Goldbarth), Iowa (Graham), Berkeley (Pinsky), Stanford (Hass), University of Houston (Hirsch), University of California, Irvine (Ryan), University of Southern California (St. John), University of Oregon (Hongo), Louisiana State University (Smith), and NYU (Gluck).

3. The *Boston Book Review* publishes the only list—so far as I am aware—of poetry bestsellers. The current list of ten poetry books (February 1998) contains *two* by Robert Pinsky: his most recent volume *The Figured Wheel* and his translation of Dante's *Inferno,* both published by Farrar, Straus and Giroux. Although the list until recently contained Graham's *The Errancy,* it is dominated by translations and books by non-U.S. poets such as Seamus Heaney and Derek Walcott.

4. Rasula, *American Poetry Wax Museum,* 432.

5. Andrei Codrescu, *Up Late: American Poetry since 1970,* 2d ed. (New York: Four Walls Eight Windows, 1991), xxii.

6. David Smith and David Bottoms, eds., *The Morrow Anthology of Younger American Poets* (New York: Morrow, 1985), 19.

7. Perloff, *Poetic License,* 60.

8. Anthony Hecht, introduction to Smith and Bottoms, *Morrow Anthology,* 33, 36, 37.

9. Ibid., 37, 38, 40.

10. Rae Armantrout, "Mainstream Marginality," *Poetics Journal* 6 (1986): 141–44.

11. See Alan Golding's discussion of these two kinds of "contemporary revisionist anthology" in *From Outlaw to Classic,* 29–35.

12. Ishmael Reed, "The Ocean of American Literature," introduction to *The*

Before Columbus Foundation Poetry Anthology, ed. J. J. Phillips, Ishmael Reed, Gundars Strads, and Shawn Wong (New York: Norton, 1992), xxiii.

13. Ibid., xvi.

14. Golding provides a very balanced account of these issues in his chapter "Provisionally Complicit Resistance," in *From Outlaw to Classic.*

15. Helen Vendler, ed., *Harvard Book of Contemporary Poetry* (Cambridge: Harvard University Press, 1988), 7.

16. Codrescu, *Up Late,* xxi.

17. McClatchy, *Vintage Anthology,* xxi.

18. Ibid., xxv.

19. For a more detailed discussion of the McClatchy anthology, see Rasula, *American Poetry Wax Museum,* 449–53.

20. *American Poetry Review* was founded in 1972 by Stephen Berg and Stephen Parker, and received funding from several granting organizations, including the NEA, CCLM, the Witter Bynner Foundation, and the Pennsylvania Council on the Arts. The journal was notable for its claim to be open to diverse audiences and different styles, but was criticized in 1977—by forty poets including Adrienne Rich and June Jordan—for failing to publish enough poetry by minorities, women, lesser-known and small-press authors, and experimental poets. *APR'*s editor, David Ignatow, resigned in protest, claiming that the journal had reneged on its duty to give a "fair representation of the poetic quality of all ethnic groups." Despite the controversy, the journal has remained remarkably successful at maintaining its market, that of the widely defined poetic mainstream. It also uses a strategy of appealing to various sectors of the poetry culture: in addition to original poems by American and other Anglophone poets, it publishes translations, essays, interviews, and memoirs.

21. Von Hallberg traces the shift both to a "weakening political consensus," which "helped make a change of literary taste seem appropriate," and to the success of Allen's anthology itself, which ironically helped not only to "publicize the avant-garde," but to "lionize" it as well by making its poets increasingly acceptable to the mainstream (*American Poetry,* 13–14).

22. Quoted in Rasula, *American Poetry Wax Museum,* 445.

23. In the case of the Heath anthology, no poetry after 1970 is given much attention, except as part of a more general multiculturalism. The introductory essay "New Directions in Literature Since 1970" does not even refer to poetry except to remark that poems by women writers "were selling well" (Lauter, *Heath Anthology,* 1783); the poetic selections themselves would suggest that there were no white male poets after the generation of Creeley, Ginsberg, and Snyder. While the anthology refers to the marginalization of women and ethnic writers whose work "deviates from what have become accepted patterns of literary representation," it totally ignores writers like the Language poets whose work deviates to a far more radical extent from these same patterns. As Hank Lazer suggests, the anthology

presents "an extraordinarily narrow range of representation," and a "deadening sameness of writing style under the auspices of the multicultural" (*Opposing Poetries*, 128, 131). Paul Lauter, the primary editor of the Heath anthology, along with the other Heath editors, provides only "a narrowly authorized version of the multicultural," a canon that is "multicultural" only in a very superficial sense, relying largely on poets trained in academic creative-writing programs and conforming to the same dominant mode of the poem as personal narrative that could be found in Morrow or other mainstream anthologies.

The Norton anthology is if anything even more egregious in its omissions and misleading information. The Norton discusses several trends in "Poetry since 1975," including academic creative-writing, regionalism, women's poetry, ethnic and minority poetry, and the use of the dramatic monologue. However, the anthology not only fails to mention any form of self-consciously experimental or avant-garde writing (such as visual poetry, performance poetry, aleatory poetry, postsurrealism, or Language writing), but it actively works against the idea of any such poetry by suggesting that the (modernist) poetic past is "now simply history . . . accepted, or perhaps ignored, but not challenged" (Richard Ellman and Robert O'Clair, eds., *The Norton Anthology of Modern Poetry*, 1st ed. [New York: Norton, 1973], 14). One would only have to read the poetic and critical work of Robert Creeley, Ed Dorn, Michael Palmer, Charles Bernstein, Susan Howe, Lyn Hejinian, Ron Silliman, Rachel Blau DuPlessis, Barrett Watten, Michael Davidson, Joan Retallack, Bob Perelman, and Johanna Drucker, to name a few, to realize the utter falsity of this claim. The anthology also makes the blanket statement that "only four of the more prominent post-1945 writers [Ashbery, Ammons, Merrill, and Rich] have continued to develop and change," which seems not only a ridiculous claim on its face, but a pointed attack on the poets of the "New American Poetry," such as Creeley, Duncan (still active as of 1988), Ginsberg, Snyder, and Levertov, not to mention African American poets such as Amiri Baraka and Audre Lorde.

24. Von Hallberg, *American Poetry*, 13. Whether von Hallberg would include the Language poets in this sweeping generalization, given the historical limits of his study (1945–80) is not clear, although by the time his book was published in 1985, Language poetry had already established itself as "the most visible and energetic avant-garde movement of the 1970s and 1980s" (Golding, *From Outlaw to Classic*, 93), and Language poets had clearly articulated most of their theoretical and aesthetic positions. Even if von Hallberg were not including Language poetry in the historical rubric of his study, however, he would have had to consider emergent 1960s and 1970s avant-gardes of various kinds: the later phase of the New York school (Ted Berrigan, Clark Coolidge, Bernadette Mayer, David Shapiro, Joe Brainerd, John Godfrey, Jim Brodey, Ron Padgett, Alice Notley, Barbara Guest), a feminist avant-garde (Beverly Dahlen, Kathleen Fraser), an avant-garde based in aleatory work (Jackson Mac Low, John Cage), an avant-garde of performance-

oriented poetry (Anne Waldman, John Giorno, Bob Holman, Jayne Cortez, Victor Hernandez Cruz), a Jungian or "whole earth" avant-garde (Clayton Eshleman, Robert Kelly, Nathaniel Tarn), an avant-garde associated with the oral poetics movement (Jerome Rothenberg, David Antin), a minimalist avant-garde (Larry Eigner, Robert Grenier), a surrealist avant-garde (Philip Lamantia, Ivan Arguelles), a visual or concrete avant-garde (Richard Kostelanetz, Dick Higgins), and an African American avant-garde (Amiri Baraka, Clarence Major).

25. Rasula, *American Poetry Wax Museum*, 453. As Rasula points out, McClatchy's selection included the vast majority of eligible Pulitzer and National Book Award winners since the 1950s.

26. David Lehman, foreword to *The Best American Poetry, 1992* (New York: Simon and Schuster, 1992), x.

27. Ashbery's 1988 issue included Coolidge, Mayer, Palmer, Perelman, and Scalapino, as well as several others affiliated with Language poetry and the second-generation New York school; from the "mainstream" he includes midcareer poets like Graham, Hass, and Pinsky, along with well-known figures from the poetry establishment such as A. R. Ammons, Anthony Hecht, John Hollander, Richard Howard, Donald Justice, Philip Levine, and James Merrill. Rich's 1996 issue appeared after this chapter had been written, and I have not had the chance to review it carefully. I am skeptical, however, that Rich's attempt to "reflect the richness and range of the best American poetry" in the volume will set any sort of trend in *Best American Poetry* annuals. Rich's more diverse and politically active selections are acknowledged by Lehman in the book's foreword as a significant departure from past issues — "representing women and gays and Latinos and poets outside the mainstream more amply than previous books in the series" — but her choices are clearly presented as a precedent for future issues. "*The Best American Poetry* cannot settle all the questions in the poetry world," Lehman writes, but it can enter the "contested site" of American poetry "with an olive branch in its mouth, like the dove announcing the end of the deluge to Noah" (Rich and Lehman, *Best American Poetry, 1996*, 11, 13). If this rather ambiguous image is meant to suggest that the choice of Rich as an editor of the current volume will put an end to the conflicts over the disputed territory of American poetic culture, Lehman is probably mistaken.

28. Richard Howard, the eighth editor of the series, appears to recognize this incongruity when he vows to depart from "what in seven years had become anthological orthodoxy" by restricting the selections to poets who had not appeared three or more times and by excluding previous series editors. This ostensibly more democratic spirit did not, however, prevent Howard from including several poems from each of the two journals of which he is currently poetry editor: the *Paris Review* and *Western Humanities Review*. Howard's claims to openness might be more credible had he also excluded work from journals he himself edits, both of which are well-established organs of the mainstream literary establishment.

29. Bernstein, *A Poetics,* 5.

30. Silliman, "Canons and Institutions," 22.

31. Rasula, *American Poetry Wax Museum,* 86. The importance of nonpoetic context is even clearer in Ransom's actual letter of explanation to Duncan: Ransom wrote that while he "originally . . . found [the] poem very brilliant," he reassessed the poem's merit when he discovered that its meaning was actually "defined" as "an obvious homosexual advertisement." The irony of this is that Ransom—despite his New Critical ideology—based this latter judgment not on any intrinsic qualities gleaned from close reading of the poem itself, but on the external or contextual evidence of an essay, "The Homosexual in Society," which Duncan had published in the journal *Politics.*

32. Eliot Weinberger, ed., *American Poetry since 1950: Innovators and Outsiders* (New York: Marsilio, 1993), xi.

33. Paul Hoover, introduction to *Postmodern American Poetry: A Norton Anthology* (New York: Norton, 1994), xxv.

34. See Silliman, *New Sentence,* 61. These include the group manifesto "Aesthetic Tendency," published in *Social Text;* the collaborative prose work *Leningrad,* by Michael Davidson, Lyn Hejinian, Ron Silliman, and Barrett Watten; the collaborative poem *Legend,* by Bruce Andrews, Charles Bernstein, Ray DiPalma, Steve McCaffery, and Silliman; and *Individuals,* by Lyn Hejinian and Kit Robinson.

35. This distinction is also manifested in the kind of nonpoetic writings by the poets of the two groups. While most of the articles and books written by mainstream poets have been traditional single-author or group studies of modern and contemporary poets, the writers of the experimental canon have published in more diverse fields and are less interested in discussing the work of individual poets than in engaging in a more general discourse concerning the relationships between poetry, language, politics, and society. Howe, for example, has published on the textual politics of Emily Dickinson, on captivity narratives, and on the politics of literary marginalia. Bernstein has written on philosophy, critical theory, and cultural history. Hejinian has published on poetics and feminist theory; Perelman on the intersections of poetry and politics; Silliman on the relationship of social and cultural theory to the field of literary production; Davidson on the San Francisco Renaissance (as a social movement as well as a poetic one); Andrews on language and society.

36. See for example Golding, who writes that "the transparent, quasi-realist rhetoric of the contemporary free verse lyric can be seen not only as a canonical aesthetic but as an ideology, designed to appear natural and to conceal its own constructedness" (*From Outlaw to Classic,* 167).

37. Ron Silliman, introduction to *In the American Tree* (Orono, Maine: National Poetry Foundation, 1986), xx. This explosion has been even greater in the decade since Silliman's anthology, as evidenced by an e-mail discussion list

with nearly four hundred subscribers, most of whom are poets of experimental or avant-garde persuasion. The Language movement has by now spawned a second generation, which has been labeled both "post-language" and "G2." This emergent generation of avant-garde poets, which appears to be numerically larger than its predecessor, is beginning to produce its own culture, with its own journals (both print and electronic), its own anthologies, and its own vocabulary. At times, the efforts of the 1990s generation poets to differentiate themselves from their elders (who themselves reacted similarly to the New American Poetry in the 1970s) have resulted in personal attacks and excessively dogmatic rhetoric. Mark Wallace, in the first essay to date on this phenomenon, refers to a "post-language crisis" in which "emerging avant garde poets" seek with varying degrees of difficulty to "establish their own identity in the face of the success of language writing." According to Wallace, these difficulties can be "crippling" for some poets and a source of anxiety for many others. See "Emerging Avant Garde Poetries and the 'Post-Language Crisis,'" *Poetic Briefs*, no. 19 (St. Louis Park, Minn.: 1995). For a partial record of the current generation of post-Language writers, see Dennis Barone and Peter Ganick's anthology *The Art of Practice: Forty-five Contemporary Poets* (Elmwood, Conn.: Potes & Poets, 1994); the collection of essays entitled *A Poetics of Criticism*, ed. Juliana Spahr, Mark Wallace, Kristin Prevallet, and Pam Rehm (Buffalo: Leave Books, 1994); and the two-volume anthology *Writing from the New Coast: Technique*, ed. Peter Gizzi and Juliana Spahr (Providence, R.I.: O-blek Editions, 1993), comprising the final issue of *O-blek* magazine.

38. Silliman, *In the American Tree*, xxi.

39. At two of the institutions where I have taught, both with prominent MFA programs in creative writing, there has been a significant awareness on the part of students of an alternative to the prevailing workshop poetic, though many students have only a vague idea of what that alternative is. At one school, a split developed between "traditionalists" who favored a more straightforward narrative lyric, and a significant "experimentalist" faction who sought to challenge that mode through devices similar to those deployed by Language poets. As a growing number of students are drawn to more "experimental" modes of writing rather than the narrative lyric or postconfessional style, the tensions within academic creative writing will no doubt lead to new, and possibly fruitful developments.

40. Given her status as the most celebrated poet of her generation, Graham is a particularly interesting instance of a career that began in the more mainstream mode of the workshop lyric and has moved gradually toward a greater affiliation with the experimentalist camp. Although Graham has continued to publish her poems in mainstream journals like the *New Yorker*, the *Yale Review*, the *Threepenny Review*, *Parnassus*, *APR*, *Antaueus*, *Ploughshares*, and the *Kenyon Review*, her more recent work has also appeared in such "avant-garde" publications as *Sulfur*, *Grand Street*, *New American Writing*, and *Volt*. Yet despite the fact that her poems are more formally and conceptually ambitious than the majority of main-

stream poetry, Graham does not cross the border into what I would consider the poetic avant-garde: her work does not interrogate the transparency of language or the fundamental coherence of the lyric self in the way Ashbery or the Language poets do.

Chapter Five

1. Von Hallberg, *American Poetry*, 25; Perloff, "Poetry Doesn't Matter," 7.

2. In fact, the editors of the first edition do not appear to have considered their designation of a canon to be enough of an issue to address it in the book's preface. The primary editorial concerns expressed were the anthology's time frame ("where to begin a selection of modern poets") and its inclusiveness (whether to include lesser-known poets as well as the "major figures"). The seemingly crucial question of *how* the editors chose what poets to include from the "considerable abundance [of] poetry written since the Second World War" is left unanswered.

3. Richard Ellman and Robert O'Clair, eds., *The Norton Anthology of Modern Poetry*, 2d ed. (New York: Norton, 1988).

4. Biggs, *A Gift that Cannot Be Refused*, 73. Of the five most highly regarded poets, Adrienne Rich was named on only 25 percent of the ballots, Galway Kinnell on 23 percent, Denise Levertov on 20 percent, Gary Snyder on 18 percent, and W. S. Merwin on 16 percent. From there the consensus dropped quickly; no other poet was listed by more than 11 percent of the poets surveyed.

5. For a list of poetry anthologies of the 1980s based on some form of "identity politics," see Golding, *From Outlaw to Classic*, 178 n. 21. Golding lists anthologies based on such groupings as African American women, Chicanos, poets of the American West, Asian Americans, Native American, Arab Americans, poets with disabilities, gays and lesbians, and poems in response to AIDS and breast cancer.

6. Vickie Karp, "When Words Combine—the Evolution of a Television Series on Poetry," *Poets and Writers*, July/August 1995, 19.

7. Helen Vendler, "Poetry for the People," *New York Times Book Review*, 18 June 1995, 14. The article has a more affirmative subtitle, no doubt provided by the Times staff in order to counterbalance the negativity of Vendler's review: "Bill Moyers's enthusiasm is democratic, pluralistic, and multicultural."

8. Rich's point about the corporate co-optation of poetry through programs such as Moyers's PBS series can in fact be demonstrated through a concrete example. In a promotional publication advertising the upscale Orange County shopping mall Fashion Island, copies of *The Language of Life* were prominently displayed on a page advertising the Barnes and Noble bookstore. In this way, poetry was displayed as an attractive commodity alongside ads for cashmere sweaters, lingerie, and tennis-wear.

9. Moyers, quoted in Karp, "When Words Combine," 23.

10. The comments by Ward and Gonzalez are summarized from the panel discussion "Anthologies and the Canon," held at Poets' House in New York City on 19 October 1993.

11. Jennifer Gillan, introduction to *Unsettling America: An Anthology of Contemporary Multicultural Poetry,* ed. Maria Mazziotti Gillan and Jennifer Gillan (New York: Penguin, 1994), xix, xxv

12. Raymond Patterson, "What's Happening in Black Poetry," in *A Gift of Tongues: Critical Challenges in Contemporary American Poetry,* ed. Marie Harris and Kathleen Aguero (Athens: University of Georgia Press, 1987), 149; Roberto Marquez, quoted in Martin Espada, "Documentaries and Declamadores: Puerto Rican Poetry in the United States," in ibid., 258.

13. Marie Harris and Kathleen Aguero, *An Ear to the Ground: An Anthology of Contemporary American Poetry* (Athens: University of Georgia Press, 1989), xxiii, 7, xxii.

14. Ibid., xxi, xxii. We might contrast these approaches with a book like Michael Bérubé's *Marginal Forces/Cultural Centers,* which despite its decidedly "institutional" approach to the canon, does succeed in promoting the work of a single previously neglected writer, the African American poet Melvin Tolson.

15. Ibid., xxi.

16. Harris and Aguero, *A Gift of Tongues,* x.

17. Clare Kinney, "Postscript from the Canon's Mouth," *Callaloo* 17, no. 2 (1994): 586.

18. Alison Booth, "Feminist Criticism at the 'English' Track Meet," *Callaloo* 17, no. 2 (1994): 560.

19. Eric Lott, "The Aesthetic Ante: Pleasure, Pop Culture, and the Middle Passage," *Callaloo* 17, no. 2 (1994): 546.

20. For Vendler, see "Poetry for the People."

21. Perloff, *Poetic License,* 2–3.

22. Vendler did, in fact, play an important role in the production of the *Voices and Visions* series of the 1980s, which examined the lives and work of canonical American poets.

Chapter Six

Bob Holman's discussion of changes in the role of poets and poetry are from my interview with him, 29 July 1995.

1. I have used first names in this section in order to preserve the more personal and spontaneous quality of the slam itself: all the "contestants" were introduced by first names only.

2. This is already the case in New York, where spoken-word poetry is variously combined with techno-ambient music, with burlesque, and with various kinds of jazz.

3. Davidson writes, "The poetry reading is an occasion on which to place the poet physically before his or her readers—in Ferlinghetti's words, to get the poem off the page and into the street. The reading also foregrounds the oral impulse of so much contemporary poetry in which the poem draws from physiological and muscular resources (Olson's 'breath line') and engages the reader as a collective whole or tribe. . . . Whereas during the 1940s and 1950s, the poet had been exiled from the poem by Eliot's impersonality or through New Critical ideas of irony and distantiation, he or she reemerges in the most physical way in the poetry reading" (*The San Francisco Renaissance: Poetics and Community at Mid-Century* [New York: Cambridge University Press, 1989], 20).

4. Ibid., 150, 203.

5. The connections between the current spoken-word culture and the Beats are unmistakable. Ginsberg was himself a supporter and elder statesman of the slam and spoken-word scene, and of the Nuyorican in particular. While some poets downplay the connection with the Beats—preferring to emphasize the influence of popular and multicultural forms such as comedy, rap, hip-hop, and MTV—others freely acknowledge their debt to Ginsberg and Beat poetry. John S. Hall, spoken-word poet and leader of the alternative rock band King Missile, takes pride in "ripping off" Ginsberg; Paul Beatty studied with Ginsberg at Brooklyn College; and Maggie Estep, who studied for two years at the Naropa Institute's School of Disembodied Poetics, can be placed in a lineage of a Beat poetics of performance from Ginsberg to Anne Waldman. If we include the overall impact of a generation that includes William Burroughs, Jack Kerouac, Lawrence Ferlinghetti, Gregory Corso, and Amiri Baraka, as well as the jazz poetry of Kenneth Patchen and others, the sense of the current performance scene as a reflowering of the Beat ethos is even more apparent. While the spoken-word poetries of the 1990s are inflected quite differently from the work of their Beat predecessors, the sense of poetry readings as liberative antiacademic performances and the poetics of accessibility, raw emotion, and common speech are descended from the Beats' bohemian rebellion against the New Critical poetry establishment of their day.

6. Wolf Knight quoted in *Slam* 1, no. 6 (1993).

7. Shutup Shelley, interview with author, 28 July 1995.

8. Yet even such antiacademic outrageousness can become institutionalized. The Taos Poetry Circus, with its "World Championship Poetry Bout," is an annual event with obvious similarities to the slam but with more mainstream inflections. Now in its fifteenth year, the "circus"—which advertises itself as "America's Premier Literary Event"—includes readings of spoken-word, regional, and multicultural poetry, as well as poetry films and videos, seminars, and the championship bout itself. One recent "bout" pitted defending champion Quincy Troupe

against challenger Bobbie Louise Hawkins in a ten-round contest modeled on a boxing match (complete with "referee, round bell, judges, ring girl, and all").

9. Jim Collins, "Appropriating Like Crazy: From Pop Art to Meta-Pop," in *Modernity and Mass Culture,* ed. James Naremore and Patrick Brantlinger (Bloomington: Indiana University Press, 1993), 221; Geoffrey Nowell-Smith, "On Kiri Te Kanawa, Judy Garland, and the Culture Industry," in ibid., 78; John Frow, *Cultural Studies and Cultural Value* (New York: Oxford University Press, 1995), 13, 146.

10. See John Fiske, "Popular Discrimination," in Naremore and Brantlinger, *Modernity and Mass Culture,* and Jostein Gripsrud, " 'High Culture' Revisited," *Cultural Studies* 3, no. 2 (1989).

11. Kirk Vandernoe and Adam Gopnik, *High and Low: Modern Art and Popular Culture* (New York: Museum of Modern Art, 1990), 409.

12. Frow, *Cultural Studies and Cultural Value,* 68. See, for example, Simon Frith, "The Cultural Study of Popular Music," in *Cultural Studies,* ed. Lawrence Grossberg, Cary Nelson, and Paula Treichler (New York: Routledge, 1992), 17–75, on the importance of a relatively sophisticated understanding among rock fans of such questions as musical genre, historical development, and influence.

13. We need only think, for example, of such television programs as *Twin Peaks, The Simpsons,* and *Beavis and Butthead;* of a wide range of experimental techniques in music videos; of bands like Talking Heads and performers like David Bowie, Patti Smith, and Laurie Anderson; and of any number of culturally self-conscious films, from *Brazil* to *Blue Velvet* to *Slacker* to *Wayne's World.* As E. Ann Kaplan remarks of MTV, "video artists are often playing with standard high art and popular culture images in a self-conscious manner, creating a liberating sense by the very defiance of traditional boundaries" (*Rocking around the Clock: Music Television, Postmodernism, and Consumer Culture* [New York: Methuen, 1987], 47).

14. It is also different from the New York school of Frank O'Hara and other poets of the 1950s and 1960s, a scene that, despite its celebration of the spontaneity of daily life in the city, was much more inflected by the "high art" culture of the New York museum and art world.

15. For a delineation of rap's influences, see Tricia Rose's *Black Noise: Rap Music and Black Culture in Contemporary America* (Hanover, N.H.: Wesleyan University Press and University Press of New England, 1994). Rose finds continuities between rap and specific African American cultural forms such as breakdancing, urban blues, rock 'n' roll, bebop, and folklore, as well as African American cultural practices such as toasting, signifying, and boasting.

16. Ibid., 4. While she quotes no statistical evidence such as comparative sales figures, Rose cites at least one claim that rap makes from 50 to 70 percent of its sales to white teenagers. Further support for rap's capacity to cross over cultural and aesthetic boundaries, as well as racial and ethnic ones, is the degree of interest exhibited in rap by academic critics and scholars.

17. See, for example, Kaplan, *Rocking around the Clock*, 33–48. According to Kaplan, avant-garde techniques employed in MTV include "the abandonment of [the] traditional narrational devices of most popular culture," the increasing self-reflexivity of videos in framing or staging their own production or consumption, the "parody of video production as an institution," and the use of the video to examine the technology used in making the video itself. For Kaplan, the music video breaks down the dominant aesthetic discourse that had "polarized the popular/realist commercial text and the 'high art' modernist one, making impossible a text that was at once avant-garde and popular" (40). Of course, the argument could be made that the adoption of avant-garde techniques or devices does not in itself define the resulting artwork as in any meaningful sense "avant-garde" or oppositional. A sense of the potential avant-garde status of MTV could only be gained from a comparison of its reception with that of other popular forms. Since MTV is run as a commercial institution, there would seem to be little incentive to produce and televise videos that constitute any genuine critique of the medium or of music and advertising culture as a whole, or that in any radical way seek to alienate their (bourgeois) audience. These being the two most salient features of avant-garde art, it seems unlikely that MTV can ultimately be viewed as avant-garde, except in the most superficial (i.e., stylistic) sense.

18. Some poets feel that the increasingly competitive and serious atmosphere of the Nuyorican slams has detracted from the original sense of communitarian spirit; slams are no longer the tongue-in-cheek event they were in the early 1990s, but have become a forum for young poets looking for the type of success achieved by poets like Beatty and Estep.

19. Miguel Algarin suggests other possible origins for the slam, from the Greek mythological tale of Apollo and Masyas, to the African griots, to the Japanese imaginary poetry team competitions, to the Puerto Rican El Trovador tradition (*Aloud*, 16). While in the case of individual slammers these origins may be more "mythic" than real, they serve to give the slam the appearance of a more legitimate literary inheritance.

20. Algarin and Holman, *Aloud*, 9. Admittedly, some mainstream poets do write "political" poems: Carolyn Forché and Yosef Komunyakaa, for example. However, the amount of attention that has been given to Forché's handful of poems about El Salvador only indicates the paucity of direct political commentary in most other academic and mainstream poetry. For a critique of the political dimension of Forché's work, see Eliot Weinberger, "Reading El Salvador," in *Works on Paper, 1980–1986* (New York: New Directions, 1986), 120–27. Weinberger suggests that Forché's poems belong more to the genre of "revolutionary tourism" or even a kind of literary "colonialism" than to that of genuinely political poetry: "The poems are neither illuminations nor artifacts of a political reality, nor are they calls to action" (126). Although Forché's poems attempt to identify with the

suffering of the El Salvadorans, they are still located primarily within the personal or confessional voice of the mainstream lyric.

21. Bob Holman, "Making Poetry Is No Vice," *Los Angeles Times*, 4 March 1996, section F, 3.

22. Rose Salari, "The Sound of What Matters," *Common Boundary*, January/February 1996, 30.

23. Linda Yablonsky, "Hip-Hop-Notic: The Rebirth of the Spoken Word," *High Times*, February 1994, 38, 57.

24. Evelyn McDonnell, "Native Tongues," *Rolling Stone*, 5 August 1993, 20.

25. Ken Tucker, *New York Times*.

26. For examples of the first tendency, see Linda Yablonsky, Ken Tucker, and Evelyn McDonnell; for the second, see Ray Gonzalez's review of *Aloud* in the *Nation*. Yablonsky describes slammers as "show-biz-oriented, feverish, and sweaty" ("Hip-Hop-Notic," 40). While Yablonsky celebrates spoken-word poetry, she clearly identifies it as a pop-cultural phenomenon: the poetry is aesthetically suspect (not "polished" and not always "good poetry"); it is closer to popular forms such as motown and rap than to poetic tradition; it is primarily concerned not with literary or philosophical ideas but with political and personal expression; it is connected to a kind of folk culture or idiom ("the realm of oral tradition storytelling"); and it is racially or ethnically motivated.

In his piece in the *Nation,* on the other hand, Gonzalez makes the same high cultural/low cultural demarcation, but based on very different criteria. Gonzalez criticizes slam poetry, and the *Aloud* anthology in particular, as "performance texts and scripts that work for the ear, the sound of words and their deliverance, but not necessarily as written language on the page." Characterizing the work as "uneven," and even "embarrassing," he asks: "How can one capture or document the energy of so many orally dramatic poets? Confine them to audio and video? Judge their orally delivered text, when it gets set on the page, with the same criteria one applies to traditional literature?" (768). Gonzalez's evocation of "traditional literature," as opposed to the "orally delivered text" that is played for the "loudest reaction from the packed audience," is indicative of the typical response spoken-word poetry has received from the more academic or "literary" sectors of the poetry community. Gonzalez's claim that the work is "uneven" and that the poems are "embarrassing" is entirely audience dependent. As Ron Silliman suggests, the context in which a given poem is presented—whether in written or oral form—largely determines both the makeup of its audience and that audience's reaction to it. What might for one reader and in one context be experienced as embarrassing might for another reader or listener, in another set of circumstances, be experienced as exciting or empowering.

27. See Richard Middleton, *Studying Popular Music* (Philadelphia: Open University Press, 1990), 25–56.

28. The following poems are from Sirowitz's eponymous collection *Mother Said* (New York: Crown, 1996).

29. Maggie Estep, *No More Mr. Nice Girl* (recording), NuYo Records, 1995.

30. In his 1996 public radio interview on the program *Fresh Air,* Sirowitz suggests that the poems are an attempt to transcribe his mother's actual language; yet the poems certainly move beyond mere transcriptions to reveal a great deal about Sirowitz's own psychic internalization of his mother's overprotective and hypercritical behavior.

31. Patti Smith must certainly be seen as a central precursor, and her influence on Estep can be most clearly heard on songs and spoken-word pieces like "Even If" and "Paradise Lost." Estep was deeply affected by Smith's music when she first heard it at age fourteen: "It changed my life. The voice. The words. I worshipped her. I still love to go watch her" (e-mail, 21 March 1996).

32. Personal e-mail, 6 March 1996.

33. Yablonsky, "Hip-Hop-Notic," 57.

34. Ibid., 40.

35. Personal e-mail, 21 March 1996.

36. While an appearance on MTV will not guarantee a career in the popular media, Estep received "a lot of audition offers," and appeared on several national talk shows subsequent to her MTV video.

37. See Henry Louis Gates, "Sudden Def," *New Yorker,* 19 June 1995. Despite the claims of rap musicians such as Michael Franti or groups like De La Soul and Arrested Development to the status of "poets," Gates believes that rap has less in common with poetry than with other African American traditions such as toasting, playing the dozens, signifying, and rhymed storytelling. While Gates admits that rap contains poetic elements—rhyme, complex rhythms, the use of "sampling" as a form of radical intertextuality, and an often innovative play of language—he prefers to maintain the autonomy of both rap and poetry as separate though related practices. "Is rap necessarily poetry? Isn't it enough that rap is, well, rap?" (37). Gates's reservations about considering rap lyrics as poetry—or rap artists as poets—reflects more general uncertainties within the literary and critical community about the radical crossing of traditional generic boundaries that is taking place within the spoken-word and slam subcultures.

38. Baraka quoted in ibid., 40.

39. Three-time national slam winner Patricia Smith, who compared the poetry stage at Lollapalooza to a "freak show," complains of the increasing personal investment in poetry slams, where "egos run rampant" in what sometimes degenerates into a "messy muddle of self-importance, arrogance, and misguided creative goals" (editorial in *Slam* 1, no. 8 [1994]). Another performance poet often associated with the slam scene, Los Angeles–based Wanda Coleman, recognizes the important function slams play in bringing poetry to a wider audience and providing opportunities for younger poets, but rejects the competitive ethos they instill:

"I like competition as much as the next person. But there's something about the slams that smacks of one beer and one pretzel too many. People are going for what's boffo and not necessarily what's literary. Its value to me is negligible." See the interview with Coleman in *A View from the Loft* 18, no. 3 (1995).

40. Beatty, quoted in McDonnell, "Native Tongues," *Rolling Stone*, 5 August 1993, 20.

41. Ibid.

42. Beatty quoted in Yablonsky, "Hip-Hop-Notic," 57. Like Beatty, Tracie Morris is unequivocal in stating that she is "not a rapper"; Morris demands that poets from the Nuyorican and other such venues be considered "writers primarily, not performers," and that the emphasis of slams be on "the words and conveying the words" rather than on popularity or entertainment. Morris claims influences from both literary and popular culture, including Edgar Allan Poe and the rap group De La Soul. A grand slam champion and a member of the New York slam team which competed at the slam nationals in 1993, Morris has been featured on *The United States of Poetry* and on the *Word Up* CD compilation.

43. Jessica Hagedorn, cover, *Joker, Joker, Deuce*. After growing up in the Latino/ African American community of Los Angeles, Beatty attended Boston University, where he discovered poetry while studying for a degree in psychology. He then moved to the MFA program at Brooklyn College, where he studied with Allen Ginsberg, among others.

44. Some poets appear to deal with this apparent contradiction by making a distinction between two kinds of poetry: "page poetry" and "spoken word." Crystal Williams, a young African American slammer and a member of the New York (Nuyorican) slam team, defines "page poetry" as written "specifically for the word/page relationship" and as more consciously "literary," involving a more pronounced use of line breaks, descriptive imagery, symbolism, and metaphor. "Spoken-word" poems, on the other hand, are written "with the intent to get the point across," and typically emphasize the "dramatic aspects of the piece" (personal e-mail, 16 April 1996). Further study of the slam subculture would be required to determine how different poets, or different segments of the slam and spoken-word community, would make this same delineation, but it is interesting that while some poets attempt to downplay the distinction between poetry and spoken-word performance, others not only accept but actively foreground the distinction.

45. "I'm unhappy about that [decision]. . . . I wanted to call it an anthology of poems, because it is an anthology of poems: I want to take on Douglas Messerli's *From the Other Side of the Century* and Paul Hoover's *Postmodern American Poetry*. . . . I don't want to give the means for being seen as second-class. . . . But calling it 'Voices,' of course, you're playing into the whole thing people say about this book, which is, 'well, they're better when they're up on stage reading it' " (Bob Holman, interview with author, 29 July 1995).

46. This has already occurred to some extent in the case of the Nuyorican, as the communities represented by Algarin and Holman have split into two separate camps. In what Holman has described to me as a "splintering of the Cafe," he left in 1996 after a falling-out with Algarin. Ed Morales has attributed the split to a clash between Algarin's desire to preserve the Latino roots of the cafe and Holman's desire to bring the Nuyorican to a wider and more multicultural audience. Holman's slogan—"We are all Nuyoricans"—does not seem to have convinced some members of the Latino community, including Algarin, who may feel that the original idea of the cafe has been co-opted by Holman and a slicker, more MTV-oriented group of poets. See Morales, "Grand Slam: The Last Word at the Nuyorican," *Village Voice*, 7 October 1997.

47. Classes and workshops on performance poetry have already been offered at nonacademic poetry centers like the Loft in Minneapolis.

Chapter Seven

1. Bob Holman, Joshua Blum, and Mark Pellington, eds., *The United States of Poetry* (New York: Harry N. Abrams, 1996), 12. Although the television series is produced by Bob Holman and Joshua Blum and directed by Mark Pellington, and the book is "compiled" by Holman, Blum, and Pellington, it is clearly Holman who was responsible for most of the decisions concerning poetic selections and for writing most of the book's editorial text.

2. Holman's claim in the introduction to the series book that "this is the first book of poems ever to be based on a television series" (ibid., 7) is not strictly true: Moyers's book *The Language of Life*, which appeared the previous year, was also based on a series of the same name. Holman also suggests that the idea of putting poetry on television was an idea that originated with him, Roberto Bedoya, and Danny O'Neil, although the PBS series *Voices and Visions*, based on American poetry, was contemporary with their efforts.

3. In my conversation with Holman, he was reluctant to criticize the Moyers series, but clear in differentiating Moyers's project from his own: "Moyers has documented this [poetry festival] and created a traditional documentary where you see a poet read in performance and then the poet is interviewed about the work."

4. Holman, *United States of Poetry*, 11.

5. Holman told me that his principal criticism of the poets represented in the Moyers series is that "everybody in the series is a teacher of poetry somewhere."

6. Holman, *United States of Poetry*, 9.

7. Ibid., 69.

8. Between Moss's introductory segment and the rest of the poems, a rapid montage of icons and images sets the tone for the entire program. American flags

cut to a gas mask, to a crowd of faces, and finally to the disturbingly ambiguous image of a baby lying in its stroller in the desert, where flashing lights and targets connote firing ranges and atomic weapons testing.

9. Holman himself commented on the spot in a letter to me: "The whole plane of these three 'professional' poets [Moss, Cohen, and Baraka] is blown out by Narissa Diaz, who is a poet solely by virtue of having written a poem. For her, the politics is standing up to a bully, and isn't that, in different scale, part of the message of the opening three poems? This scale switch, too, is engaged by the image track: what is the deep silver shape? Slowly, the icon of everybody's grade school days, the water fountain, gets pieced together. The scale switching from Cohen's entire country, to Baraka's African American people, to Diaz's personal."

10. Holman, *United States of Poetry,* 69.

11. This refrain is spoken by three male voices: the first apparently African American, the other two white. One reading of this exchange is the inability of white America to communicate its sense of the American Dream to African American and other minority communities as anything more than empty clichés.

12. Holman, *United States of Poetry,* 69.

13. Howard Rosenberg, "Poetry Carries a Big Shtick," *New York Times,* 12 February 1996.

14. Ibid. Students in my graduate poetry seminar had similar questions about how much the poems were dominated by the arresting visuals and music.

15. Discussion on e-mail "poetics list," 4 April 1996. Obviously, this balance is different in the case of each poem. The most successful spots are those in which the visual images and music enhance the written text, allowing an interplay between the two rather than overwhelming the text.

16. Kaplan, *Rocking around the Clock,* 5.

17. A significant exception to this is the very effective presentation of Larry Eigner's poem, one of the few occasions in the series where the physical form of the poem as text is foregrounded. Other segments in which words are effectively visualized as well as spoken include Wanda Coleman's "Talk about the Money" and Emily XYZ's "Slot Machine."

18. Amato, e-mail, 4 April 1996. While comparisons between the *USOP* program and MTV are inevitable, the very purpose of MTV—to sell the recordings of the singers and groups it presents—makes it a very different kind of enterprise from *USOP,* which is less concerned with boosting the sales of individual poets than with promoting a form of expression that is decidedly marginal with respect to American culture at large. Nonetheless, a campaign for the Nike Corporation aired during the 1998 Winter Olympics used works by four poets—including *USOP* poets Matt Cook and Emily XYZ—in their ads. While the poems were in celebration of the individual athletes and not linked to individual Nike products, the connection of poetry and advertising raises important questions about the function of poetry in relation to the media, advertising, and commodification.

The poets were each paid $250 to submit a poem, and $2,500 if their poem was accepted. One of the poets who was asked to submit, Martin Espada, published an open letter in the *Progressive* citing the "brutal labor practices" of Nike, as well as their use of advertising to exploit low-income adolescents. Of the seventy or eighty poets from whom poems were solicited, however, Espada was the only one who refused to participate on ideological grounds; most poets, we can assume, see nothing wrong with attaching their work to a corporate product.

19. While agreeing to download the series to their affiliates in most parts of the country, PBS refused to schedule it on a national hardfeed (as they had done for the Moyers series) or to list it on their Web site, thus making any promotional efforts extremely difficult.

Conclusion

1. As recently as the early 1960s, none of the most important small presses now publishing poetry were in existence and most of the prominent university press publishers had not yet inaugurated their poetry series. The poetry scene was almost completely dominated by trade presses, with small press publishing on the margins and university press publishing almost nonexistent. By 1980, we find a significant change in this balance, with a fairly even representation of university, trade, and small press publishing. In Mary Biggs's survey of the "most significant" presses, the largest number were still trade presses, but university and small presses were not far behind (*A Gift That Cannot Be Refused*). As of the late 1990s, however, the importance of trade press publishing in American poetry has declined to the point where commercial presses play a far less important role, at least numerically speaking, than either university or small presses. The number of new volumes of contemporary American poetry published by trade presses, excluding anthologies, declined from more than a hundred a year in the mid-1960s to its current level of between thirty and forty titles. As Charles Bernstein somewhat hyperbolically suggests, if "all the nationally circulated magazines and trade presses . . . stopped publishing or reviewing poetry," contemporary American poetry "would hardly feel the blow." See "Provisional Institutions," 133.

2. Rasula, *American Poetry Wax Museum*, 440.

3. The summer 1996 issue of the *Iowa Review*, the collection "Some Poetries of America," somewhat inadvertently reifies this rubric. While trying to "blur rather than reinforce identifying suppositions" by arranging the issue alphabetically rather than by group, the editors divided it into "three poetries"—which are clearly experimental/Language, mainstream academic, and multicultural—and allotted "the same number of pages" to each group. While in certain cases there is some overlap between the categories (is Mei-mei Berssenbrugge meant to be experimental or multicultural?), it is generally clear to which category each

poet belongs, even though we are never told what the categories are or even given contributors' notes. This ambivalence about categorization (using fixed categories as an editorial rubric while at the same time attempting to disguise that rubric) seems symptomatic of poetic culture today.

4. Dana Gioia, "Notes on the New Formalism," *Hudson Review* 40, no. 3 (1987); Brad Leithauser, "The Confinement of Free Verse," *New Criterion,* May 1987; Philip Dacey and David Jauss, *Strong Measures: Contemporary American Poetry in Traditional Forms* (New York: Harper and Row, 1986); Robert Richman, *The Direction of Poetry: An Anthology of Rhymed and Metered Verse Written in the English Language since 1975* (New York: Houghton Mifflin, 1988); Timothy Steele, *Missing Measures: Modern Poetry and the Revolt against Meter* (Fayetteville: University of Arkansas Press, 1990); Wyatt Prunty, *"Fallen from the Symboled World": Precedents for the New Formalism* (New York: Oxford University Press, 1990).

5. Joseph Conte, *Unending Design: The Forms of Modern Poetry* (Ithaca: Cornell University Press, 1991), 274, 269.

6. Wallace, "Emerging Avant Garde," 1.

7. These include the presses Sun & Moon, Roof, Burning Deck, Edge, Talon, Hanuman, Tsunami, Potes & Poets, The Figures, Station Hill, O Books, Chax, Awede, Kelsey Street, Leave, Paradigm, Zasterle, Avenue B, and Tuumba; and the magazines *O-blek, Notus, Sulfur, Avec, Lingo, Temblor, Aerial, Talisman, New American Writing, Hambone, The World, Tyuonyi, Big Allis, Sink, Writing, Temblor, Acts, Generator, Raddle Moon, Paper Air, HOW(ever), The Difficulties, Ottotole, O.ARS,* and *Poetics Journal.*

8. Other blurbs are more revealing of what I find to be the empty center of Doty's poems. Marjorie Marks writes of *My Alexandria* that "though AIDS is a potent metaphor, the crystalline sensibility and breathtaking beauty of these poems is redemptive (on several levels) rather than depressive"; Tony Whelan comments that Doty's poems contain "no hint . . . of a social agenda," a rather strange claim to make about a book that is largely concerned with the AIDS epidemic. Based on these comments, one can only speculate that perhaps Doty's poems would have found a less enthusiastic response had his approach to AIDS been more socially engaged and less metaphorical. Doty is certainly not the only poet to write about AIDS, but he has been the most successful.

9. Doty may be thinking of Williams here, but the lines are so un-Williams-like as to make this association unlikely.

10. This particular form of stepped or graduated tercets appears to have become one of Doty's favorites in *Atlantis,* where he uses it in six poems.

11. Leonard Schwartz, introduction to *Primary Trouble: An Anthology of Contemporary American Poetry,* ed. Leonard Schwartz, Joseph Donahue, and Edward Foster (Jersey City: Talisman House, 1996), 2.

12. By 1965, the only one of the groupings identified by Donald Allen in *The New American Poetry* that could still be said to have any validity was the New

York school, and it is debatable whether the New York poets ever constituted an actual movement. It is significant that by the time they published their follow-up anthology, *The Postmoderns: The New American Poetry Revised,* in 1982, Allen and George Butterick had abandoned any attempt to categorize the poets included by movement or school, instead grouping them under the nonspecific historical rubric "postmodernism."

13. Schwartz, introduction to *Primary Trouble,* 3.

14. Wallace, "Emerging Avant Garde," 2.

15. Ibid., 3.

16. Bertholf, preface to *Writing from the New Coast: Technique,* ed. Peter Gizzi and Juliana Spahr (Providence: O-blek Editions, 1993), 3.

17. Ibid., 1.

18. In fact, Evans's only mention of Language writing comes not in the context of a poetic or literary movement, but in a sentence where Language theory is aligned with Derridean deconstruction.

19. Wallace, "Emerging Avant Garde," 7.

20. Schwartz, introduction to *Primary Trouble,* 2.

21. Ibid., 3.

22. Lazer, *Opposing Poetries,* 37.

23. Walter K. Lew, *Premonitions: The Kaya Anthology of New Asian North American Poetry* (New York: Kaya Productions, 1995), 575.

24. Since I do not have the space here to discuss other multicultural anthologies, *Premonitions* will have to stand as a synecdochal example of what I see as a larger trend toward experimental multicultural poetries. Another important—though somewhat less innovative—anthology of contemporary multicultural poetry is Kevin Powell and Ras Baraka's *In the Tradition: An Anthology of Young Black Writers* (New York: Harlem River, 1992). *In the Tradition* includes forty-one poets, most of them well under the age of forty, who write in a variety of styles—some of them more experimental than others.

25. Assembling Alternatives was an "international poetry conference/festival" held at the University of New Hampshire in Durham from 29 August to 2 September 1996. While the conference did include a few papers on Chinese poetry and Hawaiian pidgin poetry, its critical and literary emphasis was overwhelmingly on white poets.

26. These include the CD recordings *Live at the Ear* (Elemenope Productions, 1993), edited by Charles Bernstein from original taped recordings of Language poets at New York's Ear Inn; *Lingo CD No. 1* (1996), released in conjunction with issue 5 of *Lingo* magazine and containing recordings of poets David Shapiro, Michael Gizzi, Elaine Equi, Gillian McCain, Frank Lima, Chris Stroffolino, and Eileen Myles; and the CD released with the *Exact Change Yearbook No. 1* (Boston: Exact Change, 1995), which includes recordings of Michael Palmer, Barbara Guest, Kamau Brathwaite, Robert Creeley, John Ashbery, Alice Notley,

John Godfrey, Jack Spicer, Mei-mei Berssenbrugge, Kenward Elmslie, Bernadette Mayer, and Ted Berrigan.

27. Christopher Funkhouser divides electronic/computer poetry into five categories: hypermedia (including graphics, moving visual images, and sound files linked with printed text); hypercard (digital file cards linking alphabetic and visual images); hypertext (written texts with links to other written texts); network hypermedia (poems on the Internet); and text-generating software (programs that automatically arrange words and images). According to Funkhouser, future electronic poetries will exist "as a conglomeration of [these] different types of interconnective materials." See Funkhouser's essay "Toward a Literature Moving outside Itself: The Beginnings of Hypermedia Poetry," *Talisman* 16 (1996). See also the CD-ROM version of *Little Magazine* 21 (1995), edited by Funkhouser, Belle Gironda, Benjamin Henry, and Roberto Bocci.

28. Bernstein, "Provisional Institutions," 143, 144. Bernstein cites the example of Random House, whose 1993 books had advertising budgets of up to $87,000 each and *lost* up to $300,000 each. Since books that do not receive this kind of economic and institutional support stand little chance of being reviewed in the *New York Times* and similar mainstream publications, those "innovative works of literature or criticism or scholarship that challenge the dominant cultural values of institutions such as Random House" are excluded from the mainstream print media by a selection process that, ironically, is controlled by the very media conglomerates who have written off literary books as "unprofitable" (145–46). Thus "official 'high' culture" can serve as a "loss leader" for large publishing corporations that can afford to lose more on a single book than the entire operating budget of most small presses. This effect has been exacerbated by a decline in public funding for poetry at the very moment when it is most needed to offset the results of such corporate control of literary culture. One result of the decline in public spending on the literary arts has clearly been a significant shift in support from the public sector to private and university funding. It is difficult to estimate the overall financial impact of private and foundation support for poetry, since foundation support for "Arts, Humanities, and Culture" is usually listed as a single category, and is seldom broken down into its component parts (i.e., literature, museums, performing arts). It seems clear, however, that at this point the total funding for poetry from private, corporate, and community foundations is greater than that provided by the public sector. Organizations like the Mellon Foundation and the Lila Wallace/Reader's Digest Fund provide a large influx of funds for poetry writing and publishing. On the regional level, significant foundation support comes from organizations like the Lannan Foundation (Southern California), and the Bush and McKnight Foundations (Minnesota). At the same time, private organizations like the Ruth Lilly Foundation, the Whiting Foundation, and the Tanning, MacArthur, Lannan and Kingsley Tufts prizes provide a source of funds for a few prizewinning poets. The largest private funder of literary

arts in the United States, the Lila Wallace/Reader's Digest Fund, has alone given over $30 million since 1989 to nonprofit public organizations that promote poetry and individual poets. It is too soon to know how this change from government support to private patronage will affect such areas as small press publishing, little magazine and journal publishing, and poetry readings, but it is probable that increased privatization will continue to have the effect of centralizing the channels of power and influence within the poetry community.

29. If the academy is the single most influential institution for poetry in America, the system of prizes, awards, grants, and fellowships is the most visible source of cultural legitimation and economic support for American poets. In the case of awards like the MacArthur, Lila Wallace/Reader's Digest Fund, Ruth Lilly, Lannan, Kingsley Tufts, Guggenheim, and Whiting, the cash prize is over $30,000, and sometimes far more. The most lucrative prizes awarded to poets on a regular basis are the Tanning ($100,000), the Lila Wallace/Reader's Digest Fund ($35,000 annually for three years), the Ruth Lilly ($75,000), the Lannon ($75,000), and the Kingsley Tufts ($50,000). Even bigger money is potentially available: Amy Clampitt's 1992 MacArthur was for $375,000, and in 1993, John Ashbery won the $150,000 Antonio Feltinelli International Prize for poetry. Yet the range of poets for whom such lucrative prizes are even a possibility remains frustratingly narrow, especially at a time when public funding for poetry has become increasingly limited in the United States.

Bibliography

Adams, Kate. "Academe's Dominance of Poetic Culture Narrows the Range of American Poetry." *Chronicle of Higher Education*, 18 May 1988.

Adorno, Theodor. "Culture and Administration." *The Culture Industry: Selected Essays on Mass Culture*. New York: Routledge, 1990.

———. "Lyric Poetry and Society." *Telos* 20 (1974).

Algarin, Miguel, and Bob Holman, eds. *Aloud: Voices from the Nuyorican Poets Cafe*. New York: Henry Holt, 1994.

Allen, Dick. "Shrinkages and Expansions." *Hudson Review* 40 (1987).

Allen, Donald, ed. *The New American Poetry, 1945–1960*. New York: Grove, 1960.

Allen, Donald, and George Butterick, eds. *The Postmoderns: The New American Poetry Revisited*. New York: Grove Weidenfeld, 1982.

Altieri, Charles. *Self and Sensibility in Contemporary American Poetry*. New York: Cambridge University Press, 1984.

Andrews, Bruce. *Paradise and Method: Poetics and Praxis*. Evanston: Northwestern University Press, 1996.

Armantrout, Rae. "Mainstream Marginality." *Poetics Journal* 6 (1986).

Barone, Dennis, and Peter Ganick. *The Art of Practice: Forty-five Contemporary Poets*. Elmwood, Conn.: Potes & Poets, 1994.

Beatty, Paul. *Joker, Joker, Deuce*. New York: Penguin, 1995.

Bedient, Calvin. "The Retreat from Poetic Modernism." *Modernism/Modernity* 1, no. 3 (1994).

Bernstein, Charles. *Content's Dream: Essays, 1975–1984*. Los Angeles: Sun & Moon, 1986.

———. *A Poetics*. Cambridge: Harvard University Press, 1992.

———. "Provisional Institutions: Alternative Presses and Poetic Innovation." *Arizona Quarterly* 51, no. 1 (1995).

Bertholf, Robert. Preface to *Writing from the New Coast: Technique*, ed. Peter Gizzi and Juliana Spahr. Providence, R.I.: O-blek Editions, 1993.

Bérubé, Michael. *Marginal Forces/Cultural Centers: Tolson, Pynchon, and the Politics of the Canon*. Ithaca: Cornell University Press, 1992.

Biggs, Mary. *A Gift that Cannot Be Refused: The Writing and Publishing of Contemporary American Poetry*. New York: Greenwood, 1990.

Booth, Alison. "Feminist Criticism at the 'English' Track Meet." *Callaloo* 17, no. 2 (1994).

Bourdieu, Pierre. *The Field of Cultural Production: Essays on Art and Literature*. Ed. Randal Johnson. New York: Columbia University Press, 1993.

Brodsky, Joseph. "An Immodest Proposal: Why American Poetry Belongs in the Supermarket." *New Republic*, 11 November 1991.

Burger, Peter. *Theory of the Avant-Garde.* 1974. Trans. Michael Shaw. Minneapolis: University of Minnesota Press, 1984.

Clark, Hilary. "The Mnemonics of Autobiography: Lyn Hejinian's *My Life.*" *Biography* 14 (1991).

Codrescu, Andrei, ed. *Up Late: American Poetry since 1970.* 2d ed. New York: Four Walls Eight Windows, 1991.

Coleman, Wanda. Interview. *A View from the Loft* 18, no. 3 (1995).

Collins, Jim. "Appropriating Like *Crazy:* From Pop Art to Meta-Pop." In *Modernity and Mass Culture,* ed. James Naremore and Patrick Brantlinger. Bloomington: Indiana University Press, 1993.

Cornford, Adam, James Brook, Iain Boal, and Tom Clark. "Political Poetry and Formalist Avant-Gardes: Four Viewpoints." *City Lights Review* 1 (1987).

Culler, Jonathan. *Framing the Sign: Criticism and Its Institutions.* Norman: University of Oklahoma Press, 1987.

Damon, Maria. *At the Dark End of the Street: Margins in Vanguard American Poetry.* Minneapolis: University of Minnesota Press, 1993.

Davidson, Michael. *The San Francisco Renaissance: Poetics and Community at Mid-Century.* New York: Cambridge University Press, 1989.

Dean, Lance. Review of *Can Poetry Matter?* by Dana Gioia. *American Literature* 66 (1994).

Digest of Education Statistics. Washington, D.C.: U.S. Dept. of Health, Education, and Welfare, Education Division, 1994.

Dimock, Wai Chee, and Michael T. Gilmore, eds. *Rethinking Class: Literary Studies and Social Formations.* New York: Columbia University Press, 1994.

Directory of American Poetry Books. 3d ed. New York: Poet's House, 1995.

Disch, Thomas. *The Castle of Indolence: On Poetry, Poets, and Poetasters.* New York: Picador, 1995.

Dobyns, Stephen. *The Balthus Poems.* New York: Atheneum, 1982.

———. *Black Dog, Red Dog.* 1984. Pittsburgh: Carnegie Mellon University Press, 1990.

———. *Body Traffic.* New York: Viking, 1990.

———. *Cemetery Nights.* New York: Viking, 1987.

———. *Velocities: New and Selected Poems.* New York: Viking, 1994.

Doty, Mark. *Atlantis.* New York: HarperCollins, 1995.

———. *My Alexandria.* Urbana: University of Illinois Press, 1993.

Eagleton, Terry. *Literary Theory: An Introduction.* Minneapolis: University of Minnesota Press, 1983.

Ellman, Richard, and Robert O'Clair, eds. *Norton Anthology of Modern Poetry.* 1st ed. New York: Norton, 1973.

———. *Norton Anthology of Modern Poetry.* 2d ed. New York: Norton, 1988.

Epstein, Joseph. "Who Killed Poetry?" *Commentary* 86, no. 2 (1988).

Evans, Steve. Introduction to *Writing from the New Coast: Technique,* ed. Peter Gizzi and Juliana Spahr. Providence, R.I.: O-blek Editions, 1993.

Fiske, John. "Popular Discrimination." In *Modernity and Mass Culture,* ed. James Naremore and Patrick Brantlinger. Bloomington: Indiana University Press, 1993.

Foster, Hal. "What's New about the Neo-Avant-Garde." *October* 70 (1994).

Fredman, Stephen. *The Grounding of American Poetry: Charles Olson and the Emersonian Tradition.* New York: Cambridge University Press, 1993.

Frith, Simon. "The Cultural Study of Popular Music." In *Cultural Studies,* ed. Lawrence Grossberg, Cary Nelson, and Paula Treichler. New York: Routledge, 1992.

Frow, John. *Cultural Studies and Cultural Value.* New York: Oxford University Press, 1995.

Fulton, Len, ed. *Directory of Poetry Publishers.* 10th ed. Paradise, Calif.: Dustbooks, 1994.

Funkhouser, Chris. "Toward a Literature Moving outside Itself: The Beginnings of Hypermedia Poetry." *Talisman* 16 (1996).

Garrett, George. "The Future of Creative-Writing Programs." In *Creative Writing in America,* ed. Joseph Moxley. Urbana: National Council of Teachers of English, 1989.

Gates, Henry Louis. "Sudden Def." *New Yorker,* 19 June 1995.

Gilbert, Sandra. "Feminist Criticism in the University: An Interview." In *Criticism and the University,* ed. Gerald Graff and Reginald Gibbons. Evanston: Northwestern University Press, 1985.

Gillan, Jennifer. Introduction to *Unsettling America: An Anthology of Contemporary Multicultural Poetry,* ed. Maria Mazziotti Gillan and Jennifer Gillan. New York: Penguin, 1994.

Ginsberg, Allen. Foreword to *Out of This World: An Anthology of the St. Mark's Poetry Project, 1966–1991,* ed. Anne Waldman. New York: Crown, 1991.

Gioia, Dana. *Can Poetry Matter?* St. Paul: Graywolf, 1992.

Golding, Alan. *From Outlaw to Classic: Canons in American Poetry.* University of Wisconsin Press, 1995.

———. "Language-Bashing Again." *Mid-American Review* 8, no. 2 (1988).

Gonzalez, Ray. Review of *Aloud: Voices from the Nuyorican Poets Cafe,* by Miguel Algarin and Bob Holman. *Nation,* 19 December 1994.

Graff, Gerald. *Professing Literature: An Institutional History.* Chicago: University of Chicago Press, 1987.

Greenblatt, Stephen, and Giles Gunn, eds. *Redrawing the Boundaries: The Transformation of English and American Literary Studies.* New York: Modern Language Association, 1992.

Greer, Michael. "Ideology and Theory in Recent Experimental Writing; or, The Naming of 'Language Poetry.'" *Boundary 2,* no. 16 (1989).

Gripsrud, Jostein. " 'High Culture' Revisited." *Cultural Studies* 3, no. 2 (1989).

Hall, Donald. *Death to the Death of Poetry: Essays, Reviews, Notes, Interviews.* Ann Arbor: University of Michigan Press, 1994.

――――. *Poetry and Ambition: Essays, 1982–1988.* Ann Arbor: University of Michigan Press, 1988.

Hall, Donald, Robert Pack, and Louis Simpson, eds. *New Poets of England and America.* New York: Meridien, 1957.

Haraway, Donna J. *Simians, Cyborgs, and Women: The Reinvention of Nature.* New York: Routledge, 1991.

Harris, Marie, and Kathleen Aguero, eds. *An Ear to the Ground: An Anthology of Contemporary American Poetry.* Athens: University of Georgia Press, 1989.

――――. *A Gift of Tongues: Critical Challenges in Contemporary American Poetry.* Athens: University of Georgia Press, 1987.

Hartley, George. *Textual Politics and the Language Poets.* Bloomington: University of Indiana Press, 1989.

Hejinian, Lyn. *The Cell.* Los Angeles: Sun & Moon, 1991.

――――. "If Written Is Writing." In *The L=A=N=G=U=A=G=E Book,* ed. Bruce Andrews and Charles Bernstein. Carbondale: Southern Illinois University Press, 1984.

――――. *My Life.* Rev. ed. Los Angeles: Sun & Moon, 1987.

――――. *Oxota: A Short Russian Novel.* Great Barrington, Mass.: The Figures, 1991.

――――. "The Rejection of Closure." In *Writing/Talks,* ed. Bob Perelman. Carbondale: Southern Illinois University Press, 1985.

――――. "Strangeness." *Poetics Journal* 8 (1989).

Holden, Jonathan. "American Poetry: 1970–1990." In *A Profile of Twentieth-Century American Poetry,* ed. Jack Myers and David Wojahn. Carbondale: Southern Illinois University Press, 1991.

――――. *The Fate of American Poetry.* Athens: Georgia University Press, 1991.

Holman, Bob. "Making Poetry Is No Vice." *Los Angeles Times,* 4 March 1996.

Holman, Bob, Joshua Blum, and Mark Pellington, eds. *The United States of Poetry.* New York: Abrams, 1996.

Hongo, Garrett, ed. *The Open Boat: Poems from Asian America.* New York: Doubleday, 1993.

Hoover, Paul, ed. *Postmodern American Poetry: A Norton Anthology.* New York: Norton, 1994.

Howard, Ben. "World and Spirit, Body and Soul." *Poetry* 158 (1991).

Howard, Richard, and David Lehman, eds. *The Best American Poetry, 1995.* New York: Simon and Schuster, 1995.

Huyssen, Andreas. *After the Great Divide: Modernism, Mass Culture, Postmodernism.* Bloomington: Indiana University Press, 1986.

Jarman, Mark. "Journals of the Soul." *Hudson Review* 46 (1993).

Jarraway, David R. "*My Life* through the Eighties: The Exemplary L=A=N=G=U=A=G=E of Lyn Hejinian." *Contemporary Literature* 33 (1992).

Kalaidjian, Walter. *American Culture between the Wars: Revisionary Modernism and Postmodern Critique.* New York: Columbia University Press, 1993.

Kaplan, E. Ann. *Rocking around the Clock: Music Television, Postmodernism, and Consumer Culture.* New York: Methuen, 1987.

Karp, Vickie. "When Words Combine—the Evolution of a Television Series on Poetry." *Poets and Writers,* July/August 1995.

Kinney, Clare. "Postscript from the Canon's Mouth." *Callaloo* 17, no. 2 (1994).

Kinzie, Mary. *The Cure for Poetry in an Age of Prose: Moral Essays on the Poet's Calling.* Chicago: University of Chicago Press, 1993.

Kuzma, Greg. "The Catastrophe of Creative Writing." *Poetry* 148, no. 6 (1986).

Lauter, Paul, general ed. *The Heath Anthology of American Literature.* Lexington, Mass.: Heath, 1990.

Lazer, Hank. *Opposing Poetries.* 2 vols. Evanston: Northwestern University Press, 1996.

Lew, Walter K. *Premonitions: The Kaya Anthology of New Asian North American Poetry.* New York: Kaya Productions, 1995.

Lott, Eric. "The Aesthetic Ante: Pleasure, Pop Culture, and the Middle Passage." *Callaloo* 17, no. 2 (1994).

Lux, Thomas. Review of *Cemetery Nights,* by Stephen Dobyns. *Western Humanities Review* 42 (1988).

McClatchy, J. D., ed. *Vintage Book of Contemporary American Poetry.* New York: Random House, 1990.

———. *White Paper: On Contemporary American Poetry.* New York: Columbia University Press, 1989.

McDonnell, Evelyn. "Native Tongues." *Rolling Stone,* 5 August 1993.

McPhillips, Robert. "The Year in Poetry." In *Dictionary of Literary Biography Yearbook, 1992,* ed. James W. Hipp. Detroit: Gale Research, 1992.

Messerli, Douglas, ed. *From the Other Side of the Century: A New American Poetry, 1960–1990.* Los Angeles: Sun & Moon, 1994.

Middleton, Richard. *Studying Popular Music.* Philadelphia: Open University Press, 1990.

Moyers, Bill, and James Haba, eds. *The Language of Life.* New York: Doubleday, 1995.

Myers, Jack, and Roger Weingarten, eds. *New American Poets of the Eighties.* Green Harbor, Mass.: Wampeter Press, 1984.

Nealon, Jeffrey T. *Double Reading: Postmodernism after Deconstruction.* Ithaca: Cornell University Press, 1993.

Nelson, Cary. *Repression and Recovery: Modern American Poetry and the Politics of Cultural Memory, 1910–1945.* Madison: University of Wisconsin Press, 1989.

Noland, Carrie. "Poetry at Stake: Blaise Cendrars, Cultural Studies, and the Future of Poetry in the Literature Classroom." *PMLA* 112, no. 1 (1997).

———. "Rimbaud and Patti Smith: Style as Social Deviance." *Critical Inquiry* 21, no. 3 (1995).

Nowell-Smith, Geoffrey. "On Kiri Te Kanawa, Judy Garland, and the Culture Industry." In *Modernism and Mass Culture*, ed. James Naremore and Patrick Brantlinger. Bloomington: Indiana University Press, 1993.

Ohmann, Richard. "The Shaping of a Canon: U.S. Fiction, 1960–1975." *Critical Inquiry* 10 (1983).

Parrinder, Patrick. *The Failure of Theory: Essays on Criticism and Contemporary Fiction*. Totowa, N.J.: Barnes and Noble, 1987.

Patterson, Raymond. "What's Happening in Black Poetry." *A Gift of Tongues: Critical Challenges in Contemporary American Poetry*. Athens: University of Georgia Press, 1987.

Perkins, David. *A History of Modern Poetry: Modernism and After*. Cambridge: Harvard University Press, 1987.

Perloff, Marjorie. *Poetic License: Essays on Modernist and Postmodernist Lyric*. Evanston: Northwestern University Press, 1990.

———. "Poetry Doesn't Matter." *American Book Review* 15, no. 5 (1993).

———. *Radical Artifice: Writing Poetry in the Age of Media*. Chicago: University of Chicago Press, 1991.

———. "Theory and/in the Creative Writing Classroom." *AWP Newsletter*, November/December 1987.

———. "What We Talk about When We Talk about Poetry: Some Aporias of Literary Journalism." *PNReview* 23, no. 5 (1997).

Peters, Robert. "The Present State of Poetry." Part 4: "The Mammoth Cloth Beast of Poetry." *New York Quarterly* 30 (1986).

Pinsky, Robert. *The Situation of Poetry*. Princeton: Princeton University Press, 1976.

Powell, Kevin, and Ras Baraka. *In the Tradition: An Anthology of Young Black Writers*. New York: Harlem River, 1992.

Radway, Janice. "The Book-of-the-Month Club and the General Reader: On the Uses of 'Serious' Fiction." In *Literature and Social Practice*, ed. Phillipe Desan, Priscilla Parkhurst Ferguson, and Wendy Griswold. Chicago: University of Chicago Press, 1989.

Rasula, Jed. *The American Poetry Wax Museum: Reality Effects, 1940–1990*. Urbana: National Council of Teachers of English, 1995.

———. "Literary Effects in the Wad: Handling the Fiction, Nursing the Wounds." *Sulfur* 24 (1989).

———. "Part of Nature, Part of—Us? The Role of Critics and the Emperor's New Clothes in American Poetry." *Sulfur* 9 (1984).

Reed, Ishmael. "The Ocean of American Literature." In *The Before Columbus*

Foundation Poetry Anthology, ed. J. J. Phillips, Ishmael Reed, Gundars Strads, and Shawn Wong. New York: Norton, 1992.

Rich, Adrienne, and David Lehman, eds. *The Best American Poetry, 1996.* New York: Simon and Schuster, 1996.

Rose, Tricia. *Black Noise: Rap Music and Black Culture in Contemporary America.* Hanover, N.H.: Wesleyan/University Press of New England, 1994.

Rosenberg, Howard. "Poetry Carries a Big Shtick as PBS Seeks Pulse in America." *New York Times,* 12 February 1996.

Ross, Andrew. "The New Sentence and the Commodity Form: Recent American Writing." In *Marxism and the Interpretation of Culture,* ed. Cary Nelson and Lawrence Grossberg. Urbana: University of Illinois Press, 1988.

———. "Reinventing Community: A Symposium on/with Language Poets." *Minnesota Review* 32 (1989).

Roth's American Poetry Annual, 1990. Great Neck, N.Y.: Roth Publishing, 1990.

Salari, Rose. "The Sound of What Matters." *Common Boundary,* January/February 1996.

Schwartz, Leonard, Joseph Donahue, and Edward Foster, eds. *Primary Trouble: An Anthology of Contemporary American Poetry.* Jersey City, N.J.: Talisman House, 1996.

Semansky, Chris. "Discourse, Institution, and Profession: A Profile of Creative and Critical Practices." PhD diss., SUNY Stony Brook, 1993.

Shaw, Robert. Review of *Cemetery Nights,* by Stephen Dobyns. *Poetry* 150 (1987).

Shelnutt, Eve. "Notes from a Cell: Creative Writing Programs in Isolation." In *Creative Writing in America,* ed. Joseph Moxley. Urbana: National Council of Teachers of English, 1989.

Shetley, Vernon. *After the Death of American Poetry: Poet and Audience in Contemporary America.* Durham: Duke University Press, 1993.

Silliman, Ron. "Canons and Institutions: New Hope for the Disappeared." In *The Politics of Poetic Form: Poetry and Public Policy,* ed. Charles Bernstein. New York: Roof, 1990.

———. *The New Sentence.* New York: Roof, 1987.

———. ed. *In the American Tree.* Orono, Maine: National Poetry Foundation, 1986.

Sirowitz, Hal. *Mother Said.* New York: Crown, 1996.

Smith, Barbara Herrnstein. "Contingencies of Value." *Critical Inquiry* 10 (1983).

Smith, Dave. *Local Assays: On Contemporary American Poetry.* Urbana: University of Illinois Press, 1985.

Smith, Dave, and David Bottoms, eds. *The Morrow Anthology of Younger American Poets.* New York: Morrow, 1985.

Smith, Patricia. Editorial. *Slam* 1, no. 8 (1994).

Spahr, Juliana, Mark Wallace, Kristin Prevallet, and Pam Rehm, eds. *A Poetics of Criticism.* Buffalo: Leave Books, 1994.

Stitt, Peter. "Writers, Theorists, and the Department of English." *AWP Newsletter,* September/October 1987.

Tanner, Ron. "How to Be an Artist in the Anthill of Academe." *AWP Chronicle,* March/April 1991.

Vandernoe, Kirk, and Adam Gopnik. *High and Low: Modern Art and Popular Culture.* New York: Museum of Modern Art, 1990.

Vendler, Helen, ed. *The Harvard Book of Contemporary American Poetry.* Cambridge: Harvard University Press, 1985.

———. *The Music of What Happens: Poems, Poets, Critics.* Cambridge: Harvard University Press, 1988.

———. "Poetry for the People." *New York Times Book Review,* 18 June 1995.

Von Hallberg, Robert. *American Poetry and Culture, 1945–1980.* Cambridge: Harvard University Press, 1985.

Wallace, Mark. "Emerging Avant Garde Poetries and the 'Post-Language Crisis.'" *Poetic Briefs,* no. 19 (St. Louis Park, Minn.: 1995).

Webster, Grant. *The Republic of Letters: A History of Postwar American Literary Opinion.* Baltimore: Johns Hopkins University Press, 1976.

Weinberger, Eliot, ed. *American Poetry since 1950: Innovators and Outsiders.* New York: Marsilio, 1993.

———. *Works on Paper, 1980–1986.* New York: New Directions, 1986.

White, Harrison, and Cynthia White. *Canvases and Careers: Institutional Change in the French Painting World.* New York: Wiley, 1965.

Wilbers, Stephen. *The Iowa Writers' Workshop.* Iowa City: University of Iowa Press, 1980.

Wilson, Edmund. "Is Verse a Dying Technique?" *The Triple Thinkers: Ten Essays on Literature.* New York: Harcourt Brace, 1938.

Yablonsky, Linda. "Hip-Hop-Notic: The Rebirth of Spoken Word." *High Times,* February 1994.

Index

multicultural poetry, 7–9, 28–30, 77,
88–89, 95, 97, 99–100, 102, 108–
16, 118, 149, 151, 153, 155–57,
171–72, 180, 184–86, 218, 220
   African American, 7, 12, 14, 89, 100,
101, 103, 108, 114, 120, 130–31, 143,
146–48, 159, 161, 164, 215, 217, 220
   Asian American 7, 101–2, 108,
113–14, 184–85
   Caribbean dub, 153
   Chicano/Chicana, 100, 112, 157, 164
   feminist, 7, 90, 97, 115, 143
   gay and lesbian, 14, 35, 90, 97, 100,
102, 157, 164
   Hawaiian pidgin, 153, 169
   Hispanic American, 101, 103
   Italian American, 101
   Jewish American, 14, 15, 101, 120, 135
   Latino/Latina, 7, 100–102, 111–14,
119–20, 125, 130–31, 153–54, 164,
215
   Lebanese American, 101
   Native American, 7, 12, 100–101,
103, 109, 113–14, 164
Mura, David, 102, 104–5, 109–10, 184
Murphy, Bruce, 194
Mutabaruka, 153
Myles, Eileen, 87, 220

Naropa Institute, 92, 156, 171, 210
National Endowment for the Arts
(NEA), 6, 8, 36, 60, 85, 88, 96, 177,
203
Nealon, Jeffrey, 57, 191
Needell, Claire, 183
Nelson, Cary, 10–11, 13, 128
Neruda, Pablo, 60, 85
New American Poetry, 7, 77, 86, 89,
94, 171, 181, 183, 206
New Criticism, 2, 7, 15, 24, 33, 59, 91,
93–95, 124, 142, 171, 210

New Formalism, 7, 17, 20, 28, 52, 171,
173–74
Newman, Randy, 115
New York school, 7, 46, 88, 90, 92,
171, 183, 205, 211
Noethe, Sheryl, 154
Noland, Carrie, 189, 194
North, Charles, 87
Northrop, Jim, 156, 164
Notley, Alice, 87, 204, 220
Noto, John, 182
Nowell-Smith, Geoffrey, 126
Nuyorican Poets Cafe, 7, 36, 119–49,
151–52, 157, 210

O'Brien, Geoffrey, 87
official verse culture. *See* mainstream
poetry
O'Hara, Frank, 181, 211
Ohmann, Richard, 2, 83, 191, 200
Olds, Sharon, 45, 83
Oliver, Mary, 172, 177
Olson, Charles, 8, 77, 90–91, 181
O'Neil, Danny, 152, 216
Owen, Maureen, 87

Padgett, Ron, 87, 204
Palmer, Michael, 66, 76, 87, 172, 204,
205, 220
Park, Gloria Toyun, 35, 185
Parker, Stephen, 203
Parrinder, Patrick, 32
Patchen, Kenneth, 210
Patterson, Raymond, 112
PBS, 101–2, 107, 115–16, 150, 152, 154,
168, 216
Perdomo, Willie, 153, 157
Perelman, Bob, 71, 87, 172, 198, 204–6
Perkins, David, 39
Perloff, Marjorie, 17, 26–28, 32, 50–51,
55, 68, 74, 80, 86, 99, 116, 192–93,
201